AF353180

WINGWAVE COACHING

Like the Beat of a Butterfly's Wings

By

CORA BESSER-SIEGMUND,
LOLA A. SIEGMUND & HARRY SIEGMUND

Castle Mount
Media

2020

In Cooperation with

Besser-Siegmund-Institut GmbH
Mönckebergstraße 11
20095 Hamburg
www.besser-siegmund.de

Bibliographic Information from the German National Library can be found under http://dnb.d-nb.de.

Printed for International Distribution in the United States of America and in the United Kingdom

Book design by Marites Bautista

ISBN 978-3-948615-00-0 (Paperback)
ISBN 978-3-948615-01-7 (eBook)

COACHING AWARD

In May 2014 in London, the British *Association for Business Psychology* nominated the *Wingwave Coaching Method* for their "Workforce Experience Award," and wingwave coaching was awarded the finalist's trophy in the category of "Excellence in Coaching or Training of Specialists." The concepts and methods submitted for this award have been used by companies such as Jaguar, McDonalds, and Unilever. No doubt, the excellent findings of research on wingwave coaching also proved to be a plus factor.

Upon completing this book, we received the news that wingwave coaching got the internationally recognized ISO-certification DIN EN ISO 29993 from TÜV-Nord (Technical Inspection Agency - North) due to the high quality of training for coaches. We hope that this book will be another contribution to the sustainability of this methodological quality.

TABLE OF CONTENTS

*The word "psyche" does not only mean
breath, soul, and life force;
it also means butterfly.*

WHAT DOES THE NAME "WINGWAVE" MEAN?

In the physics of chaos theory, the beat of a butterfly's wings can change the weather on the other side of the earth. If the wings beat at precisely the right time and in the right place, their motion can have a huge impact. The philosophy of our short-term coaching method is that it gets maximum coaching results with minimum effort. The precise use of this method can create a positive emotional state in a person's psyche at an astoundingly fast pace. This describes the reference to the word "wing."

The word "wave" is derived from the term "brainwave." This refers to the synchronized electrical pulses in the brain from neurons communicating with each other. It also refers to a flash of insight, a brilliant idea, or an epiphany. It is precisely these brainwaves that are triggered by wingwave coaching to give performance-enhancing energy and emotional balance to our clients.

INTRODUCTION

A little exercise:

Please let your eyes wander from left-to-right and from right-to-left between the butterflies for a gentle REM (rapid eye movement) experience. Choose a comfortable pace or simply try different speeds.

In the late 1980s, American psychotherapists and neurolinguistic programming (NLP) experts began researching rapid eye movements to gently encourage a cognitive change process in the subconscious mind. They wanted to test the therapeutic efficacy of the rapid eye movement technique for effective stress reduction, and their research showed amazing results. This intervention is referred to as the "Eye Movement Integrator." These eye movements happen naturally during sleep, especially during deep dream sleep phases. Sleep specialists have long observed the rapid eye movements (REM), that help us process information we collected through our sensory nervous system and stored in our subconscious as we go about our day.

For example, imagine returning home from a wonderful shopping spree. The first thing you do after returning home is to place everything you bought in the entryway of your house. From a neurobiological perspective, the entryway is, metaphorically speaking, your limbic system, which acts as a temporary storage area. In the brain, new sensory impressions are temporarily stored in the hippocampus, which is where short-term memory is stored. Unfortunately, these memories cannot stay there for long. As you experience new memories, the older memories need to be stored elsewhere. Back to the shopping metaphor, we start putting the items we bought away by stowing each item in its own designated place. The toothpaste goes in the bathroom, the butter in the refrigerator, and the fruit in the fruit basket. Only after we complete these tasks is our house tidy again.

In the same way the entryway is being cleared, our brain loads the new memories into the cerebrum (right and left hemispheres) – the large memory system in the brain – and distributes the information accordingly. Our sensory information is processed, and the body experiences it emotionally as a pleasant, tidied-up feeling.

Sometimes, however, our shopping bag is too heavy, and it remains in the entryway where it blocks our way. The same happens with personal experiences that overstrain the nocturnal processing capability of the brain. The memories are too bulky, too complex, too perplexing, and do not fit into the existing order of our neurobiology or our world experience. We cannot process the situation, and the experiences "get stuck" in our system. We feel blocked by these memories and feelings.

People with post-traumatic stress disorder (PTSD) describe this phenomenon quite clearly. Even years after an experienced trauma, they suffer the distressing recurrence of images, feelings, and recollections from the event. They cannot just get over it. The memory does not fade, but remains actively entangled in their short-term memory as if the event happened yesterday. In such a case, consciously using REM phases in an intervention can cause the beneficial "cleaning-up" process to be initiated, where the trauma gets processed and successfully incorporated into the neurobiological system.

In the early 1990s, American psychotherapist Francine Shapiro further developed consciously applied REM intervention into an independent method for the treatment of PTSD and gave it the name Eye Movement Desensitization and Reprocessing (EDMR). This became very well known throughout the USA and Europe, and people were fascinated by this new idea of being able to simply "wave away" mental blocks.

As with EMDR, the rapid finger movements in front of the client's eyes also plays a significant role in the wingwave method. Wingwave therapists trigger eye movements by waving their fingers left and right in front of their client's face, while the client follows the motion with their eyes. This method is among the most effective and well-researched psychotherapeutic methods for dealing with PTSD following life-threatening experiences, such as abuse, natural catastrophes, war, and acts of violence.

Illustration 1: The Application of "Awake REM Phases" (© Besser-Siegmund)

After many years of experience with this method, we are continuously amazed at how quickly and sustainably EMDR can help with psychological injuries. A person who was psychologically and emotionally secure before a trauma occurred often needs only a few sessions to begin to feel emotional, psychological, and physical relief from the traumatic experience.

Upon observing the powerful effects of EMDR, it seemed obvious that this intervention could be a useful method in the processing of everyday stress. We, therefore, further developed this originally therapeutic approach for the coaching context. We combined EMDR intervention with elements of neurolinguistic programming (NLP), the myostatic muscle test, and music which has been specifically composed to enhance the coaching results. Since 2001, we have been calling this method wingwave coaching®, and the precise use of language in the wingwave process is referred to as Neurolinguistic Coaching (NLC).[1] Today, wingwave is successfully used internationally by thousands of coaches in many different sectors, such as performance sports, the bank industry, the insurance sector, corporate enterprises, learning and teaching environments, and even in dentistry for the management of den-

[1] In the autumn of 2015, the following book was published: Besser-Siegmund, C. & Siegmund, L.: Neurolinguistisches Coaching – NLC. Paderborn: Junfermann.

tal phobia/anxiety. We call our approach "Emotion Coaching" because the coachees do not necessarily need to develop any new skills; instead, through this process they create an emotional flexibility, which allows them to use their existing skills to achieve the positive results they strive for.

The feedback from our clients is extremely positive. Mental blocks transform into a plethora of creative ideas; depression can develop into a sustainable self-confidence.

One of our clients said, "If I come across a setback in my job, the thought of the existence of this method comforts me."

"When I have to give a new presentation, I prepare myself by using wingwave in order to feel confident and self-assured beforehand," an actress said describing the benefits of wingwave.

A managing director said, "I know that by using wingwave, I can quickly find a sound solution even in messy situations." The latter statement is very important. Neither EMDR nor wingwave coaching® supports any repression techniques. On the contrary, these techniques ensure that people are able to cope with a situation using resources that they already have.

In areas where there is a pressure for peak performance, people are exposed to a wide variety of stressful situations and challenges, whether it is of a health, social, or economic nature. These positions range from senior executives, professional athletes, to artists and writers. Stressful experiences are not often related to external catastrophes but an internal conflict where stress can accumulate. A world can come crashing down or an inner turmoil can be the result of internal personal pressures. In most cases, there is no recovery from the stress imprinting. Over time, the events start to hurt and it takes longer for the physical, psychological, and spiritual sources of energy to flow.

Imprints of performance and peak performance stress could arise because of:

- Areas of tension within a team, with superiors, or with customers
- Spotlight stress due to public appearances, competitions, or attention by the media
- Preparing for and taking an exam
- Setbacks on the way to a goal

- Chronic troublesome projects
- Creative blocks
- Unexpected disappointments or setbacks
- A professional dilemma, such as having to terminate an employee
- Lack of focus within the scope of important conflicts
- Lack of sleep
- Stressful experiences such as a turbulent flight or a threatening situation during a stay abroad
- Work-life balance topics for the coordination of professional and private life

Although the above situations have detrimental effects on an individual, we do not refer to these as traumas in a coaching context. We refer to them as "topics." We also use the terms "stress imprinting" or "mini trauma." Although the situations are classified as stressful, they can be easily reduced so that an individual can cope and realize that their life is *not* in danger. For these everyday traumas and internal conflicts, the EMDR founder Francine Shapiro used the term "small-t" trauma. The term refers to stressful situations in which a person does not suffer any physical harm, but the psyche cannot seem to heal from the incident.

In reference to small-t trauma, we use the term Performance Stress Imprinting (PSI), which means people in peak performance situations can become resistant to normal stress responses. The term PSI allows us to categorize experiences which are subjectively described by those affected as unpleasant and obstructive as stress imprints instead of immediately referring to them as clinical trauma. We no longer use the word "post" when referring to post-traumatic stress disorder because many stress reactions in the field of performance also relate to the future, to orbital moments, which lie ahead: examinations, competitions, job interviews, premieres, marriage proposals, etc. By definition, performance stress imprinting is resistant to proven methods of reducing mental and physical stress moments. Rest, distraction, conversation, reasonable thinking, argumentation, and even time, which otherwise "heals all wounds", fizzles out in its effect. The stress spine continues to act, blocking and annoying.

Sometimes clients are satisfied with their emotional response to a situation and do not feel any significant stress. They may instead wish to enhance their performance ability and to be better versions of themselves, and in wingwave we can assist them. On a scale of 0 to 10, a person may perceive themselves to be a 5 and wish to move toward 9 or 10. In such cases, we introduce interventions which bring individuals to an optimum source of strength. In addition, we introduce the possibilities of Belief Coaching using the wingwave method. The subjective belief in our potential is driven by our performance capabilities, our self-assurance, and our inner balance—especially in the face of the challenges that exist in the world.

In the spring of 2001, our first wingwave training group on the topic of EMDR in Coaching took place. Since then, we have been joined by several thousand professional wingwave coaches internationally in countries such as Germany, Switzerland, Austria, the United Kingdom, Denmark, Norway, France, Italy, Spain, Mexico, Russia, and the USA. We are pleased that in recent years, wingwave Coaching has become increasingly popular in Serbia and Croatia, and methods are very frequently reported in the media in these countries. Furthermore, it gives us great pleasure that our book has been published in Spanish, Russian, Hungarian, and Croatian.

As you read, we hope you discover a fascinating coaching approach for your professional objectives. Of course, this book does not replace in-person coaching, but it will teach you how these methods can help you address your individual strengths. At the end of chapters, you will find tips you can use for your personal management. Perhaps you will want to try wingwave! If so, you can find the location of wingwave coaches on our website: www.wingwave.com.

Whether you are a coach, trainer, or therapist, you will gain beneficial insight from this book that will enrich the services you offer. Information about how you can become a wingwave coach can be found in the appendix to this book.

We wish our readers not only interesting insight, but a lot of fun while reading this book!

Cora Besser-Siegmund, Lola A. Siegmund, & Harry Siegmund

PRACTICAL TIPS FOR READERS

This book is for individuals who are interested in self-coaching/personal development and for coaches who offer (or intend to offer) wingwave to their clients. To use wingwave as an intervention tool, it is compulsory to successfully complete professional wingwave training in the appropriate country. If, after reading this book, you wish to undergo a coaching with the methods presented here, know that every wingwave coach is well-trained in these interventions as part of their professional training. Throughout this book we have collected a few practical tips for our readers.

Self-Coaching Tips

This information relates to the general subject-matter, as well as to the wingwave training music, which you will find in the appendix of this book. These are only brief descriptions and short exercises you can try with the aid of the music.

Note for Coaches

Since we see this book as a reference for individuals training to become a wingwave coach, current coaches will find suggestions and recommendations for the application of methods. They can also be considered as the supplementation of the detailed script, which the coaches are provided during their training.

1

SUCCESS FACTOR OF EMOTION COACHING

Do you know the term *homo economicus*? According to Wikipedia, *homo economicus*, or economic man, is "the portrayal of humans as agents who are consistently rational, narrowly self-interested, and who pursue their subjectively-defined ends optimally." It also mentions that this is merely an archetypical character created for academic study. Interestingly, the discourse about the *homo economicus* model in modern economic theory is often criticized, because the possession of these characteristics is rare—even in business or other performance-related contexts. A professional who is organized and well-prepared might have difficulties defending themselves in a verbal dispute, yet following the dispute, they remember all the things they wished they had said. They have had this knowledge all along, but because stress blocked their thought processes, they could not access the information while participating in the verbal dispute. Examination candidates, artists, and professional athletes can experience this blockage, and despite preparation, they are often unable to think or act as optimally as they do during their rehearsals or trainings.

Trainers, managers, and teachers know that people perform best when positively motivated in their environment. This is not solely about the fundamental value of ethics; it is about the perceived benefits of the environment in which they are working. Since the 1930s, there have been innumerable studies in the fields of sociology, business management, psychology, and pedagogy on this topic and the results show the importance of having a healthy, positive work environment. Employees tend to get sick significantly less when they feel comfortable in their job. Students retain information and achieve higher grades in a positive emotional atmosphere, and athletes performing practiced movement sequences are more precise when they are trained in a positive atmosphere. In numerous recent neuropsychological studies, brain research has confirmed this from a medical point of view. People may be more productive under stress for a short time, but on a long-term basis, stress will likely cause them to fall sick and lose momentum.

It follows that a *homo economicus*, in his capacity as a manager or an executive, would have to cultivate a conducive motivational style to motivate his employees to achieve the best possible result. Situations in everyday life, however, can interfere with this behavioral consistency. "When under stress, I seem to forget my good intentions and am just curt. I can see on the face of my employees that it's not okay, but it just takes over me," admitted an experienced manager during a coaching session.

Illustration 2: Positive Motivation (Drawing: Harry Siegmund)

In addition to effective interpersonal communication, a successful leader should inspire those around them with positive, role-model behavior. This also applies to managers, teachers, sport-coaches, and of course to parents around their children. Therefore, it is not just about the external behavior—such as punctuality or manners—but also the expectations of positive emotions. When we read about the systemic effect of important role-models, we often come across a list of desirable managerial emotions. They should be fearless, determined and goal-oriented. The benefits of positive role-model behavior are well known, but this knowledge is overlooked in everyday life. One department head complained, "Since our sales figures dropped so low last year, our team manager has been unbearable. It would be so important for our team right now if he could show a bit of optimism." In this example, the stress caused by low sales may have triggered anxiety, feelings of helplessness, or even anger. These negative emotions can carry over and appear at times unrelated to the situation.

On the contrary, emotions which are subjectively perceived as positive could jeopardize long-term successes or could have equally destructive effects. For example, someone who wants to lose weight and who knows the detriments of eating a chocolate bar can still find it a challenge to lose weight. Despite being aware of its detriments, if this sweet temptation is found lying on the table, it may be quickly consumed by the person trying to lose weight. In contrast to the health benefits of ignoring the chocolate—which were fully understood at a cognitive level–eating the chocolate is associated with a positive emotional response. The person knows that it is an unhealthy choice but chooses to eat it anyway.

If we consider the financial crisis of 2008 with its long-lasting negative effects on the global economy, the significance of emotional factors in business and performance sectors becomes particularly clear. Analysts of this event agree that it was, above all, excessive positive emotions—euphoric confidence, feelings of power and greed—that were responsible for the breakdown of the financial system. This emotional energy emanated from several economists, whose thoughts and actions were far from *homo economicus*. Since then, economic experts have been working intensively on the topic of Behavioral Finance. Behavioral Finance research shows that people who are active in business do not always think and act as rational *homo economicus*, but that those involved—managers, employees, investors, or consumers—are guided not just by intellect, but by their emotions.

Our topic is not only about positive and negative emotions, it is about finding the optimal dosage of all emotional energy so that a person may succeed in a long-term performance context. The aim of emotion coaching in business and for performance behavior is to integrate the cognitive and professional resources of the coachee with an optimally and precisely-dosed emotional balance. This way, the coachee can successfully progress toward, and eventually reach a targeted objective. Optimal performance behavior is rarely easy. Most of the time it is a balancing act. To be successful over time – even in their model – managers, for example, must constantly reconcile professional know-how, communication fitness, conflict stability, creativity, and determination, and they must coordinate these skills to achieve a balanced harmony.

Do you know how you feel walking across a fallen tree trunk or balance beam? First, you stand on one end of the tree trunk or the beam. Instinctively, you do not immediately start to walk across it: you begin to get in touch with your sense of balance, then you hold your arms out straight. If you stop midway, you may wobble or nearly fall off. If you try to rush, you may lose your footing. Yet, if you take sufficient time to find your balance and the correct movement, it ultimately saves time and effort. With the perfect poise and preparation, we can quickly and safely walk to the other end of the trunk or the balance beam.

This balancing metaphor is taken from the management consultant and author Sibylle Nagler-Springmann from her research in Emotion Coaching in Performance-Related Context. We have been working intensively with her research at the Besser-Siegmund-Institut since the end of the 1990s.

As the above example shows, a perfect balance can be achieved only by using carefully prepared movements. Through these movements, we can succeed in pursuing an objective, even on difficult terrain or with difficult obstacles. If we are to succeed—to be successful and achieve great things for ourselves or our team—we must apply this principle of carefully prepared movements to carefully prepare our emotions to support our goals. The secret to success lies in the optimal sequence of movements and preparation.

But what does emotion have to do with movement? The word emotion is derived from the Latin prefix *e*, meaning "from" or "out of" and *motio* meaning "motion" or "movement." So, emotion literally means "out of (from) motion or movement." We experience this movement through emotions by external sensory experiences coming either from external stimuli or from our internal thought processes. We then react to the internal or external events, not only through our cognitive perception, but with noticeable physical responses. These physical responses are called body echoes, and they trigger measurable physical waves, which we refer to as physiological parameters. These physiological parameters can be measured quite clearly from a medical perspective through vascular reactions, cardiac and circulatory activity, muscle tone, body temperature, and brain activity. These physical responses can support us by giving us energy to reach our goals or give us have additional stress which then inhibits our performance ability.

Emotions which cause excessive stress or block our emotional response can jeopardize our inner balance.

Illustration 3: Effect of Stressful Emotions

Targeted, focused, and measured emotions through Emotion Coaching help us remain inwardly balanced so that we can reach our goals.

Illustration 4: Effect of Emotion Coaching

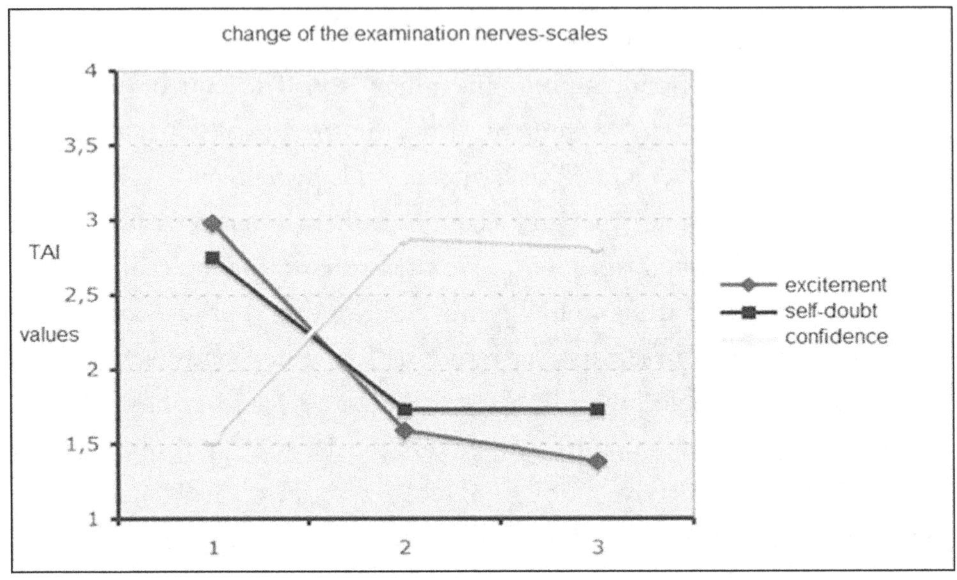

Illustration 5: After Two Hours of Wingwave Coaching: Less Anxiety and Self-Doubt, More Confidence (Nadia Fritsche, University of Hamburg)[2]

Emotion coaching using EMDR and the wingwave method is always based on the premise that the coachee has all the resources they need to achieve their goals. The objective of this approach is not concerned with what a person does, but how they can access these resources as easily and selectively as possible. The Hamburg-based psychologist Nadia Fritsche investigated the effects of wingwave coaching on emotional stability in performance-related contexts, including examples of test anxiety in students. Apart from their exam stress/anxiety, these students were otherwise well prepared for their examinations. All the examination students had to go through a test prior to any intervention. An immediate follow-up survey showed that the results of their anxiety levels had not changed. Subsequently, all the study participants were given an average of two hours of wingwave coaching, and through this, they were able to overcome their test anxiety. They did the next test with considerably more confidence, a positive sense of wellbeing, and markedly reduced fear.

---

[2] TAI: Psychological test for the measurement of various anxiety and stress factors

The first point of measurement shows the uncoached status of the first test, the second shows the coached status after two hours of wingwave coaching and the third point of measurement reflects the retest one month after the successful examination.

This successful result was still stable after one month and the trend was in line with the results of another study done by the Hannover Medical School (Medizinische Hochschule Hannover (MHH)) on "Wingwave in Method Comparison." Marie-Luise Dierks, Professor of Public Health at the MHH, reported separately in the final chapter K on the results of the study mentioned above.

2

EMDR AND WINGWAVE IN THE COACHING PROCESS

Coaching is professional training in personal and social competence. We've already discussed what psychological methods are predominantly used. When selecting wingwave methods, it must be acknowledged that coaching clients, irrespective of the process in which they find themselves, are always psychologically stable. Inhibitions and stress phenomena should always be considered normal and generally comprehensible responses of a healthy person in the context of high-performance. EMDR and wingwave are ideal methods to rapidly strengthen and expand the mental and creative resources which already exist in a psychologically healthy person. Using these interventions, personal resources can be tapped into and anchored by means of focused emotion coaching.

Example: Leo

Leo has been a successful professional musician for twenty years. He regularly composes and writes new songs for himself and for colleagues. Last year, he suffered from writer's block: "I just wasn't able to think of anything. There was complete mental silence. It didn't get any better when I focused on composing the music."

Although generally satisfied with his overall success, this creative block disturbed him. From previous coaching on different topics in the past, Leo already knew about the de-stressing and liberating effect of the awake REM intervention. During the course of his next coaching session, Leo was introduced to the concept of self-coaching with the help of wingwave music. The music is designed so that an alternating left-right rhythmic tone is played directly into the inner ears through headphones. While listening to the alternating rhythmic tones, the eyes of the user make involuntarily minor eye movements, as if they were following the beat to the left and right. This produces a gentle de-stressing effect that is similar to the effect of "waving" directly in front of the eyes. In addition, just by listening, the auditory left-right input seems to release the blocked mental processes and bring them back into motion.

Leo decided he wanted to continue with the wingwave music to overcome his writer's block. Leo played the wingwave music on his MP3 through headphones while doing various chores in his garden. Leo explained that after only 2 hours he received many flashes of inspiration and within 14 days he wrote 30 new songs and had many more creative ideas: "I had to keep my notepad nearby so I could keep writing!" The music was clearly an invaluable asset to Leo as a passionate musical artist. Wingwave music can help many others, too.

Leo's example proves that the use of EMDR can be incorporated into a coaching and self-coaching context. This is why wingwave is so effective. More information on the self-coaching method using wingwave music will be described later in this book. Wingwave music can be introduced to clients after a practical introduction to the method. The prerequisite is a sufficient understanding of the mode of action of the interventions and of their neurobiological explanatory model. Using the process described above and by reading this book, you will broaden your understanding of the phenomenon called Performance Stress Imprinting (PSI), and experience the effectiveness of the awake REM phases. We will then discuss how the concept of wingwave coaching developed from the expansion of the pure application of EMDR. Finally, we will describe procedures you may apply to activate your resources and creativity in a professional context, just as we have already seen in Leo's example.

Interestingly, overcoming mental blocks and furthering professional and personal growth occur in wingwave coaching equally. Many of our clients wish to overcome performance blocks, but most people, such as Leo, are generally satisfied with their current situation and simply wish to seek further professional and personal growth. Clients can work on several topics at the same time, and all the case studies in this book relate to people who can be evaluated as mentally healthy and stable. This is certainly one of the reasons why EMDR and wingwave coaching often work so fast. In therapeutic situations and treatment of psychological disorders, a similarly quick response cannot always be expected.

All coaching examples used in this book come from our practice and all the names have been changed for confidentiality. In this book, we refer to our clients by their first name. In the coaching itself, we address our clients formally.

Self-coaching tip: Composure and creativity through wingwave music

For self-coaching, we invite you to put on your stereo headphones and let the music influence you. Embedded in a pleasant melody, the beat moves to the left and right, back and forth. Leo uses the wingwave music to relax his eye movements, and he therefore activates a gentle awake REM rhythm in his brain. The eyes spontaneously follow the left and right sounds with minimal searching movements. There is no need to give conscious instructions for the eye movements as the effect takes place automatically. The auditory change of beat inspires the brain hemispheres to combine the auditory experience which creates a gentle balancing coordination.

Illustration 6 shows the de-stressing effect of wingwave music.

The measurement was taken using the Porta Bioscreen unit and illustrates the harmonizing and calming effect of the wingwave music. Electrodes were placed on both hands to measure skin resistance. Skin resistance is an indicator of the state of excitation of our entire neurobiology and, consequently, of our brain. After listening for just five minutes, a distinct relaxation sets in. This explains why the music especially composed for wingwave serves to produce a general calming effect and stress reduction, and is also helpful for memorization or in sports. The effect supports endurance and well-being at the intellectual and behavioral level.

The de-stressing effect of the wingwave music visibly reduces the arousal level of the client. This effect has a calming impact and ensures an effective inner balance and reduction of stress. These skin resistance measurements were taken with the Porta Bio Screen. The skin resistance was measured with the left hand (red) and with the right hand (blue).

Illustration 6: How Wingwave Music Works

A study conducted by the German Sport University Cologne (Deutschen Sporthochschule Köln) proved that the performance of physical activity with wingwave music induced a lower pulse rate than physical activity being performed without music. This is immensely beneficial for any sports training. Furthermore, the pulse rate during an activity is lower when listening to the wingwave music than when listening to classical music.[3]

---

[3] Nasse, A. (2013): Der Einsatz der wingwave-Musik bei körperlicher Aktivität hinsichtlich objektiver sowie subjektiver Belastungsparameter [The use of wingwave music during physical activity with regard to the objective, as well as subjective stress parameters]. Bachelor Thesis, German Sport University Cologne.

You may even wish to listen to the wingwave music while reading this book. It may help you absorb and retain the content more efficiently because the REM activation of your brain helps in the awake state when storing newly learned content. Many actors quietly listen to the wingwave music while memorising their lines, because it helps them more effectively learn and retain their text.

Listen to the wingwave music whenever you are looking for new, bright ideas and inspiration. Listen while resting, walking, or doing automatic activities, such as cleaning, cooking, etc. The effect occurs even if you turn down the volume so low that you can even talk at the same time. We know a team within a training company who uses the wingwave music during joint brainstorming sessions: "It does look a bit funny when each of us carries our MP3 player into the meeting, although no one really pays attention to the music. We are enormously creative in the process and very quickly get into an excellent flow," the team leader told us.

2.1 Not Being "In the Flow"—Where is the blockage?

A coaching client came to us with the following issue: For quite some time, he was not enjoying his work. Everything had become routine. It was actually incomprehensible for him because he had achieved some great professional successes during that same year, but for some reason, he no longer felt like himself.

Many clients experience changes in themselves which are unfamiliar to them: "I just do not function smoothly, as if my energies are not flowing as usual." Some clients even express that they are experiencing a side of their personality that they do not know. In such a case, one or more events during a peak performance situation can leave a trace of stress in their memory, which cannot be relieved on its own. Even minor triggers can cause stress imprinting and thus disturbingly trigger an emotional response.

The description of a before and after in their own evaluation of the experience and behavior makes them stop and take notice. Clients who have blockages caused by performance stress often wish to tap into the sources of strength which they had previously experienced and could access on command. They feel that a familiar flow of energy is no longer accessible to them. It is not a change that is necessary but a return to accessing their ideas, strengths, and talents. Often, clients do not have to look far when searching for those inhibiting experiences which virtually choke the positive flow. We've often heard statements like, "Actually, I began being very cautious when the chairman of our board unfairly criticized me publicly." Or, "…when we lost the championship for which we had prepared for two long years."

There are people who constantly have a latent feeling that they are not reaching their potential, or they have difficulty "coming out of their shell." "I am sitting in a meeting, listening to my colleagues, and thousands of ideas and responses come to mind," complained a coaching client, "but I do not utter a word! Only when the others talk to me do I speak, and then I get to hear: 'Why didn't you say that much earlier? You always hold back your opinion!'" There are athletes who, despite the intense preparation and great talent, only achieve second or third place. These people are an enigma, standing in their own way, helplessly shaking their heads and doubting their abilities. "Sometimes, I just wish that I had an unfair boss or an envious colleague," complained a coaching client. "But everyone is so nice to me that I always break into a sweat whenever I have to give a presentation in our meetings!" In this case, the so-called hidden stress triggers start revealing themselves. The coachee is unable to name the trigger of this unpleasant performance inhibitor, but it plays out nevertheless—even in a safe or comfortable environment.

The trigger can even be hidden in everyday activities, activities which, on the surface, appear normal. For example, one of our clients received an email, which served as a trigger. "The email of this customer annoyed me a lot when I received it, but I don't understand why it caused this reaction! In the course of my career, I have received countless such emails. Or did it affect me more strongly than I thought? We had worn ourselves out on this assignment, and every contact with this customer seemed to trigger an emotional reaction." In this case, the client was trying to find the source of their trigger on their own. Even seemingly small triggers can become a thorn in the flesh of general well-being and performance capability. The trigger itself seldom works on its own, rather in combination with other aggravating factors, as we are going to discuss in the following examples.

In our first coaching example, we are going to introduce a managing director who can precisely name the trigger of his stress. We will then demonstrate how we deal with the topic of blockages in coaching in which the clients are unable to explain satisfactorily what their triggers or blockages may be. Issues of stress where a client knows the triggers–we call these specific stress triggers—can be treated using the EMDR method. For the irrational blockages, supported by hidden stress triggers, the wingwave approach is invaluable, because in applying the waving technique within the framework of neurolinguistic coaching, we are able to locate the unknown triggers that are causing the blockage.

The same applies to resource coaching in which the clients do not primarily desire stress reduction, but an increase in performance as their goal. In such cases, it is imperative to discover which strengths should be anchored through emotion coaching. Does this person need more determination or restraint in order to be successful? Does he need courage or humour to progress? Perhaps he needs enthusiasm or patience? The coach and the coachee work together to achieve effective results. Together, we search for the ideal performance triggers, which we refer to as positive resource anchors. Before we start describing this procedure with the hidden stress triggers and success anchors, we will first describe a coaching process based on a specific stress trigger.

Note for coaches: Which method for which blockage?

It happens more in coaching than in therapy that clients are unable to pinpoint the cause of their blockage, or they do not know what mental resources they need as an ideal performance anchor to perfect their craft. In this situation, it is important to begin by finding and naming both the hidden internal stress triggers and the positive resource anchors. The client does not have a massive disorder; they live a perfectly normal life and are simply looking to improve their performance in certain situations. They are looking for that certain ingredient to make them better or stronger. Similar to a good recipe, which might already taste satisfactory, we look for that single spice that will give the entire recipe a special something. This small factor can make that famous one-hundredth of a second possible that makes an athlete a winner. In a coaching setting, clients wish to invest as little time as possible, but to have the greatest possible benefits. This is what makes choaching significantly different from therapy sessions, which take longer and focus on really getting to know the client.

Coaching clients want precise procedures, which can quickly provide them keys to great success. In wingwave coaching, the coach and the coachee accomplish this by working together. Using the muscle feedback test, they can find the stress triggers quicker than in a therapeutic investigative conversation. We will describe this test in detail in the chapters on the wingwave process. The muscle test is part of the wingwave coaching process and is likened to a compass which guides the coach by testing the accuracy of the topic at hand. This, in turn, ensures that the coachee feels and remains emotionally secure.

As a coach, you may know the difference between EMDR and wingwave coaching methods, but we will explain it now: EMDR is suitable for known causes of a blockage or challenge–thus effective for dealing with specific triggers. Wingwave coaching can help to pinpoint *subconscious* blocks and inhibitors and dissolve those hidden stress triggers. It can help find those additional ingredients in as resource anchors for a tasty recipe for personal success.

2.2 Coaching Example with a Specific Stress Trigger: Is the Managing Director a Mimosa?

Karsten W., 45 years of age, is a managing director of a medium-sized and successful press agency. For the last four years, he has had a particularly creative employee. The graphic designer, Sönke A., joined the company as a young professional and turned out to be extremely talented. Karsten W. took him under his wing and encouraged Sönke to undertake assignments, which he thought Sönke would not be capable of completing. Sönke soon developed into an "all-rounder" and at the same time, into an ever-changing source of ideas. This was due to his talent and personal abilities, but also to the opportunities the company offered him.

With a convincing presentation, the agency eventually prevailed over well-known competitors and acquired a major client with an enormous budget. In the midst of the euphoria from gaining this contract, and only two days after giving the winning pitch, Sönke turned in his resignation. He had been planning a career transition for almost a year. Sönke believed 4 years with the same company was far too long for someone ascending their career. He praised Karsten for everything and thanked him for his support: "Thanks for everything. It was a great start!"

Sönke played a leading role in this new and labour-intensive project because a significant part of the concept and design came from him. It would not be easy to fill this gap in the team. Karsten tried not to feel upset with Sönke. He did not want to hold Sönke back, and it was clear that moving on would be good for Sönke's career growth. Despite this, two months later, Karsten noted that Sönke's resignation "still irked" him; he felt "wounded and hurt" and "just couldn't get over it." In coaching, he said: "It seems the resignation affected me, I was not at all prepared for it and somehow it still rattles me." However, Karsten gets angry over his reaction: "It is so silly; this should not actually happen to a professional like me, to let a common-place incident, such as a resignation bother me. I can't just sit around and mope like a frustrated child!" It was clear that this incident was consuming him emotionally, and a colleague recommended that he try wingwave. So, he came to us with the hope of having his frustration waved away.

During his coaching, Karsten discovered that he is suffering from a minor form of post-traumatic stress, which we call stress imprinting. "That's what my colleague thought. But this only applies to people who have experienced an earthquake, an abduction or something like that?" he asked. Yet, he could not overcome the situation; the resignation scene was burned in his memory. He also noticed a bitterness in himself which he was directing at other employees, and he condemned himself for these destructive thoughts and behaviors.

We began the coaching with an introduction to performance stress imprinting.

2.3 Performance Stress Imprinting: When Time Does Not Heal the Wounds

Throughout our lives, we often feel hurt, angry, or shaken, but we are also accustomed to the fact that these emotions do subside. We know that we will get over it. The emotions that are subjectively unpleasant are considered processed when the body feels balanced again while remembering the triggering event.

Our offices are located in the center of downtown Hamburg, and we can see the parking area of our building clearly from our balcony. As a result, we have often witnessed sporadic outbursts of anger as drivers battle for a parking space. We are certain that if we were to ask the angry drivers the day following their outburst if they still felt angry, they would likely respond: "No, I have forgotten about it." More often than not, that person would no longer feel angry and might even laugh about the incident.

Please consider the act of reading the daily newspaper: you read about plane crashes, illnesses, and violent acts without heart palpitations and without breaking into a sweat. The "grey cells"–the bastion of our brain–process the information at the level of perception. At this level, we also assess the events and naturally, we condemn a the perpetrator of violence or consider donating to the victims of natural disasters. In the process, our amygdala for the most part remains remarkably calm. This almost inconspicuous part of the brain—it is as small as an almond seed–is very aptly described by several brain researchers as the "alarm bell of the brain." If our instinctive perception assesses an incoming sensory stimulus as threatening or stressful, the amygdala responds by releasing extra doses of stress hormones. Everyone knows the feeling of an adrenaline rush.

A few days following the event, we might laugh about the stressful experience. It is a similar scenario to the case of people looking for a parking space. Another example might be parents who get angry at the sight of chaos in their children's bedroom and who, then, after a brief period of time, feel nothing but a deep-felt love for their offspring. The alarm bell calms down. The anger disappears, and the positive feelings remain thoroughly preserved. This enables us to gather a wealth of learning experiences in life without becoming psychologically dented with every negative event or shocking news that comes our way. If we were not able to process these events without becoming emotionally scarred, we would become emotionall paralyzed.

In more than 95 percent of cases, we reduce stress, anxiety and excitement in our life through our own mental strength. We find our psychological equilibrium and overcome the issues or experiences on our own. Although we do not necessarily forget these events, we can perceive that the emotional experience is a thing of the past. It can be likened to someone who has walked over a patch of grass in the landscape of our soul. For a while, you can see footprints, then the blades of grass straighten up again, and, with time, it is as if the footprints never existed.

In these situations, we benefit from time. The memory is blurred, fades away, and eventually no longer affects us. With time, one can remember the incident and speak about it without feeling hurt. The experience is now integrated, as psychotherapists say, and can has transformed into a usable treasure trove of experience. Francine Shapiro compares daily mental traumas with minor physical injuries, for example, the prick of a rose's thorn. The finger bleeds and hurts, but the pain does not not last. At the moment of the injury, we know through our experience that this pain will heal in one or two days.

This daily psychological healing process goes back to our first coaching example, the case of Karsten and his disappointment with the colleague who resigned. The sting remained to remind him of the injury. In this case, time has not healed the wound. The pain remains and constrains Karsten's daily activities. The footprints in the landscape of Karsten's psyche remain, thus a challenging stress imprinting is formed.

2.4 How Does the "Shock Gets Stuck in our System"? Or: What are the Effects of Stress Imprinting and Post-traumatic Stress?

The fascinating film titled *How the Nerve Cell Learns the Pain* is about nerve cell memory and pain research. A researcher at the Max-Planck-Institut, Walter Zieglgänsberger, has been successful in filming the reaction of an isolated nerve cell using a jagged curve. A nerve cell fires an impulse when it shows a reaction following a stimulus. Correspondingly, it is possible to observe an action spike in each experimental stimulation of the cell. However, if the nerve cell is stimulated very intensively or frequently, it begins to independently react. The nerve initiates a continuous firing of impulses without getting stimulated externally and is thus active without any external cause. On the basis of the results of this research, Walter Zieglgänsberger was able to explain the phenomenon of phantom pain, a condition in which an amputee experiences pain in the limb which has been amputated, regardless of the fact that there is no limb there to casue the pain.

Until this research, phantom pain was a mystery in the medical field. Now we know that brain cells are capable of learning pain. They can send signals of pain sensations even if the cause of the pain has ceased to exist. One might speak of a "memory of pain" or even neuronal plasticity. Neurons and nerve cells learn the sensation of pain like a song that gets stuck in your head. This kind of pain is now called neuropathic pain. Walther Zieglgänsberger believes that his research will also be able to clarify the neuronal patterns of phobias and post-traumatic stress.

Due to a flooding of the nervous system with stress hormones, fear causes a physical perception that is just as strong as the pain: muscles become tense, breath becomes shallow or short, blood circulation rushes, vision becomes rigid, blood vessels alter, the stomach and intestines feel cramped. If such a shock or fright is too intense for the nervous system, it derails the natural processing of information. The body remains in shock, even though the danger is long gone. One might describe it as phantom pain in the mind. Each emotion that becomes chronically independent is a "neuropathic emotion." Some examples of this are fear, rage, anger, grief, disgust, or shame. Then there are the opposite emotions: a lack of feeling, not being affected, which is often perceived as being a little confusing.

Since we are accustomed to the dissipation of negative emotions, the trapped emotions can cause a feeling of helplessness. Familiar conscious or subconscious processing possibilities, such as distraction, sports, or conversation, no longer fulfil their usual function of processing—the neurological integration process of our experiences and emotions. Perhaps you remember the term *emotion* holds the Latin word for movement: *motio*. This movement comes to a halt and manifests as post-traumatic stress disorder or stress imprinting. The emotion becomes rigid and, consequently, remains stuck.

In a case like this, even the old remedy of sleep fails to aid in processing these negative emotions. One often hears, "Just sleep on it for a night, and tomorrow everything will look completely different." Sleep and brain researchers agree that we process a large part of our experiences while dreaming. However, in the case of persistent stress imprinting, dreaming does not perform this processing function. Just like a CD with a scratch, the processing gets stuck at a particular spot and will not move any further. This dream blockage does not lead to a pleasant resolution, but rather to a tormenting nightmare, which frightens the affected person until he wakes.

Too little is known about the exact neurological effects of clinical trauma or PSI to make a universal statement. One can only pick up the individual pieces of the puzzle and fit them into the big picture. This includes the images of the brain functions of phobics, people who have strong chronic anxiety reactions associated with specific situations, objects or animals. These images show in bright colours the activities of the brain experiencing and consequently reacting to a phobia. In the movie titled *Phobia–The Naked Fear*, broadcast by Vox in BBC's exclusive series, you can see the remarkable corresponding images. They show that the amygdala (the brain's alarm bell) rings when individuals are shown pictures that every person would classify as stressful or frightening (such as a grotesque face from a horror movie).

Shortly after this presentation, however, the amygdala immediately switches off once again.

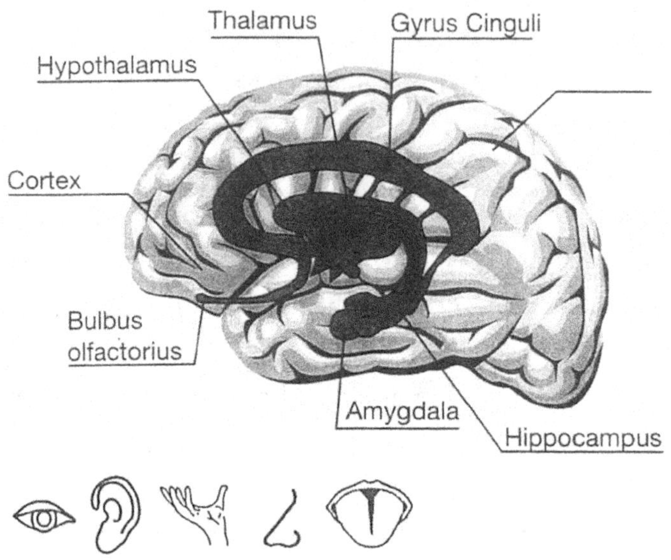

Illustration 7: Limbic System with the Hippocampus

However, if they are shown an image related to the subject of their phobia, the amygdala and the left hippocampus light up at the same time. The hippocampus is a part of the brain that is closely linked with our memory. Interestingly, this reservoir of memory remains virtually mute in the case of shocking images like a grotesque face. In contrast, the image of the phobia sets off the "alarm bell", and the memory of the feelings associated with the object re-surfaces. An overdose of stress hormones is then released.. This is aggravated by the fact that our sensory perceptions have to pass through the limbic system—our emotional brain—before they are transmitted to the cortex—our cognitive brain. This transmission takes from ½ to ¾ of a second. First and foremost, the thalamus assesses the new information against the background of our overall experiences and immediately informs the amygdala if it considers an incoming sensory stimulus as threatening or particularly important. Only then is the cerebral cortex informed.

That is why fear sets in from ½ to ¾ of a second earlier than the reasoning. And once the fear is triggered, it is close to impossible to have a clear mind to analyze the situation in a rational way. The Bremen-based brain researcher G. Roth states, "Unfortunately, because the amygdala passes on the signal to the cortex, the cortex either says nothing in return or something, but very reluctantly."

The limbic system, including amygdala, runs at full-speed when positive stimuli come in, for example, when you see a great pair of shoes (or some other object that you love) on sale that you cannot afford. The emotions dominate the assiduously warning mind. It gets lost in a sensual frenzy, and your credit card somehow wanders across the counter. Later, the cerebral cortex wonders to how this pair of shoes came to be in the shopping bag. It was switched on half of a second too late once again. Even the stock market fever functions according to the same principle.

The research results mentioned above are consistent with the findings in research studying severely traumatized people. For example, in the case of war veterans or people who have experienced violence or abuse, a significant reduction of the left hippocampus can be found vis-à-vis the non-traumatized person—as if this area has been exhausted over the years due to the permanent connection with the alarm bell system. Moreover, the clear mind seems to be of no benefit to a severely traumatized person: he continues to live in fear, although he knows perfectly well that he is no longer in danger.

We pass on this information to our coaching clients, but we distinguish their issues from the problems faced by the severely traumatized people. Nevertheless, this information explains and relieves the effects of PSI. If we look back a Karsten's example, he was relieved to know that it was normal that he could not solve his problem on his own through his own sheer willpower. Once he understood the process which had taken place in his brain, he could better understand how to find a solution.

This is an extremely important aspect of our work. For years, we have been cautiously dealing with sentences such as: "If you have the will, you can move mountains." This is like saying to an injured person, "You only have to] want it, and the bandage will wrap around the injury on its own," Or to a person lost in the forest, "You only have to want it, and you will find your way home" when a map or a compass would be more helpful. The emotions or stressors being imprinted and described here do not need therapy. They do, however, need a targeted coaching know-how, so the persons affected can effectively process the events that have occurred and overcome their situation.

Example:

Imagine for a moment that someone comes to you with the following request: "I noticed that a helicopter has landed in front of my car, but I need to drive away right now. Could you fly it away so that I can get out? The pilot is nowhere to be found, and I have to make an important telephone call." You could answer "do it yourself;" however, as a polite person, you reply: "I am sorry, but I don't know how to fly a helicopter." They then respond: "What a load of nonsense! You just need to *want* to do it!" In this context, you would be responding without the feeling of failure: "Wanting to do it is not the issue. I have simply not learned how to fly a helicopter. I do not know how it works. I lack the know-how."

In this example, you are not avoiding change or development due to a lack of willingness. The problem is simply that you don't have the skills and knowledge to fly the helicopter. The problem is not that you lack the will-power to fly the helicopter away. All the coachees who seek our advice want to solve their problems, otherwise they would not have made an appointment. Because know-how plays a leading role in every learning experience or change process, we commence each coaching session with a detailed description of the neurobiological model of this particular coaching tool.

For instance, we provided information to Karsten about the scientific studies on the subject of rejection and exclusion by fellow human beings. It has been established using brain scan images that experiences of this kind are accompanied by high activity in the pain center. Thus, rejection and exclusion really hurt—even at the neurobiological level. Externally, there is no injury, but internally, our nerve cells experience real pain. The term "it hurts" is, therefore, not a metaphor at all. In this context, it rather describes the experience somatically. These studies have led to the term: social pain.

Further studies show that even figures of speech such as he/she is "as cold as ice" or "warm-hearted" correspond to a neurobiological truth. Test subjects who were shown scenes depicting rejection or marginalization perceived the temperature to be colder than those assessed by the control subjects. Without this influence, and after the presentation, they almost always chose hot beverages to recover from the "coldness" shown in the movie.

Karsten responded very thoughtfully to this information: he was comfortable in his chair and appeared visibly relaxed. The information helped him better understand his issue and to classify it cognitively.

Note for coaches: The importance of methodical transparency and psychoeducation for successful coaching.

This terminology originated from classic behavioral therapy and means the inclusion of a human being in the theoretic models and considerations, which explains the meaning of psychologically substantiated intervention. This not only includes the explanation of the approach vis-à-vis a patient, a coachee, or a group of people, but also the comprehensible presentation of the model of further discussion, with which therapists, coaches, or trainers may explain their theories on the origination of these psychologically problematic knots and their solutions.

It is important to inform the coaching clients that the theoretical backgrounds of the procedures do not relate to the universally accepted scientific facts, but are only models which have proven their worth for positive change processes. Studies in behavioral therapies have shown that the corresponding content preparations not only ensure the methodical transparency, but also the positive expectations of people who have already turned these measures into further intervention. In his book, "Psychological Therapy", the behavioral therapy expert, now deceased, Klaus Grawe, stated that 30% of therapeutic success is dependent on the positive expectations of the patient, which is aroused triggered by an excellent content-based preparation by the therapist before conducting the therapy.

The clients being coached really appreciate it, especially when the coach can explain at any given time during the process just what is happening and which strategic considerations need to be used so the respective interventions can be applied. As part of their training, all wingwave coaches are given considerable illustrative material about the method in the form of PowerPoint presentations and informative texts, as well as numerous stories and metaphors, with which they are able to explain to their clients the theoretic considerations of wingwave coaching. For individual coaching, most of the coaches keep the printed copy of the material at hand and ready for their clients.

Here is an example:

Using wingwave, we were able to help a client who had, three weeks before our first session, survived a helicopter crash during a sightseeing trip over Hamburg. Fortunately, she and her friend survived the crash without any physical harm, but the young woman suffered from sleep disorders and panic attacks after this incident. We explained to her the neurobiological backgrounds of post-traumatic stress. We described the meaning and purpose of the planned application of the method, and then planned the actual wingwave intervention at a later appointment. She then informed us that after this preparatory conversation, she immediately started sleeping much better at night: "It was comforting to know what was actually wrong with me, as I was able to explain the sleep disorders to myself. It was the vivid images that allayed my fears that something unusual had happened to me, which I couldn't control."

Although the client still had panic feelings during the day, psychoeducation and methodical transparency elicited a positive effect in itself. The actual intervention four days later was successful and only lasted 1 hour and 30 minutes. This coaching was filmed and shown as part of a four-part television series on the topic of wingwave coaching.

Although this example is not about any classic coaching topic, it shows that methodical transparency and the explanation of problem and solution models has an expedient changing effect on the coaching clients.

2.5 PSI and the "Inner Sleeping Beauty's Castle"

The Brothers Grimm fairytale *Sleeping Beauty* is a wonderful metaphor for resistant stress imprinting. It has vibrant and flourishing landscapes with villages and cities, at the heart of which is an enchanted castle entwined in a thick, thorny hedge. Time stands still in this castle because an evil fairy has put it and its inhabitants into a one-hundred-year sleep. Everything remained exactly as it was when Sleeping Beauty injured herself by pricking her finger with the spindle belonging to the evil fairy. Even the cook, who was about to slap the kitchen boy's face for meddling with the soup, stood still with his hand raised in the air. The daily routine that had flowed before became an eternal still image. No processes and, consequently, no processing whatsoever could take place. Over decades, many princes attempted to penetrate the castle to reach Sleeping Beauty, but they were all caught in the thorns of the hedge surrounding the castle.

In the case of people with stress imprinting, this frozen castle stands for the landscape of the psyche or of those billions of interlinked brains cells. Life pulsates everywhere; it will act, react, and further develop—but not in this castle which has become a frozen in time. Most people with PSI are aware of their possibilities and talents—as long as they do not come into contact with their inner thorny hedge, which isolates the stressful experience. They can get stuck and become unable to progress any further. In coaching, this phenomenon is called the isolated blockage: everything is marvellously in order, except for that one thing.

In our metaphor of *Sleeping Beauty* if the awake REM phases take affect, the thorny hedge opens up and life returns to the castle. The processing of endogenous emotional healing begins and with it, consequently, a sense of creativity, sources of strength, and feeling returns to the person who had been inernally frozen in time. Through the intervention, the person can relax and allow healing to take place. There is, however, still the issue of the cook slapping the kitchen boy. When the spell is broken, he naturally carries this out immediately, and the kitchen boy cries out, "Ouch!" For a moment, put yourself in the place of the kitchen boy: would you prefer to stay frozen for decades and not move forward, or experience the brief pain of a slap and take part in life once again? This metaphor has become familiar in wingwave coaching as the "kitchen boy effect."

When working with our clients, we prepare them by using similar metaphors and analogies. This enables the wingwave coaching to be an emotional procedure. For this reason, we also use the term emotions coaching. A wide variety of emotions may emerge and vanish again in rapid succession. Often, feelings flow up and out of the body—these are the feelings that should have been processed during the specific stressful event. For an example a feeling of rage or revenge can take root after being insulted. If it subsides during an REM intervention, it may be followed by a feeling of sadness, a feeling that one has not felt before in light of the insult, but which also has a psycho-logic. Similar to the slap of the kitchen boy, the frozen emotion flows and hits the coachee during the intervention. Many coaching clients are extremely surprised by the variety of emotions and the rapid succession of the emotional experience that may occur during the process. The positive emotions which emerge at the end of the intervention can be just as intense: relief, joy, enthusiasm, or feelings of competence, strength or determination.

Are the oaches well prepared for the kitchen-boy phenomenon? Can they go through the feeling, and at the same time correctly categorize its importance at a mental meta-level? The surge of emotions has nothing to do with events in the present, they emerge for the erasure of the stress imprinting, which are signals from the past.

For a moment, compare this perception at the meta-level with an entirely normal hiccup. This is actually quite an intense physical sensation; you gasp for breath, utter uncontrolled sounds, and the torso is shaken by a spasm. In spite of this acute drama, people affected can usually both hiccup and laugh at this physiological phenomenon.

Our clients do not laugh, but they do keep calm while the body experiences the emotion in a super time-lapse. These intense spell can dissolve very quickly; it can take as little as a minute for each set of waves.

After the intervention, the feeling in the body is often perceived as very pleasant. Many people feel relieved and relaxed, but also tired or pleasantly exhausted. Some clients yawn more often. There is a metaphor for this as well: when you are carrying heavy shopping bags, you are able to tolerate the weight for as long as it takes to reach your apartment. You then put the bags down, drop into a chair, let arms and legs hang, take a few deep breaths, and say: "Phew, glad that's over!" At the same time, you sigh and say: "Oh dear, that was strenuous!"

It is only when the shopping bags are put down that you allow yourself to assess how exhausting it was. The same applies to emotional burdens, which one has just laid own. For this reason, we always advise our clients to take some time for themselves after the coaching sessions, if possible, to go to sleep early or just relax their mind by doing something pleasant.

The effects described here demonstrate that with each session, our clients grow more confident in using the method and begin to address more and more issues. These are issues that they did not wish to address before, as they were afraid of getting emotionally caught in the traumatic hedge of thorns. Once, a client came to their third coaching session with a small list: "I would like all of this waved away as well." This choice of words may alarm many experienced psychotherapists, as one cannot simply wave away stressful experiences. Careful preparation is required. This applies to the psychologically stable coaching clients, as well as to the clients with post-traumatic stress disorders. It is only with careful preparation that the frozen and tormenting emotions can be melted away using a simple-looking intervention–similar to the deliverance from the traumatic spell in "Sleeping Beauty."

The preparation before the wingwave intervention also includes the establishment of an inner safe place between the coach and coachee. We will describe these in detail in Chapter 4. An overview of individual phases of the process will be given in that chapter as well. In the following section, you will read a live-scene of how the awake REM phases are applied. First, you may be interested in a self-coaching exercise, and by using this you can prevent a "kitchen-boy effect" in the stresses of everyday living.

Self-coaching tip: Stress prevention through awake REM phases and by using the wingwave music

Under no circumstance should you have to wait to see if an everyday stress will be relieved on its own or whether it will result in a stress imprinting. If you are frightened, angry, or even injured, consciously try to avoid the kitchen-boy effect by making rapid eye movements immediately or listen to the wingwave music.

For example, if you bumped your elbow tripping or falling down while jogging, you will notice that you start moving your eyes rapidly. You collect your thoughts at lightning speed and are able to quickly process what just happened. As a result, you mitigate your pain memory, relaxing the entire musculature with ocular muscles and thereby facilitating better blood circulation. This indirectly provides the injured area with curative substances.

Think for a moment how people who have experienced something bad are portrayed in movies and on television: In close-up shots they always show the eyes bulging with fear and staring. The facial expression makes it abundantly clear that something surprising, unpleasant, stressful, or even disgusting has just happened or will happen. Just as the kitchen-boy stands paralysed with fear of the slap. Across cultures, humans interpret this look in a similar way. When in real life we react as these actors do, with bulging staring eyes, we become paralyzed. This short exercise of rapidly moving the eyes back and forth relieves of the paralysis and calms our emotional reaction to whatever just happened.

If your best customer shocks you with an entirely unsubstantiated accusation, you should not start with the intervention of awake eye movements, as that would seem ridiculous and would result in further complications. But when you are alone, perform a few sets of awake REM phases or put on your MP3 player headphones and go over that event a few more times, until you feel "in the flow" once again.

2.6 Coaching Unit: The Use of Awake REM Phases

After the appropriate introduction, we ask Karsten to think about the resignation situation with Sönke.

Coach: "When you remember this event, what is the worst and the most stressful moment for you today?"

Karsten: "I see Sönke sitting in front of me. Instead of telling me something about our tremendous success, he tells me that he is resigning. What disturbs me most is his friendly face, which does not suit the context of the message."

Coach: "How do you feel?"

Karsten: "Somehow betrayed and, above all, like an idiot."

Coach: "What and how would you prefer to think about yourself?"

Karsten: "I am competent, I am a professional, and I have done everything right. But that idiotic feeling is simply stronger."

Coach: "If we could rate sentences on a scale of one to seven on how believable they are, how would you rate this statement? For example, number 1 means: "Great sentence, but, unfortunately, I cannot believe it at all. It just does not correspond to my feeling." Number 7 indicates: "I strongly agree, this sentence is 100% true in the case to my self-assessment." At the present moment, how would you rate the sentence "I am competent" with regard to your memory with Sönke?"

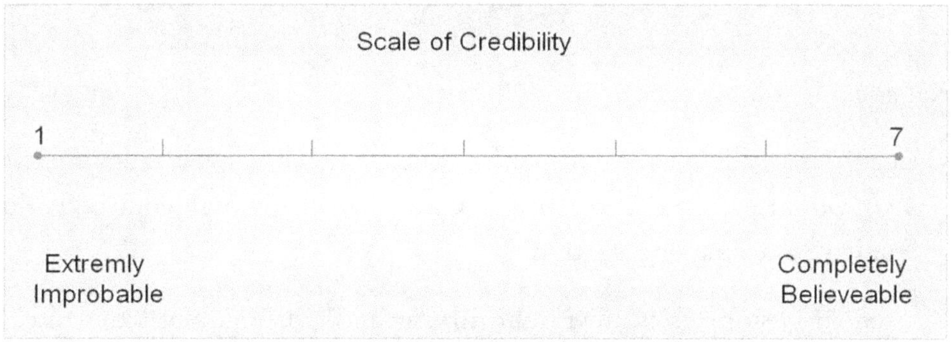

Illustration 8: Scale of Credibility

Karsten: "At 1, because, as I said, it does not reflect my emotional state at all."

Coach: "Now, please think about the stressful scene of resignation. Which emotion is center stage at the moment?"

Karsten: "I feel disappointed and humiliated."

Coach: "What is troubling you more?"

Karsten: "I feel ashamed that I invested so much in this person and was naive enough to have expected some special gratitude. That's the worst thing! Although the disappointment is there, it's not so much in the foreground as the feeling of pain."

Coach: "How strongly do you feel that your sense of well-being is affected now when you reflect on this scene? Please rate your subjective discomfort on a minus scale of 0 to -10."

<table>
<tr><td>Level of Subjective
Unease</td><td></td><td>Level of
Wellness</td></tr>
<tr><td>- 10</td><td>Neutral</td><td>+ 10</td></tr>
<tr><td>Strongest perceivable
Unease</td><td></td><td>Strongest Perceivable
Experience of Strenght
and Sense of Well-being</td></tr>
</table>

Illustration 9: Scale of Subjective Experience

Karsten: "It still bugs me a lot, I will say -8."

Coach: "Please allow your body to feel it exactly. We call this empathy the *body scan* or even the *search for the physical echo*. Where in your body do you have a feeling or sensation?"

Karsten: "My stomach is downright turning and twisting. Not like nausea, but more like a spasm. Just like a punch in the stomach."

It is only after this detailed exploration has been completed that the waving starts. The coach waves in front of the client, who accordingly follows the waving with his eyes in both directions, horizontally back and forth every second: half a second back, half a second forth. These induced rapid eye movements are similar to the REM patterns (Rapid Eye Movements) in the dream phase during sleep. The coachees must be well prepared for this waving. Initially, most of them have the feeling that the coach is waving too fast. There is good reason for this because most of the emotions, which we subjectively evaluate as unpleasant, involve a strong muscle tone to the eyes.

In the case of sad or depressed people, one can likewise see only minimal eye movements. However, low muscle tone is the reason for this. Using the waving technique, the muscle tone, which is too high must be relaxed, and the muscle tone which is too low must be revived. As a practitioner, one can clearly see that initially the client's eyes follow the finger movements abruptly and sluggishly, and that the corresponding movement becomes fluent only after prolonged waving. Accordingly, the finger movement must be fast enough to get the eye movement into motion, but slow enough that the client's eyes remain in contact with the beat of waving.

When we observe this flow, we stop the first sequence of waving after the first physiological change in the facial expression and body language of the coachee. What appears is a typical symptom for the transformation of the stress activation into a parasympathetic, relaxed physical activation. These could be: A deep breath, swallowing, a spontaneous change in the sitting position, a stomach sound, or even a laugh or a sudden idea that the person spontaneously expresses. EMDR therapists recommend performing approximately 20 back and forth movements in each set. We have, however, noticed that individual retrieval of their spontaneous reactions by various people leads to faster results. Some coachees exhibit the first physiological change in the desired direction after ten waving units, others, only after 30.

After the first aforementioned change of the sympathicotonic physical activation (stress, tension, vascular constriction) in the direction of parasympathicotonic activation, the first change check is discussed. Even Karsten suddenly took a deep breath. The coach lowered his hand.

Coach: "Think about the scene once again. Feel into your body. How do you feel now?"

Karsten: "My stomach is no longer cramped and feels much more relaxed."

Coach: "How do you feel now?"

Karsten: "Suddenly I am very peeved."

Coach: "How and where do you feel that?"

Karsten: "In my arms, especially in my hands." (He clenches his fists).

Coach: "Think about the scene once again and feel how your anger is located in your hands."

We further explain to the client that they can think of this as the stress scene, completely focusing on it as well as on the emotions and physical sensations associated therewith, only before and after the waving sequence. It is absolutely clear that the stress scene can be focused on less intensively during the waving process because the waving also works as a diversion.

After another sequence of 20 waving movements, Karsten took a deep breath. Now, we can verbally assess the interim status once again.

Coach: "Please make again the bodyscan: what now do you feel?"

Karsten: "The anger is completely gone. At the same time, this sentence is going through my head: 'Don't reveal your true feelings!'"

Coach: "How does it feel if you don't reveal anything?"

Karsten: "It is as if the body temperature has dropped."

Coach: "And where in your body do you feel particularly cold?"

Karsten: "In the stomach."

Coach: "Stay with the sentence, 'don't reveal your true feelings.' Think about the scene and feel the 'coolness' in your stomach."

At this point, the process appears to be repeating itself and is stuck in a phenomenon called the loop. From set to set, Karsten'perceptions always swing back and forth between anger and keeping cool. At this point, the coach moves on to verbal intervention.

Coach: "Why can't you let your feelings show?"

Karsten: "That is simply self-pity!"

Coach: "What is wrong with that? Don't you believe that anyone in your situation would have been affected?"

Karsten: "You think so? But one should not have self-pity!"

Coach: "And if it is fully justified and appropriate? Think about our conversation once again concerning rejection, social pain, and social exclusion. After all, you are not angry because your tie has fewer polka dots. In that case, self-pity would indeed be ridiculous. You just felt extremely hurt because of your personal commitment to Sönke and, for that matter, you had absolutely normal and completely honest feelings."

Karsten had to slightly smile at the word honest. The coach continues further: "Why should a person not be allowed to observe such a thing? Think about it for a moment, and follow the movement of the finger." This is followed by another set.

It is apparent that the coaching process does not only consist of waving. The above-mentioned waving sequence, which lasted only 30 seconds, is called cognitive interweaving. In a brief verbal intervention, the coach selectively adds a broadening perspective to the perceptual world of the client and consequently expands his scope of evaluation. Apparently, Karsten had a personal belief that might read: "A professional must not show any feelings." The coach does not initiate any conscious discussion on belief, rather only offers a new thought or idea, which opens the mental boundaries. If the remark makes the client contemplate, the waving is immediately continued further. This accelerates the integration of the new information in the processing.

During an introduction, the client is prepared and made aware that the coach will speak as little as possible during the process and that even in the case of a verbal sequence, the waving will continue as quickly as possible. The technique of cognitive interweaving requires a coach to possess high competence in the recognition of resource-inhibitive beliefs and in the formulation of permissive and ego-strengthening beliefs and doctrines. Since this part of the coaching work is so immensely important for the activation of resources in the subjective experience of a person, we have dedicated an extra chapter to this topic later in the book: "Belief Coaching: The constructive handling of beliefs."

But let us get back to Karsten: In the middle of this waving set, suddenly, he looks like someone who has had a surprising inspiration. He makes the stop sign, and the coach stops the waving. In the introduction, the raised hand is usually agreed upon as the stop sign. In addition, we agree upon yet another signal to continue the waving because a lot of coaching clients, who are familiar with the method, intuitively feel how much "waving energy" they require to get over an important point or to sufficiently increase their sense of wellbeing.

Coach: "What now do you feel?"

Karsten: "I simply tell him."

Coach: "What do you mean by that?"

Karsten: "In my thoughts just now, I calmly told him to his face: 'Sönke, of course, you have every right to resign, but for me, at the moment, it is quite a blow. I need some time to think about it first. Therefore, I would rather like to continue this conversation tomorrow, when I am calmer.'"

Coach (enters the 'film'): "And how does he react to it?"

Karsten (laughs): "That smirk finally disappears and now the situation is embarrassing for him."

Coach: "How do you feel now, when you think at this kind of performance?"

Karsten: "Relieved."

Coach: "Where in the body do you feel the relief most clearly?"

Karsten: "In the shoulders and most of all in the ribcage. I can now breathe deeply."

Karsten sat upright and expanded his chest. Thereby, we twice heard a soft crackling sound of the blockages being released in the neck and back area. We will discuss this phenomenon of the liberating physical responses in greater detail later.

Coach: "Feel this pleasant feeling and follow the movement of the finger again."

This is followed by another set, in which the coach is now waving very slowly. It has become apparent that because of the slow eye movement, the pleasant physical perception is increased. We can explain the varying use of the fast and slow waving speed with the following thoughts: By waving as fast as possible, we flush the traces of stress and then disperse them; by waving slowly, we would like to interweave positive feelings in the landscape of the soul and intensify them there.

It has become apparent that the application of awake REM phases leads every subjective state of mind toward a positive and pleasant experience. This applies not only to the unpleasant, but also to the pleasant physical and mental states, which can be significantly strengthened by means of intervention. Thus, the intensity of complacency can be rated with +2 on the scale, which then increases to +6 or +7 by means of slow "pleasure waving."

Karsten: "That positive feeling is now flowing throughout the body."

Coach: "Please think about the situation once again. How is it now?"

Karsten: "The positive feeling is there and, suddenly, I am thinking quite differently about Sönke." (Calmly, he looks at the recollected scene with the facial expression of a musing observer).

Coach: "Can you express that in words?"

Karsten: "Suddenly I can empathize with Sönke, and I believe that Sönke was not at all cool, but simply insecure. It was certainly uncomfortable for him to tell me that he was leaving. Instead of showing it, he blurted out the news in a nonchalant manner. He just behaved clumsily; well, he is still quite young. Now the whole scene is not bothering me anymore."

At this stage, Karsten has reached exactly that emotional level which he had consistently wished for in the preceding weeks. He wanted to react to the situation in what he felt should be the mature way, the way that an experienced executive would react, not as a self-pitying snowflake. But this wish, controlled by the mind, did not find its way into Karsten's emotions. Only the coaching intervention provided a perceptible connectivity between the desire and emotion and/or between the cortex and the limbic system. The amygdala now behaves calmly and when Karsten thinks about the scene with Sönke, alarm bells are not ringing anymore. He can now creatively work on his own initiative using his entire brain.

It is interesting that by restoring his emotional flow, Karsten has subconsciously and intuitively chosen a different emotional way as the painless solution to the problem. In this case, he has established contact to his feelings and used his mirror neurons to overcome his own interpersonal problem.

The term 'mirror neurons' refers to the brain cells which become active in human beings when we put ourselves in the emotional place of another person. Brain scans were performed on people who had to watch how a person close to them was pricked with a needle. They not only winced briefly, but the pain center of their brain lit up as well. The mirror neurons became active in this region. They reported a pain due to an injury, which the brain's owner did not have to suffer at all. In his book, *Warum ich fühle, was du fühlst (Why I Feel What You Feel),* the German neuroscientist Joachim Bauer describes how we are constantly cross-linked through our mirror neurons in the systemic contact with our fellow human beings. Karstens approach also led through this systemic cross-linking.

Coach: "Now, think about the scene once again and, at the same time, envision the sentence: 'I am competent.' To what extent can you believe this sentence now?"

Karsten: "It feels correct now. I feel like a professional once again. I could further add to the sentence: 'I can competently deal with my feelings.' What's more, there is also this thought: 'My feelings are OK!', which I find important as well."

Coach: "What effect does this sentence have: 'I am an idiot'?"

Karsten: "It is completely false, it is not correct at all."

In the coaching process, we no longer remember the original negative cognition. Even in conclusion, we avoid the initial negative sentence and focus Karsten's attention on the strength of the positive sentence. Karsten appears relieved and confident now that the coach brought the first sentence back into play as a test.

But why do we prefer to allow the statement with negative cognition to fall into oblivion? In wingwave coaching we take into consideration the important fundamentals arising from neurolinguistic coaching, which, among other things, is about the brain-friendly dealings with the language. Here is a simple example: "Dear reader, please do <u>not</u> think of a crocodile now!" What happens? Of course, the crocodile appears in your mind's eye.

Illustration 10: Crocodile

The brain promptly responds to words and ignores negations such as "no" or "not." Therefore, the choice of words is particularly important in wingwave coaching. We consciously use words to anchor in the desired target state and speak of optimal formulation of goals. A goal should be formulated in such a manner that it can be realized by the person using his own abilities. In other words, it should be realistic. An example of apoorly constructed goal might be, "I must be able to learn Chinese or French in two weeks." Ultimately, the sense of disappointment and failure would be pre-programmed no matter how diligently a person could learn. Likewise, just wishing that "my superior would be nicer to me" is of little use. More helpful is the question: "How can I think, act, and feel differently myself, so that the probability of motivating him to become more friendly increases?"

After this glimpse into the world of the optimal formulation of goals, here is the closing scene of the coaching with Karsten.

Coach: "Finally, think about the original scene once again, visualize it with all of your senses. Earlier, your assessment stood on the minus side of the scale at -8. How do you feel now when you think about the scene?"

Karsten: "Neutral, therefore at 0. But if I think about it further, I feel actually quite good about the situation and thus at a rating of +2. Sönke has actually learned a lot from me, and I can also be proud of that. I am actually a good coach, I think."

In his enthusiasm, Karsten slapped the back of the chair with the palm of his hand. He seemed very animated. This positive effect was reinforced by yet another set as Karsten thought about the scene in the context of the sentence "I am competent." We refer to the positive area of the state of mind as the "scale of wellness." Sometimes, additional waving sets can bring about yet another intensification of an overall positive state.

The intervention described here lasted 45 minutes and the introduction prior to that, just as long. Along with the debriefing, we took almost two hours. Karsten had already achieved his goal with this session. He once again felt motivated and resourceful and was finally able to deal with his employees frankly and humorously.

It is important to note that Karsten's stress reaction was not solely caused by the disappointing experience with the young employee. It was also related to the preceding stress at work that he had had for days and even weeks before the employee's resignation. Performance stress does not make you strong, but sensitive. We will discuss this in Chapter 5.2. Before that, we will discuss how to get acquainted with further details of the wingwave method.

2.7 What are the Effects of Waving?

During the application of the awake REM phases, the coaching process takes place with very little content-related suggestions from the coach. An exception is cognitive interweaving, during which the coach expands or resolves the beliefs which restrict personality development and quality of life, with the aid of mental inspirations. In the case of Karsten, it was the subconscious law: "I may not have any self-pity." This sentence will remind many readers of statements such as: "No pain, no gain" or "Big boys don't cry", these attitudes, in the case of social pain, have an inhibiting effect on self-acceptance and consequently on internal processing.

All other processes are based on the client's creativity, which has been activated through intervention. For instance, in Karsten's process, the coach would not say: "What could you have said to Sönke in this situation?" The idea of a target-oriented dialogue evolves from Karsten's existing pool of ideas for the solution to the problem. For this reason, in our opinion, this approach belongs to the humanistic personality model, which correspondingly works on the following assumption: "Every person possesses his own resources, which enable him to achieve his goals – they just need to be activated." The mental energies released by the awake REM activation can manifest themselves in a variety of effects, which are not suggested by the coach, but which the coachee develops on his own. They happen in processing and occur suddenly—often to the surprise of the client. It can be likened to a movie playing in your head. One of our clients made reference to this phenomenon when he stated, "I sit in the front row and admire my own personal development."

2.7.1 Memory Fades

In the case of PSI, almost everyone affected suffers from perennially occurring internal images of mortifying or threatening memories or futuristic fantasies. It often translates to, "I cannot get it out of my head" or, "I cannot get rid of it." The technical term for this phenomenon is "intrinsic image" or "intrinsic imaginative experience." The images throng on to the screen of mental consciousness and because the person affected is unable to exercise control over them, the individual feels at their mercy. The power of these images arises through their quality: they are clear, close, predominantly coloured, and loud. Often these are not even images, but three-dimensional inner representations. Due to the intensity of the internal image quality, the brain acts as if the scene is not a memory or a playful imagination, but an event that happened today and one which will inevitably happen again (one example is, the image of oneself homeless under the bridge, resulting as a fear of being unsuccessful).

Waving results in the following changes—often in a matter of seconds:

- The image becomes pale and one-dimensional
- The imagined scene flickers or wobbles by fading-out or fading-in
- Many coachees are no longer able to produce the previously threatening images after one or two sets of waving
- The image moves away for the person, so that it is only vaguely remembered
- The entire scene gets smaller
- The voices, sounds, and noises of loud images soften or become silent

In neurolinguistic programming (NLP), one speaks of the change of submodalities. There are sensory modalities, such as seeing, hearing, feeling, smelling, and tasting. Each senseory modality has its respective miscellaneous qualities of representation, for example, sight, which is characterized as colored or black and white, high-contrast or blurred, small image or large image, dark or light, etc. To some extent, you can compare these visual submodalities with a television and its remote control: just by clicking a few buttons, you can change the setting. The same applies to the other sensory channels. With the auditory sensory channel, for example, you can play with the submodalities of sounds sounds and noises in your head. You can make a sound or voice in your head become louder or softer, higher or lower in pitch, faster or slower in tempo, etc. If an accident has left stress imprinting, often the sounds—for example screeching brakes—is still left ringing in the ears. It is a huge relief and a pleasant feeling when these memories either soften or fall completely silent.

Many NLP interventions work with the conscious change of submodalities. "For a moment, try to take the colour out of the image." "Make it a two-dimensional representation and project it onto a screen." These methods are extremely effective on the subjective experience. It is amazing that under the influence of the awake REM phase, the coachees perform a work of submodalities with themselves without any further psychological guidance and without any theoretical know-how. They hold within themselves this wisdom to change and they unlock this potential with conducive brain activation on their own.

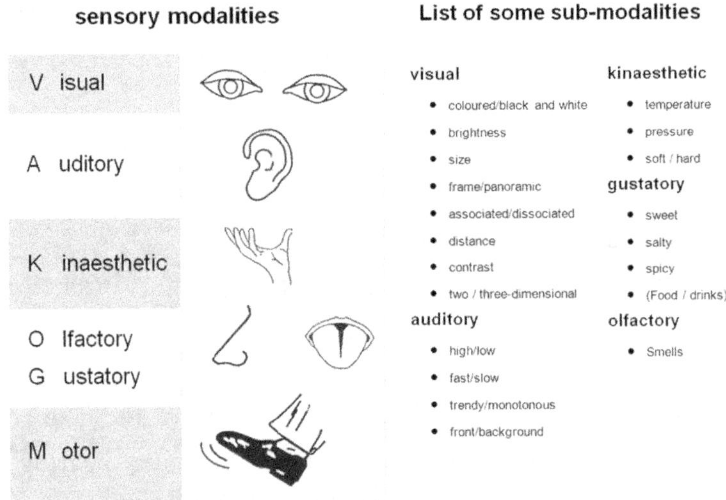

Illustration 11: Modalities and Submodalities

By changing these settings in the truest sense of the word, the waved person quickly gets his sense of time back. Many formulate sentences, such as: "I'm over it now" or, "It's a thing of the past now." Some suddenly start thinking about today as tomorrow and sometimes about completely trivial things: one client said, "It just occurred to me that I need to buy bread later." He then added, "Why am I thinking of such a thing now?" It seems that time, which had stood still for him for so long, had begun to flow again. His mental energy can deal with life again in the here and now.

2.7.2 Changing History or Redesigning the Experienced Content

During this technique the recollected scene develops a new psychodynamic with regard to its content by continuing to play the sequence of the experience or by simulating it afresh. For example, Karsten imagined how he could give a satisfactory reply to Sönke. Other clients describe that they turn around suddenly and leave the situation, or that instead of getting affected by it, they react calmly or even humorously. Sometimes, it's violent: "I just want to smash the swine right in the face!" Such fantasies do not change the fact that the real experience has taken place in its original version. However, one is able to suddenly imagine the behavioral alternatives, which were not available in the original scene because of internal blockages or restrictive beliefs.

The abolished blockage now frees up resources in the imagination which can be used spontaneously in a similar situation later on. Even Karsten reported in the next session that it is easier for him to now show his personal dismay in an appropriate manner when a counterpart exceeds his emotional boundaries.

The example of aggressiveness mentioned above ("punching the swine in the face") has rarely anything to do with real physical aggression. It is rather that such imagined scenes symbolize the change in fatal subconscious beliefs, such as, "I may not be able to defend myself" or "it's my fault this happened to me." New beliefs could be formed "I am worthy of being treated well." The behavioral outcome can be a completely new perception in the area of verbal communication.

2.7.3 The Daydream Symbolism

Similar to the case of change history, the memory of the stress-imprinting scene is interwoven with new psychological moments of experiences. However, these are unreal fantasy elements, as one only knows them from the realm of dreams. They always have a corresponding symbolic character. For example, a client started to expand her imagination and looked down at her surroundings from high above, seeing that the persons facing her reacted with fear and intimidation. Her spontaneous comment was "now I feel that I am able to cope with such people." Likewise, people can transform into animals, or suddenly it starts raining pink confetti, or the eagerly anticipated tournament cup suddenly floats from an attainable distance and hovers over the athletes in a close-up shot. These phenomena conspicuously remind us of the real dream phase and are accompanied by rapid eye movements. The awake REM phases effectuate a similar processing mode in the brain as in the case of insightful and processed dreams. This analogy applies to the internal world of visual experiences.

2.7.4 Relieving Physical Reactions

Stressful memories have an adverse impairing effect because you feel unpleasantly impacted when they appear on the screen of your consciousness. In EMDR and in wingwave coaching, the physical center of the negative feeling or sensation is explicitly requested. Clients are even requested to thoroughly check the body for an unpleasant feeling when recollecting a problematic memory. Karsten described his impairment as a cramping feeling in the stomach. Others describe pressure on the chest or shoulders, feelings of weakness in the legs or arms, or phenomena such as sweating and feeling hot or cold. The descriptions are always subjective.

With waving, it is not only the internal images but also the unpleasant physical sensations or feelings that fade away. This comes with an exceptional feeling of relief. Interestingly, the paraesthesia could wiggle around in our body for some time before disappearing completely. In the case of one female client, an unpleasant stomach feeling shifted ten centimetres higher during each waving set. Finally, some pressure was felt in the throat and during the last waving set, she had to yawn a few times, which cleared the throat. This particular client invented a term for this: body spook. "Spooky because everything happens so unbelievably fast. Had I not experienced it in my own body, I would not have believed it."

Due to the specific sensations and feelings, we can experience this kind of emotion coaching as a body therapy whereby the body itself becomes a success barometer in this scenario. The recollection of a memory or thoughts of a future scenario can only be overcome and processed when the nervous system, muscles, and organs feel well and healthy again. Due to this experience, many coaching clients often book a waving set with the aim of increasing physical complacency. This is because even positive feelings and sensations can be further intensified with waving. The feeling of lightness is further enhanced and a sense of power flows strongly after one set of waving. Such an intervention is an activation of resources in coaching.

2.7.5 The Frog Prince Phenomenon

You might remember that with Karsten we heard a soft crackling sound at the end of the coaching session as he straightened up his neck, shoulders, and back. Such auditory and perceptible clearance of blockages in the joints frequently occurs during an emotions' coaching session with awake REM phases due to changes in posture. However, unlike physiotherapy, clients are not encouraged to do this. Instead they are encouraged to respond to the pleasant mental energy intuitively, which often manifests as an impulse to move the body. A fairy tale by the Brothers Grimm wonderfully describes how the relief from a psychological trauma can be connected with an audible clearance of blockages.

In "The Frog Prince", a witch transforms a prince into an ugly frog. The servant of the young prince, the loyal Henry, places "three iron bands" around his heart to prevent it from "breaking through grief and sorrow." After the prince is released from the spell, Henry picks up the transformed prince and his wife, a beautiful princess, in a magnificent carriage. The prince hears a cracking sound and shouts: "Henry, the carriage is breaking apart," whereupon Henry replies:

"No, my lord, the carriage it's not,
but one of the bands surrounding my heart,
that suffered such great pain,
when you were sitting in the well,
when you were a frog."

These words speak for themselves. Incidentally, the Frog Prince has also become a metaphor of neurolinguistic programming. "Frogs into Princes" is the original title (in German: "Neue Wege der Kurzzeit-Therapie [New ways of short-term therapy]") and is the most famous standard reference work of the NLP founders Richard Bandler and John Grinder.

Illustration 12: The Frog Prince

2.7.6 Effects in Everyday Life

Most clients, particularly during coaching, feel free and relaxed after successful emotions' management—as demonstrated by Karsten. This relates not only to the specific issue in question, but also to their general health, as every de-stressing process relieves the nervous system and enhances the feeling of well-being. Clients also describe that they feel exhausted in a pleasant way. Some clients have to repeatedly yawn for a few more hours after the intervention or feel the need to breathe deeply.

Even a light trance phenomenon can occur because the synapses in the brain are spreading the word, so to speak, as the stress imprinting disappears from the physical body. Incidentally, the brain needs four to six weeks for the change to arrive into each cell. We request that our clients allow daydreaming as often as possible, for example, not to read a newspaper while waiting in an airport departure lounge, but to let their eyes wander and allow their thoughts to survey the scene. Today, although we know that our brain stores the imprints mainly at night, light daydreams and states of trances are also minor storage processes.

Physiologically considered, spontaneous everyday trances are states that are similar to a specifically applied hypnosis. However, there is a difference: Hypnosis is planned. Because of optimal brain activation, hypnosis is used for positive suggestions, pain and stress relief, the planning of successful future events, memory activation, and for creative processes. We pass on this knowledge as well, so that the coaching clients, who are too busy most of the time, can indulge in everyday trances with a clear conscience.

Many clients also report vivid dreams after such a session, which is the sign of a subconscious continuation of the creative problem-solving process that has been triggered into motion by the intervention. One can compare this phenomenon using an example of an over-sized email, which, owing to the complex amount of data it contains, gets stuck on the server. Often, further events occur in life, which thematically fit into the memory that has been processed. These can be processed additionally so that the trace of a stressful memory calms down comprehensively. Translated into the realms of psyche and depending on the types of emotions, one can remember memories of being generally anxious, angry, disgusted, or hurt, and these can be released during intervention. However, we will discuss the importance of emotional past experiences in more detail later.

Self-coaching tip: Open the stress window with eye movements

You can gain from the de-stressing effect of the relaxed eye movements at all times by simply using them for general relaxation. Whenever you are sitting idly–in a supermarket queue, at a traffic light–let your eyes consciously move a little bit. This stimulates and relaxes six muscle pairs, which control our eyeballs and thus, our vision. In civilized everyday life, our vision is sentenced to freeze all too often: when reading, watching television, or looking at the PC monitor.

This constriction of vision to the monitor is strongly reminiscent of the so-called stress window given in pilots' language. Here, the compact arrangement of action symbols and windows have an important function in an emergency situation. Even in the case of experienced pilots, an emergency situation can trigger stress and lead to tunnel vision: The vivacity of vision is lost, the pilot stares in front of him, and is thus restricted in his capacity to only find and operate the most important switches and levers for a smooth landing. That is why these are arranged in a small area centrally within the field of vision. No important switch is installed, for example, on the side of the seat, or right on top of the console, because a stressed person's field of vision has a limited radius.

After the eye movements, keep your eyes open as if you were daydreaming and let them take a rest. Gently look into the distance and, while doing so, defocus your vision. You will now notice that you have a very wide field of vision and can observe the periphery quite a long way to the left and right without any eye movements. Therefore, this daydream look is also referred to as peripheral vision, to which even your fellow human beings subconsciously respond in an extremely positive manner.

Let your eyes rest completely detached from eye contact and observe the entire peripheral frame, which surrounds the person opposite you. Your conversation partner will experience being looked at in this manner as friendly, interested and warm. Alternatively, it has been found in experiments that a fixed, stressful gaze can trigger tensions or even anxious feelings in the person with who you are speaking. Hence, the relaxed look also helps in facilitating a pleasant atmosphere when communicating.

Thus, the detached and the lively look make you pleasantly awake, relaxed, and also increase the radius of perception and open other possible stress windows for you. It automatically has a relieving and calming effect. In addition, focused eye movement is mental refreshment while sitting at your desk. If vision is in flow, thoughts, feelings, and conversations will start to flow again optimally.

2.8 Why do Awake REM Phases Work?

There are several theories on the working principles of the awake REM phases, all of which have still not been conclusively proven to date. Some observers assume the long-known principle of desensitization. In his thoughts, the client exposes himself to a stressful memory or imagination, and thus to an aversive and unpleasant stimuli. According to theory, the simultaneously performed eye movements distract from the thoughts and thus cause an unlearning—the memory is increasingly linked to neutral emotions and feelings.

In the case of classic desensitization process, the confrontation with the unpleasant stimulus is usually combined with a previously learned relaxation technique. However, as experienced therapists, we–like many of our colleagues–are able to report that although this pure confrontation, in conjunction with an additional, neutral task can bring about relieving effects, it is no match for the effectively relieving EMDR and wingwave process. Actual relief only takes place when rapid eye movements or other forms of stimulation of the sensory channels rapidly alternating between the left and the right are applied. We will discuss other forms of bilateral stimulation in detail shortly.

In the case of classic desensitization interventions without the use of bilateral stimulation, it often happens that clients do not find any relief at all through repeated confrontation. They are consistently affected by their painful memory or stressful situation over and over again. Even repeated narration of a stressful memory does not help and it is felt by many clients who are suffering with disturbing stress imprinting as painful or can also bring the trauma back. Effects such as the creative ideas of the treated persons or spontaneously relieving physical experiences occur at a reliable frequency, and their intensive effects only appear with the application of the awake REM phases or a comparable process.

Interestingly, the effects described above occur not only by waving, but also with an auditory input of a comparable kind. For example, if you make a snapping sound in sync with the original rhythm close to the left and right ears of the client, they will oftem experience a similar positive result as with eye movements. The same applies to tactile stimuli: alternate tapping on the left and right shoulders or the left and right palms. Many EMDR and wingwave practitioners try it out with their clients to find out on which sensory channel intervention is most effective. The EMDR founder, Francine Shapiro and many neuroscientists, such as Bessel van der Kolk, believe that the awake REM phases act as "bilateral stimulations", and thus accomplish optimal cooperation of the right and left-brain hemispheres. It results in sweeping activation of neuronal networking, which releases an intensive mental remedial and healing process on the basis of the existing resources of the client.

During a dream-sleep-phase, the brain integrates our experiences of the day in its large memory, this process is always accompanied by rapid eye movements and this rapid ocular motor function belongs to the successful processing and storage of our neurobiological data. The eyes are naturally attached to the brain so eye stimulation is always our first choice of sensory stimulation. In our experience the processes take place rapidly, intensively, and lead to the desired goal.

Even sleep research shows that from the eye movement patterns, you can determine a person's ability to concentrate and their reaction speed. If the mental capabilities slow down due to excessive tiredness, a person can only move his eyes with a jerk and can no longer move them smoothly. The importance of this knowledge is discussed in regard to the driving safety of motorists and professional drivers. The development of assistance systems is being considered, which would sensitively measures the eye movements of the driver and switch to a warning function if the movement pattern becomes slow and jerky to avoid the dangers of nodding off.

The very core of the bilateral hemispheric stimulations, such as the awake REM phase, is non-verbal. The path to change leads across rhythmic, bilateral sensory experiences and eyes move left and right alternating auditory or tactile stimulations. As a result of this intervention, the neural pathways re-awaken, which ensure communication between the right and left-brain hemispheres function, and thus restore the full performance capacity of the brain. The processing blockage is remedied and the new experiences can be smoothly uploaded to the cerebrum by the limbic system. If mental strengths are fully and holistically reactivated, the brain can find its own creative solutions within the sense of healing information processing of the memory that is blocked and stuck in the nervous system.

This restored connectivity remains effective even when the client deals with their experiences on their own later on. If the emotional blockages can be removed in the coaching or therapy sessions once, the client can consistently work his way out of the emotional traces of his experiences using his own neural strengths.

With these statements, we would like to recall that as human beings, we enjoy this relieving and sustaining effect often, without paying much attention to it. Throughout the course of our lives, we are reliably removing innumerable traces of stress during our night-time sleep over and over again. It is only in individual cases that night-time dreams are not sufficient on their own to overcome stressful emotions. These then become stress imprintings: One of our clients described his subjective experience as "a thorn in the flesh." He was simply unable to cope with the fact that after months of preparation, he had lost an important golf tournament to a particular opponent two years ago. Significantly the night-time sleep can be disturbed because the affected persons become stuck in the processing of their dreams and wake up with a blocking feeling. "I dream of this experience over and over again," reported our coachee. "Most of the time, I feel paralysed and am unable to move the golf club." In this case, the emotional hurdle could only be overcome by means of bilateral stimulation in the awake state.

There are still questions surrounding bilateral interventions and whether the ocular motor function in the awake state can help relieve phantom pains. The method seems to induce the corresponding nerves to unlearn the chronic transmission of a feeling of pain and to switch back to the transmission of pleasant or neutral physical sensations. Perhaps EMDR and wingwave likewise have an unlearning effect on the neurons, which chronically maintain emotions such as fear, anger, or shame.

However, the many open questions are no reason to refrain from the application of the methods. The positive effect seems to us as a fully sufficient motive for the application, and one thing seems to be certain: EMDR and wingwave are effective. They allow us to communicate directly with the amygdala, the brain's alarm bell and to sustainably induce it to calm itself down.

Self-coaching tip: The "Butterfly Technique"

To apply bilateral stimulation yourself as a method of relaxation, you will need to have familiarized yourself with the eye movements and the use of wingwave music. As the tactile method for the emotional channel, we recommend the butterfly technique, which you can apply while lying down or in a comfortable sitting position.

Cross your forearms above your shoulders so that your fingertips are touching both your shoulders. You can touch your shoulders with the palms of your hands or fingertips with an alternating gentle tap synchronized with the rhythm of waving, thus achieving the desired neural stimulation effect.

In addition to tactile stimulation, an auditory input also takes place since the tapping naturally entails sounds alternating between the left and right ears. Interestingly, it is children who particularly like to use this method. It helps in falling asleep and in calming them down before class tests.

Incidentally, for children and adults, the butterfly technique is an excellent sedative carried out shortly before a dental treatment. It can be applied on the dental chair prior to the treatment. Feel it in your body, perceive your body echo while thinking about the treatment and after 30 seconds, a perceptibly deeper breath occurs – without any conscious assistance. Continue to tap gently and register the pleasant calming of emotions.

2.9 "Find One's Voice Again" by Using Bilateral Hemispheric Stimulation

The theory of bilateral hemispheric stimulation is supported by the unique images of the actively functioning brain. The images, which were shown in a report broadcast by the TV network "ARTE" on the topic of EMDR[4], were recorded during the night-time sleep of people severely traumatized by nightmares. People affected, such as war veterans, wake up due to the overwhelming experiences of fear and anxiety and feel themselves being emotionally catapulted back into a past traumatic experience. In trauma therapy, this is referred to as a flashback.

Brain scans demonstrate areas in the brain in which the brain cell networks are currently active. Activities in both brain hemispheres are displayed in different coloured energy centers. The above-mentioned images of the severely traumatized persons clearly show that in the flashback experience the left cerebral hemisphere and, in this case, particularly the speech center, seem as though they have been switched off—showing no kind of activity at all. Alternatively, the right hemisphere of the brain displays high activity, as if the remembered experience is being acted out in images and emotions. A stressful flashback experience seems to literally leave a person speechless. Figures of speach on this topic include: "lost for words", "jaw dropping" and, "has the cat got your tongue?" which is an expression sometimes used with shy children who do not, or cannot speak. Incidentally, children often react to traumatic memories with chronic speech disorders such as stuttering or, in severe cases, becoming mute.

This observation is of particular importance because we use language not only to communicate with other people, but for our self-management as well. Every day, thousands of thoughts go through our head where we comment on our experiences, plans, and sensitivities: "Oh, it's already seven o'clock, I have to get up now"; or we might ask ourselves: "What should I wear today?" These subconscious inner linguistic processes are called

---

[4] Das Ende der Angst [The end of fear]" by Sonja Hachenberger. arte, June 09, 2011.

automatic thoughts. They are also used to process the sensory impressions of the day: "What was that rustling sound I heard? Gosh! I was startled. Oh, that was just a little bird in the bushes–completely harmless." Thus, we use automatic thoughts to consistently moderate our experiences and consequently, our feelings. It is only this interpersonal linguistic moderation that ensures the fear is relieved.

If required, we transfer the knowledge acquired in our thoughts through conversation, reading, or contemplation, which is accessible to us by means of inner speech. When a war veteran goes to bed at night, he can tell himself: "Everything is alright. I am at home now, the war happened many years ago." However, at night, this linguistic self-calming effect no longer works because of the speech center being temporarily unavailable. Even the other regulative capabilities of this now-switched-off cerebral hemisphere, such as analysing, thinking in numbers, the categorization of experiences in the internal course of time, are no longer able to repress the internal impression. The emotional experiences and the images overwhelm the psyche, and cannot be sorted by either speech or by any other system of thought. It is as though the unpleasant emotions spread out unhindered, like a genie out of the bottle when nobody knows the magic spell that will coerce him back and trap him again.

The above-mentioned results were very thought provoking for us and for many of our colleagues although the psychology is deemed to be a bastion of speech; "It's good that we have talked about it" has become a common phrase and, "Just get it off your chest, you will feel better" is considered the generally accepted remedy for the psychological mind.

In the 1980s and 1990s, practitioners were very well intentioned when we were overlooking the fears and anxieties of our clients who claimed to have a fear of speaking they wanted to overcome, or those who were afraid they might have to relive a nightmare once again. We experts simply knew what was better and guided them to speak out. But what if, in the case of post-traumatic stress and/or stress imprinting, the results of them opening up do not relieve the stress at all, in spite of the logic and good intentions? What if, in the case of this particular psychological disorder caused by stress imprinting, the networking between the speech center and the processing of emotions is blocked? In such a case, it could be absolutely true that in individual cases, conversations simply reactivate the old feelings, instead of pleasantly integrating them, and that the instinct of many people to be left alone is not so wrong intuitively as psychotherapists had previously thought.

Note for the coaches: The client-oriented approach to language and body language

Just because people can be lost for words in moments of stress, a sensitive approach with carefully chosen words from the coaches has proven its worth in the intervention process. During processing, we work only using the words chosen by our clients. The coach avoids his own analysis, interpretations, or formulation of sentences and instead repeats the wording of the client during the process. Questions are kept as open as possible: "What is happening now?"; "what are you feeling now?" The coachee then replies: "I can feel my stomach rumbling!" The coach's reply is significant: "Aha, it's rumbling. Feel that rumbling belly inside yourself and carry this feeling with you when I continue the waving now." Under no circumstances do we say: "What kind of a word is that— I am not familiar with it at all!" We also must eliminate interpretations such as: "Oh you mean the anger is building up?" because this does not correspond to the wording of the coachees.

This linguistically client-oriented approach promotes a healthy processing particularly because the person affected remains focused on their world of experience using their words. Important to note that the waving sets should follow one another as rapidly as possible to avoid any long pauses or conversations during the REM intervention because the REM speed (rapid means fast) needs to continue. Naturally, an exception to this rule is the technique of cognitive interweaving, when the process gets stuck in a loop and the coach offers the coachee linguistic stimuli to expand the perceived angles. However, we actually make these suggestions only in the situation of a loop.

The coach also follows the inputs of the coachee physically. For example, if he suddenly leans backward and presses his head into the nape of his head and looks upwards, we must quickly say: "Remain as you are and maintain this body posture in the next set." Perhaps one would then have to lean forward or even stand up. But under no circumstances should the coach say: "Sit up straight, so that we can continue to wave!" We can also ask the client to apply a kinaesthetic body movement in the set: "You have just made a circular movement using both your hands when we used the word 'easy.' Take this movement into the next set when we continue." When we incorporate the body language into the process, it results in particularly intensive and relieving positive effects.

Self-coaching tip: How to move on from conflict

In a dispute or a conflict discussion, it may be natural that you or your opponent is at a loss to find the appropriate words to free yourself seek solutions together. Often it is recommended to go out for a walk together. Just the process of walking stimulates the brain for the continuous bilateral hemispheric stimulations because the motor functions of the left and right legs must proceed in a coordinated manner when we are moving forward. By doing this, it is not only the body movements but also speech that comes back into flow.

Even when you are searching for good ideas and are not making any progress, just go for walk, go jogging, or ride a bicycle. The search for ideas takes place not just in internal images, but also in internal dialogues. Even for this, we need our speech center, which regains its flow of words because of the bilateral motor impulses.

2.10 Another Positive Outcome: The Generalization Effect

Many people report that after a wingwave coaching session there is not only an improvement in the topics they initially come for, but also in their subjective experiences, feelings, and spontaneous actions, even though these were not highlighted at all in the sessions. This can be explained by the preference of our brain to search for rules and patterns, which are hidden behind an experience and which need to be transferred to other perceptions as well. This is also used to describe family conditioning as the model of our internal world: Children not only get to know their parents inside-out, but store their role models here: "Men are like this" and "women are like that." This is also referred to as the sense of future: The recognition of rules and patterns allows the brain to make predictions about forthcoming events, for which it can optimally prepare. It then selects the best possible approachtoensure the optimal chance of survival. For a prehistoric human being it would have been important to assume the danger of a hostile creature behind a rustling sound, or to associate birdsong in darkness with the approach of the rising of the sun.

We explain this phenomenon to our coaching customers as the "tomato effect". When you read the word "tomato," you likely imagine a tomato. Most people do this immediately and close-up, right in front of their mind's eye. Now, ask yourself: "How many tomatoes have I seen in my life?" "Of course many times!" will be the answer in most cases. The consideration continues—do you know which of those many tomatoes appeared before your mind's eye when you hear the keyword? Which one was it exactly? Most people are unable to answer this question because our brain does not gather all the tomatoes as an individual image. Somewhere along the line, it creates an image of an representative tomato, which then becomes the key image for all tomatoes: It is red and round with a small green stalk in the middle, or whatever your personal created image of a tomato may be.

The brain does something similarl in the case of performance anxieties: Situations of a similar kind virtually cumulate in a type of tomato, if you will. The mind creates a type of generic scene which represents all of the performances which have gone wrong (or potentially gone wrong) and uses this representation as the go-to mental image of giving a presentation. "Since what you say is observed by others, many mistakes can occur, which can be embarrassing. You then sweat and that makes it worse." Sometimes wingwave has been successful with just one intervention in positively changing the entire key image for all the underlying scenes, so that – like waves in the sea – the effect impacts the entire "folder" of this topic in the brain. As a result, a new generalization or belief can be formed: "A presentation is something where I have the opportunity to pass on useful information that I know or understand"; "There are many people who are excited or interested in seeing or experiencing my presentation"; "If I perform well, recognition and new contacts will follow." This phenomenon of radiating positive effects is also referred to in professional circles as the "generalization" or "streamline effect."

Let's go back to our example: How could a streamline effect influence the case of Karsten? In the conflict with his counterpart, he criticized himself initially. Then, in the flow of intervention, he also scrutinized his counterpart and found weaknesses in him as well. This brought relief and shifted his interpretation of the event. Of course, this does not mean that the search for weakness in your counterpart is the ideal solution, but particularly for Karsten, this discovery ended his feeling of being hopelessly blocked. Perhaps sometime in the past, under some authoritarian influence, he had learned, as a rule, that he must always find weakness in himself. In any case, Karsten was more composure after the wingwave coaching when dealing with difficult scenarios such as the resignation of an employee.

3

WINGWAVE COACHING: THE METHODOLOGICAL ELEMENTS

40-year-old Dennis is excited about a new management position in a leading company in the cosmetic industry. Shortly after accepting the new position, he is invited to a talk show on the topic of the "ideal of beauty." Although he is an experienced speaker, he feels uncomfortable excitement at the thought of this public appearance, but he does not know the reason for his discomfort.

35-year-old Eva has been an expert in human resource management for many years. She now wants to become self-employed in the recruitment field as a headhunter. Although she is keen to make her dream come true, she has problems developing copy for her range of services and after a few failed attempts, she realizes that she has writer's block: "I have been asked by so many websites as to when my homepage will go live, but I have not written a single sentence for the last four weeks!"

Both Dennis and Eva come to wingwave coaching to gain inspiration to overcome their blockages and to enhance their performance. However, neither could name specific trigger points for their perceived stress (just like Karsten). They only had assumptions. In these cases, before waving can be applied, the coach and the coachee have to find out at which point the intervention should actually begin. The wingwave approach is ideal for precisely pulling the right lever to detect the indirect stress trigger and to activate individual resources.

In this chapter, you will learn how wingwave coaches approach issues of this nature. We will now introduce you to the methodological elements of wingwave. You are now thoroughly familiar with the methodological elements of bilateral hemispheric stimulation. Later, we will further discuss the application possibilities of wingwave music as an auditory intervention tool. Before we familiarize you with the muscle feedback test, which is used in the coaching process by the coach and the coachee as a compass on route to reaching their goal, we would like to make an important preliminary remark: Two people are always needed for the myostatic test, therefore it is not well-suited as a self-coaching option. There are people who use this test by themselves by forming a strong muscle ring with one hand and testing it by pulling it forcefully with the finger of the other hand. We are not convinced by the quality of these results because the person affected by stress and the tester are the same person.

It has become apparent that the quality of the test also requires emotional balance and inner stability from the coach. Of course, you should always demand inner stability and methodological security from a coach. As with all other methods, even this test requires at least some training, as well as methodological experience and supervision among colleagues. Even for their own issues, many wingwave coaches take advantage of coaching by a colleague experienced in this method, for example, during a joint working group or in official individual coaching sessions. Even as coaches, we are reluctant to rely on a self-test but prefer to place our trust in a colleague.

As a self-coaching option, we would rather recommend the wingwave music. Coaches also use this as an alternative in individual coaching when they are unable to apply the test (for any reason whatsoever). Wingwave music provides a type of "security blanket" in the coaching process and ensures that the coachee can intensively focus on his own mental processing material. However, in wingwave coaching, the myostatic test is actively used in over 90% of cases.

Finally, we will show you the connection between these first two methodological elements with formats arising from neurolinguistic coaching. These include the optimization of inner dialogue or the imaginative work with an inner part of the personality. No limits are set for the range of the combinations. Wingwave programmes also exist for family and organizational constellations, timeline coaching, team coaching, health training for groups, and much more.

3.1 Muscle Feedback: Myostatic Test and the Basic Strength Level

Before we start using the waving technique with our coaching clients, we need to ensure that we pinpoint and trigger both stressors, as well as the correct impulses toward achieving the goal. For that purpose, we conduct the muscle test; this will guide us through the process toward the outcome of our coaching. As shown in the illustration, the coachee forms a ring in the shape of an O using their thumb and index finger, which they hold together using maximum force.

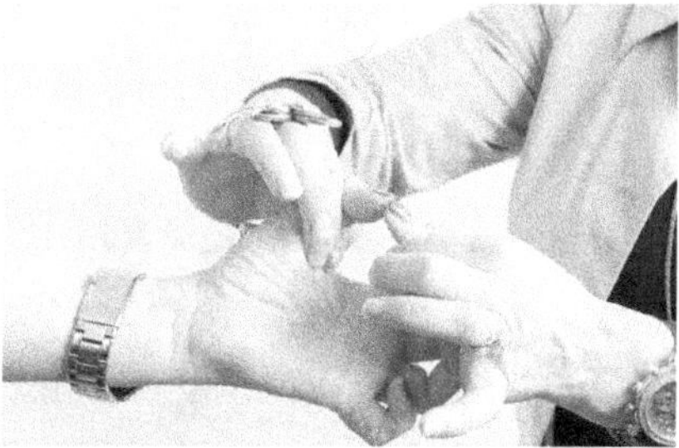

Illustration 13: Myostatic Test

During this test, the subject sits with his body in a completely symmetrical position (the legs are not crossed, the head is not tilted to one side and the subject looks straight ahead), keeping a small distance between the knees and feet. The other person, who acts as a tester, sits on the right or left next to the subject. Both of them should not wear battery-powered wristwatches. The subject should have consumed a sufficient amount of fluids and should be breathing normally. Even the coach should have taken care of his physical well-being.

The first strength test is conducted in a neutral manner. The muscle rings formed by joining the thumb and index finger, thumb and middle finger, and thumb and ring finger are tested one by one. During the process, the coach and the coachee must develop a feeling for the individual strength of the subject. The question is how quickly, strongly, and firmly the muscles contract to withstand the counteracting force in holding the fingers together. It should be obvious that the strength of a seven-year-old will be very different to that of a strong bodybuilder. However, not all of the wingwave coaches have equal strength. Accordingly, each of the finger-pair combinations can later be used as a test instrument.

When these first three tests are stable, it ensures that the subject has a sufficient level of basic strength. If one of the finger rings can easily be opened, the coachee must be stabilized by drinking something, taking deep breaths and tapping the thymus gland. This gland, which is significant for our immune system and for general physical strength, is located behind the sternum (breast bone) about five centimetres below the upper thoracic vertebrae. With a relaxed fist or with two fingers, tap this area back and forth. As a result, the bony substance begins to vibrate and the thymus gland is stimulated by this vibration.

For those who do not know how it works, just watch a Tarzan movie once again! Along with his famous scream, Tarzan thumps this important gland with his fists. Instead though, a slight tapping with one hand is absolutely sufficient for the desired effect. This power thumping is archetypally deeprooted and can be observed in our distant relatives, the apes. Intuitively, all primates occasionally thump the sternum in the area of the thymus gland. Humans also involuntarily grab this area, when they are frightened.

But let us get back to our coaching situation, where we now test the astounding effect of the thymus gland's stimulation: After tapping for only one or two minutes, the previously weak finger can now hold the muscle ring with significantly increased strength.

We can find the explanation for this in the functioning of the nervous system. The nerve impulses in the brain and body have to jump over small hurdles on their way through numerous nerve pathways and nerve cells. These nerve tracts do not continuously run from cell to cell, but are subdivided into various segments of nerve pathways. The impulse has to then jump over these segments. As a result, the nerve impulse moves through the body just as in a relay race. However, the baton is not handed over from one runner to the other, but from one segment of the nerve pathway to the other and from one cell to the other. This function is due to the chemical presence of the so-called neurotransmitters between the segments of the nerve pathways and the cells, thus they are the synapse. The thymus gland plays a significant role in the metabolism. The metabolism, in turn, guarantees the presence of the neurotransmitters, which are important for the nerve impulses.

It is understandable then that the stimulation of the thymus gland helps to spontaneously increase muscle strength. The reception of the nerve impulse is simply better because, due to its excellent metabolic situation, the relay baton is smoothly transported through the nerve pathways up to the muscle fibre.

There are a multitude of phrases that describe the connection between a good physical and mental state and our muscular reaction. The worst form of blocked cooperation between the brain and our musculature is paralysis: "I was paralysed with fear" is often said, for example. If a person wishes to express his helplessness, he always acts it out through gestures using his hands and arms: Even "I don't know!" as he shrugs his shoulders, lifts his arms and hands, and then lets them feebly fall down again visibly. We also use phrases like "weak at the knees," "lose your footing," or "hang your head." After tapping, a person feels capable of handling challenges again.

Self-coaching tip: De-stressing by stimulating the thymus gland

If you stimulate the thymus gland for three to five minutes every day, you will enhance your subjectively available physical strength and your resistance to diseases. Even your mental performance capability is stabilized by this stimulation. Many clients are skeptical, and as things like, "but can I really start tapping in front of my boss or in the middle of a lecture?" Of course not. The strengthening effect of thymus gland stimulation lasts for two to three hours. Therefore, you can perform the action 30 minutes before an important performance or event. Simply tap until you have to take a deep breath. The deep inhalation indicates the effect of stimulation.

Even children can benefit from this simple energy-booster before attending classes, sporting events, or other experiences where they wish to demonstrating their performance.

3.2 Muscle Feedback: Test the Testability

In the case of testing the strength level of the O ring, the coach now tries to open the closed thumb and finger. However, this time he offers the coachee various stressors. At this time, it is not about the coaching topic, but about the issue as to whether the muscle reaction in this tester pair is suitable as feedback. This phase is referred to as calibration.

In most cases, calibration works with words and sentences. If the ring can be opened easily, the test indicates that the person tested cannot cope with the issue associated with the statement, or they are irritated and therefore stress has been encountered. But if the ring is strong, the coachee feels he is ready to cope with the mentioned issue—he can tackle, endure, or at least react to it in a balanced and neutral manner.

Perhaps many readers are aware of muscle testing in kinesiology, for example, the laterally outstretched arm, which is pressed downwards by the tester in order to determine the strength or stress of the subjects. However, the test with fingers seems to be exceptionally sensitive in reflecting the mental state of a human being: It is not without reason that directors of crime thrillers enjoy the image of a vase or glass slipping out of a hand to show that a person affected, frightened, or highly irritated. There are several schools and theories of kinesiology which are partly based on the meridian system of Chinese medicine. These theories are not used in wingwave coaching. Our focus of interest is the close correspondence between the muscle tone of hand and fingers and the neurophysiological situation of the brain.

The hand is a completely unique organ in animate biology: It combines the sensory perceptions and fine motor skills in a unique and highly complex manner. Therefore, the hand requires a comparatively large control area in the brain —even in the cerebrum. This is not only the seat of our intellect, but our highest authority: one could argue that the conductor of our entire experience is located in the frontal lobe. Only by using it are we able to combine experiences, new knowledge, thoughts, feelings, and actions to provide a meaningful performance. If this conductor is unable to do its job, we feel irritated, confused, and out of line. This irritation can also be measured with a change of potential in the cerebrum, an effect called "P 300" and/or "N 300." The respective terms P for positive and N for negative are dependent on whether the potential goes up or down out of the rhythm.

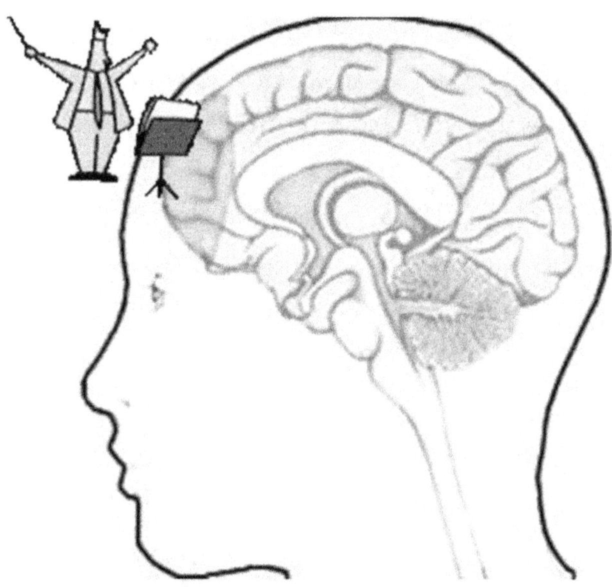

Illustration 14: Prefrontal Cortex

Even small irritations in the coordination ability of the cerebrum are reflected in the hand muscles within a fraction of a second. In the case of Eva, the coaching client with writer's block mentioned above, we begin the calibration with the following statement test: "Please form the O-ring" and we ask her to say at the same time: "My name is Heinrich." Saying an incorrect name provokes minor irritation with the change in potential in the cerebrum associated therewith because Eva is unable to hold the muscle ring together. Now, we repeat the experiment by saying the correct name and the ring is stronger.

One can also provoke the artificial irritation through other annoyances: The coach hands over to the coachee a piece of white sugar or a battery-powered quartz watch. During the test, we can also request the subjects to press the navel toward the spinal column with one hand, which likewise leads to a weaker reaction in the myostatic test. This sensitive network of nerves is located in the abdominal region and is called the vagus nerve, which immediately transmits the stress of pressure to the entire nervous system. For Eva, no further calibration experiment is needed; she had been sufficiently tested by "Heinrich" and the fingers came apart. Now that we know she can be tested, we can begin the coaching.

Within the framework of his doctoral thesis, the graduate psychologist Marco Rathschlag was able to significantly confirm the reliability of the myostatic test by objectively using a measuring machine at the German Sport University Cologne [Deutschen Sporthochschule Köln]. All the research results of this study can be found in the wingwave book "Mit Freude läuft's besser [With joy, the going gets better]." A summary of these research results can be found in Chapter 6.

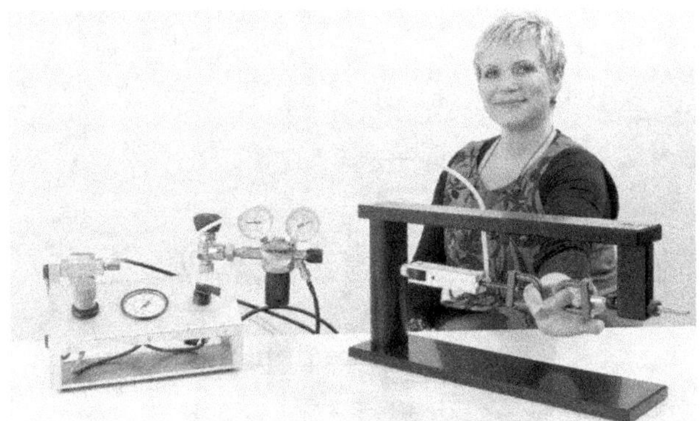

Illustration 15: Measuring Machine for the Myostatic Test

Note for coaches: Test variants for the calibration phase

In rare cases, people do not react ambiguously to the name test. Actors, for example, also react strongly to a false name because of the nature of their profession. In such a case, we use other artificial stress triggers and note which test we used on the customer card for future reference. Even nonsensical statements such as "the pizza is too hot to fly" lead to mental irritation and therefore to a weak test. We prefer statements such as stress calibration because the coachee has to speak and breathe simultaneously. Many people hold their breath during physical exertion, which, in turn, renders the test result useless because the bated breath compensates the stress stimulus for a short term. We know about this from weightlifters and from our own experiences: we often compensate the stress of exertion with bated breath.

Therefore, when you conduct the calibration test with your clients, regardless of which artificial stressor you use, always give the following instructions: "Please sit straight in a symmetrical position, look straight ahead and breathe freely." When performing the test, you, as a coach, should not wear a quartz watch because that could also falsify the result.

3.3 Coaching Compass for Muscle Feedback: Find the Stress Trigger

This section begins with important information: under no circumstances are the results of myostatic tests synonymous with the words yes and no, but rather with the words bearable and unbearable. We do not ask any questions during wingwave coaching; we present only words and statements to test the emotional charge.

We classify the emotionally effective words and statements as the "vita language" of a human being. For this purpose, here is an example taken from sports coaching: from a list of special statements, the coach says "audience's reaction" and the coachee has a weak test response to the myostatic test when confronted with this statement. Therefore, for this coachee, the statement "audience's reaction" is a vita word charged with negative emotions. So the athlete can play in top form, this stressful statement must be worked on. A strong response would indicate the athlete could emotionally cope the audience's reaction and is not irritated by this trigger.

This neurolinguistic navigation ensures that this is the issue to work on. Accordingly, stable reactions indicate that there is no need for any emotion coaching. Thus, the myostatic test contributes to the best possible outcome in coaching. In most cases the positive testing ensures strengthening of the positive motivation: "I am really glad that I tested positively on that as I wasn't sure!" commented a manager in the fashion industry with regard to her test results.

In order to search for stress triggers, we offer not only verbal statements, words and sentences, but we also bring in specific objects and illustrations, such as photographs of relevant people involved in the situation or the slide presentation, which the coachee is planning on showing when giving his presentation.

A pharmaceutical representative once brought all the packages of products, which she was planning on presenting during her visits to doctors. This enabled us to test out everything she was using in her presentation to see which of the objects might be causing a stress factor. The results surprised her. She herself was convinced that these medicines would help the patients. After we tested her with emotions coaching, however, it was revealed that she had to struggle with anger, when some doctors reacted critically to her presentation. She did not take it calmly and professionally but rather felt personally attacked because of her own enthusiasm for the products.

During tests, we follow our intuition as experienced coaches or the intuition of the coachee, which is secondary. When confronting a problem or a case history, we could run the risk of distraction from the key issue as a result of too much conscious talking. Eva's example astonishingly demonstrates how far the psychological theorization can stray from the target. Eva presented herself in coaching with writer's block. She brought not only her issue, but also the explanation for her blockage: "I assume that I am subconsciously prohibiting myself from realising my dream of self-employment. I have already come across this issue in a family constellation. I definitely have self-doubts which say: 'You are not worthy of success.' Of course, I want to change that."

It is immediately obvious that Eva is no beginner in psychology. She has completed training in coaching and in her spare time has attended seminars, training, and practiced self-awareness on topics of personality, psyche, and communication. Since she had already gained experience with wingwave coaching, she forms the ring with her thumb and index finger and holds out her hand to the coach. According to Eva's plan, we immediately test the statement: "I am worthy of success" – and the ring holds. Eva is amazed: "Then, what other reason can there be for my writer's block?"

We continue coaching with the system of the statement tree, which we will discuss in detail shortly. In the search for one or \ several stress triggers, we will examine the entire sequence in the context of a problem. "When you say: 'I try to write', where does it take place exactly?" asks the coach. "In my study" is the answer. First, we test the thought of entering the study room and the result is strong. The test of sitting at the desk was equally stable. "How do you write then? Predominantly on a computer or by hand as well?"

"Occasionally, I write notes by hand and then type the actual text onto the computer" Eva says. We test the statements "writing by hand" and "typing onto the computer", whereby the second test turns out to be weak. "Do you already have an idea as to what could be wrong with the computer?" asks the coach. "Yes. First of all, it is not really the right computer–I disposed of it four weeks ago and bought myself a small laptop, which is simply more practical for me."

"There is something with the laptop" and so we test that in the next step and there is stress feedback once again. We continue: "It's the files." "It's the contents of the files." The tests turn out to be strong. Then we test the external features: "It's the keyboard," and here we are successful.

Eva looks at her hand in amazement: "I don't believe it!" She wants to repeat the test. We do the test again, the result is the same. Eva goes into a trance for a while and then suddenly, she straightens up, makes eye contact and says: "You know what, the test is spot on! I have had writer's block since I started working with the new laptop. In fact, the keyboard is a stress for me because it is much smaller than the one on my large PC. Over and over again, I have deleted entire paragraphs because the keys are simply too close to each other. That was extremely annoying!" Although Eva has assumed a success blockage within herself on the level of self-esteem, factually, she has always been successful professionally. Eva works perseveringly, effectively and, above all, quickly. Thereby, she cannot tolerate when the technology she uses is not fast enough and is unnecessarily difficult. That goes for the telephone, computer, and even traffic jams on the motorways or delayed flights: "I hate those things!"

"Think about the small keys and the particularly annoying moment when an entire paragraph disappears at the touch of a finger. Where can you feel the anger now when you think about this glitch?" She answers, "In the neck, it's literally a pain in the neck!" We wave away the anger and after two to three sets, Eva is already able to laugh about that issue with relief. We still test the statements: "Typing with the laptop", "keyboard", and "the issue is OK now" and all the statements are strong and confirmed.

For good measure, we do a crosscheck: "We should continue to work on the issue." Here, Eva tested weakly. In wingwave coaching we interpret this result as follows: a continuation of the intervention would now be considered by the subconscious psychoneurology as unnecessary or even disruptive. From now on, Eva's perceptual and action system can deal with the issue on its own. "The grass won't grow faster if you pull it" is an apt saying on this topic—there is no need to be over-coached! Interestingly, the myostatic test not only displays information about a suitable starting point, but also about a suitable end point to the coaching process.

Eva's example illustrates the economic value of the wingwave method. Every reader can easily imagine that the hypothesis brought along by this coaching client would have provided sufficient material for several coaching hours on the topic of self-esteem, belief, and motivational work, as well as for family and learning history. But in this specific case, the detailed and professional handling of the mentioned fields could not have removed the actual blockages; thus, one would have strayed away from the issue in the coaching session. Perhaps, after discovering the keyboard as the performance inhibitor, the coach would have come up with the idea of expanding the issue to work on Eva's high expectations from the functioning of her technological environment. However, the test showed that the intervention described above was completely sufficient to end the coaching session. In the closing session, the psychological efforts were rounded off with an obvious and practical solution: the coach and the coachee came up with the idea that for her home-office, Eva would simply purchase a normal-sized keyboard compatible with her laptop and work with the small keyboard only when she is travelling. Eva is fast and effective, and right after the session she drove straight to the nearest department store, bought a large keyboard, connected it to her laptop at home and wrote five pages of text for her new homepage that ame evening. "I really enjoyed the comfortable feeling I had when writing" she said later. The writer's block has not returned to this day.

Note for coaches: Muscle test as an issue finder and process planner

Here, we summarize once again that the myostatic test checks two bodily reactions of the coaching clients.

The strong reaction means:
- ☺ "That feels good."
- ☺ "I react neutrally."
- ☺ "I can cope."
- ☺ "It makes sense to me."

The weak reaction means:
- ☺ "That feels unpleasant."
- ☺ "I am stressed."
- ☺ "That statement/thought weakens me."
- ☺ "That does not make sense to me."

A: Myostatic test as a topic finder:

When searching for issues we do not test questions, but pure statements, words, illustrations, presentations of objects etc.

1. *Weak reactions* indicate a stress trigger in the coaching topics because the coachee must be stabilized at the weak limbic points and needs to be brought back into emotional balance again. If the test result is strong, there is no need for coaching because the coachee remains energetic and powerful when speaking about the contents of the experience.

2. *In the search for resources* in which the coachee needs to achieve his goals, *the strong test indicates the topic of the coaching*. If the statement "you need humour" yields a stable test result, the coachee needs a dose of humour on his way to the successful goal. Alternatively, if these statements are weak, humour would not have a particularly stabilising effect.

B: Myostatic test as a process planner for protection from overstress:

1. You can ask *what further steps must be taken in the coaching process?* This is determined by the strength reaction of the coachee; it basically gives a green light on the way to the objective. There is also the possibility of the process planning offering greater certainty of the coaching quality. The clients know themselves to understand their resources, as well as their limitations. In this manner, one can precisely determine how much coaching input is meaningful for the client in the respective session, and perhaps which issues should not be worked or could be worked on later. One can also test time allocations, such as: "For this issue, we agree on a double session" in comparison to: for this, we need an hour-long session." The strength reaction then indicates the ideal time quota.

2. *The weak reaction* in process planning indicates that one of the proposed process steps should not be implemented, it *protects against overload or from redundant detours in the coaching.* If, for example, the test result of the statement: "We need to continue to work on this issue" is weak, any further bilateral hemispheric stimulations should be refrained. In such a case, the coach and the coachee move their chairs further apart, return to the chatting position, and carry out a debriefing of the previous session.

3.4 The Impact of Biographical Stress on Individual Performance Capability

Imagine you are in a queue and somebody bumps you slightly on the upper arm and immediately apologizes for it. Most people would say "it's all right, nothing really happened!" Now further imagine that you already have a painful bruise exactly at that spot on your upper arm. In such a case, you would cry out and hold your arm. The unsuspecting person who bumped you would not be able to understand because he only bumped you lightly. From his perspective, your reaction is exaggerated. Similar scenes take place every day in interpersonal communication. "He/she has a sore spot" is often said.

These sore spots are stress imprintings, which have become chronic. In most cases, they appear in coaching as hidden stress triggers—neither the coachee nor the coach is aware of these triggers. In the introductory chapter, you learned that unprocessed resistant stress imprinting has an unpleasant symptom of temporarily overriding one's internal sense of time. For example, a complaining customer may trigger a subconscious stress memory for a salesperson, associated with a former teacher who criticized him as a young student. The mind may then remember that same feeling which contains fear of failure or perhaps an embarrassing repetition of the school year.

Many clients are surprised at these correlations because some of the past events took place decades earlier and perhaps had little conscious significance at the time. At this point, the detailed information on stress imprinting is important once again to comprehend the current meaning of the past experiences. In wingwave coaching, we describe this as biographical stress, which impacts as an indirect and subconscious stress trigger.

Whenever we work on performance stress with our coachees, we also test for possible biographical stress, which he or she might have brought into the situation. If such stress is present (sometimes there are several points to work with), it must be dealt with jointly to make that person stable again. Sometimes our clients are already aware of their sore spots, as they have come up throughout their lives. However, sometimes they only surface in the course of the intervention. It is as if by waving, one enters a kind of associative network in which the unrelieved stress imprintings are stored. Often, similarities to the present-day event are obvious, but sometimes even clients are surprised at the scenes emerging from their past.

Our client Ines, who is very successful in her company, suffered from constant attacks from an older colleague. He had been working in the company for over ten years, had developed a certain comfortable daily routine and felt overshadowed by Ines's dynamism. Her problem was that she simply felt bad in the evenings and on weekends because she was not able to defend herself. During a session, with the aid of the muscle test, the memory suddenly surfaced: when she was five-years old, her older sister pushed her from the bed during a quarrel and she was badly hurt. The parent, who came running, then scolded both the quarrelling children, instead of protecting Ines and chastising her sister. Patterns such as this were then repeated in the family environment, whereby Ines subconsciously adopted the following rule: "I cannot defend myself against injustice—it's no use." Thus, the subconscious perception associated the envious colleague with her elder sister. Instead of defending herself, Ines constantly walked around with an unpleasant sense of helplessness, a feeling of being at someone's mercy and an impotent rage.

Often, the described associative work of the brain initially seems illogical to clients. However, our subconscious does not sort by categories, such as male or female, but is based on what "it feels similar to," thus, the sorting primarily depends on our emotions involved in biographical stress, such as fear, anger, grief, shame, disgust, helplessness, etc. If in such a case, the pattern has psychological similarities, the events are thrust into the same stress category. Just like the tomato effect, which was described earlier, they are stored in the same memory folder. As an adult, one may wonder why, for example, a childhood event can still have an effect on their present-day life: "Siblings will sometimes fight with each other irrespective of where they are", as Ines said. However, under no circumstance should one look at the younger version of oneself from the viewpoint of an adult and trivialize the child's experience of that time. As in the case of Sleeping Beauty's castle, the nervous system has frozen that emotion in exactly the way it was experienced by Ines as a five-year-old. These feelings will become active again when this sore spot is "touched" or "bumped" psychologically.

In the case of Ines, it was not just about the quarrel with her sister, but the deeply buried anger at how her parents dealt with the situation unfairly. It was this same anger that she also felt when her colleague took digs at her. After the coaching session, and when the next unpleasant incident arose, she had all of her usual quick-wittedness about her: "He again made one of his provocative remarks, I happily leaned back in my chair and said quite simply: 'You are just jealous!' I was even able to smile at him!" When this colleague wanted to protest, another colleague came forward, to the surprise of Ines: "Come on, Werner, Ines is absolutely right, it's quite obvious to everyone here that you are jealous of her." Due to her active intervention in the dialogue with Werner, Ines was lucky enough to register another experience that was different to the belief she had learned in her childhood, and as a result, she felt more empowered.

3.5 Coaching Compass for Muscle Test Feedback: Identify and Eliminate Biographical Stress

How does a wingwave coach proceed with the myostatic test on his coachee in order to discover a possible biographical stress behind his selective stress sensitivity? Most importantly, using a systematic approach. By using the example of Dennis who is preparing for his talk show appearance, we want to present the approach in a comprehensible manner.

When Dennis came for the first session concerning his issue, he had already carried out a preliminary discussion on the process of the talk show with an employee of the program. "The conversation actually went very well with this strange feeling of excitement starting thereafter. Still, this day seems like a mountain in front of me." We calibrate Dennis with the O-ring test. Then we use the test as a coaching compass. First of all, we do not test the thought of the talk show, but the memory of the preliminary discussion. We are presenting the statement testing in *italics*. The statements that tested weak are considered as emotionally negative, and these then become the topic of coaching later on.

"It is the conversation partner of the preliminary discussion."	*Strong test*
"It is about the course of the talk show."	*Weak test*
"It is about the other guests."	*Strong test*
"It is about you, yourself."	*Weak test*
"It is about your feelings."	*Strong test*
"It is about your behavior."	*Weak test*
"It is about your verbal contributions."	*Weak test*

At this point, Dennis seems irritated: "I have prepared my verbal contributions particularly well with the support of our press office. All this makes it, in fact, watertight." We continue the test:

"It is the content."	*Strong test*
"It is the way, how you present the content."	*Weak test*

Dennis still looked helplessly perplexed. "What have they discussed with you? Do you know, for instance, when it is your turn?" asks the coach. "I will be interviewed as the penultimate guest by one of the moderators, however, they have told me that I can chip in anytime even before my turn to make the episode lively and spontaneous." We continue the test.

"You are interviewed as planned."	*Strong test*
"You make intermediate remarks."	*Weak test*

"What does that mean?" asks Dennis. "We can try to test the reason", the coach suggests. In the search for an indirect stress trigger, we conduct the test going through the categories of the statement tree.

"It is about your feeling."	*Strong test*
"It is about the feelings of the others."	*Weak test*
"It is the feelings of the talk show participants."	*Strong test*
"It is the feelings of the television viewers."	*Strong test*
It is the feelings of the talk show moderator."	*Weak test*
"The moderator could be disappointed."	*Strong test*
"The moderator could become angry."	*Weak test*

"But I was explicitly asked to chip in" says Dennis. "That surely means that the moderators think it would be a good thing if I contribute in between." Since Dennis still finds the test results puzzling, we open another folder in the statement tree. We describe the communication pattern:

"Someone is angry because you interrupt."	*Weak test*
"The stress arises from the present."	*Strong test*
"The stress relates to the future TV programme."	*Strong test*
"The stress arises from the past."	*Weak test*
"It is adulthood."	*Strong test*
"It is childhood."	*Weak test*
"It is the family."	*Strong test*
"It is the school."	*Weak test*

After a few more tests on the basis of the vita sentences, which were defined in negative terms, we finally end up in the eighth year of his life and, in this case, with a Mrs. Eberhard, the primary school teacher. Suddenly, everything comes back to Dennis. "That was an eternal battle for both of us" he says. "I can still clearly see the note in my report card: 'Dennis disturbs the class.' But I simply couldn't keep my mouth shut; it somehow did not work. Over and over again, my temperament got the better of me; I did nothing but fool around. My parents had to come to the school and I always had to stand outside, in front of the door as a punishment." While remembering, Dennis presses his lips together into a thin line, just like someone who is really trying to keep his mouth shut. "This teacher was also very boring. In the third grade, she had a baby and we got a new class teacher. I found him to be really cool. With him, I had no problems."

While he thinks about the angry teacher, Dennis explores the question: "Where in your body do you feel this memory of Mrs. Eberhard being full of anger toward you?"– It actually feels as if I am near a ticking bomb" says Dennis. "My neck is all tense." He presses his lips together once again; he keeps quiet while recollecting this memory. This process is again related to the topic of mirror neurons. In case of conflicts, many people sensitively perceive the of their opponent. After we are able to successfully wave off this stress transfer, we test again:

"The anger of the teacher."	*Strong test*
"The situation is now OK."	*Weak test*
"It is about your own feelings."	*Weak test*

After relieving the stress transfer, which emanates from another person, very often, the clients' own feelings surface, feelings that had been previously hidden because they were experienced from their counterpart's perspective.

"It is fear."	*Strong test*
"It is shame."	*Weak test*

"I would have never admitted it at that time, but I know that I did not like myself for my behavior. I felt really bad, especially when my parents were summoned to the school. Even these negative statements on my report card did not bother me at that time. Time and again, I went to school full of good intentions, then messed around with my friends and suddenly, I couldn't keep my mouth shut. Then, I was ashamed of myself once again. Standing-in-front-of-the-door was just embarrassing. When I remember it, my guilty conscience gives me an uneasy feeling in my stomach: It's a bit like my stomach is turning over." After the stress imprinting of the guilty conscience was waved off, the feeling of anger against the teacher was still tested: "She did not have a clue as to how to deal with children!" After this anger had subsequently evaporated with the aid of the awake REM phases, the memory is tested stable. As a final test, we again concentrate on the upcoming event.

"You can intervene during the talk show."　　　　　　　　　　*Strong test*

In the debriefing, it became conspicuous to Dennis that he had never had problems with speeches and presentations, he did however feel inhibited in discussions: "That would have almost become a problem for me in an important assessment center. At least, the observers told me later that I should spontaneously take part in discussions of this kind." This dilemma often emerges through one's learning history: people learn in school that keeping their mouth shut leads to good grades, recognition, and success. Later in life, as managers for instance, they have to actively voice their opinions and are rewarded for doing so. Because of this, our subconscious is confused and no longer knows which rule of success is actually correct; in short, we feel blocked. Dennis reported to us later that after coaching, he was able to express himself much more freely even in lively meetings and discussions.

But let us get back to the initial situation: after Dennis was able to activate the permission to chip in at the subconscious level as well, we continued the test.

"The talk show topic is entirely OK now."　　　　　　　　　　*Weak test*

Clearly there are still more hidden stress issues with regard to the television appearance. In the following tests, we are not able to discover anything in the specific talk show situation. Once again, we concentrate on the modalities of the process.

"You wake up on the morning of the talk show."	*Strong test*
"You go through the day."	*Strong test*
"You drive to the studio site."	*Strong test*
"You enter the studio premises."	*Weak test*

In further testing, we do not end up in emotional stress this time, but in the issue of physical stress. In wingwave coaching, we describe it as stress imprintings, which are caused by the physical overload, such as, pain, fatigue, hunger, cold, exhaustion, overexertion etc. In this case, overexertion tested weak.

The series of tests lead us once again to Dennis's childhood. This time we end up in the year twelve of his life, again in the context of school. This time, the subject of sports turns out to be the biographical stress. Specifically, we come to the topic of Federal Youth Games [Bundesjugendspielen], an annual sporting event, in which students from all over the nation compete in athletic disciplines, such as running, long jump, and throwing events. "We had fought hard for weeks in training, we had competed against each other and we had exhausted ourselves physically." Dennis is still athletic and therefore knows that "according to present day criteria, we had done everything wrong. We were always in the area of physical stress and trained till our muscles ached. Today, it is understood that muscle soreness is not healthy and it indicates a microtrauma of the muscle fibres." Dennis can still visualize the big sports ground and most of the students of various age groups, who were cavorting around the ground that day. "Large groups were standing around everywhere and were cheering each other on." Here, his subconscious perception has found a connecting factor: that large studio ground, that trial of strength in quick-witted repartee, and the talk show and the desire to perform well in front of a crowd—the studio guests, the moderator, the television viewers and, above all, his colleagues.

In the next round, we ask Dennis to think of an event in which he had completely exhausted himself earlier on the sports field. He thinks of the running event immediately. "If you feel it inside yourself now, where do you have your physical experience that could have stored the overexertion?" "I can actually feel the burning sensation in my lungs once again, and I can clearly feel how my entire jaw tensed up." "Bring it along" says the coach, and they starts the waving. After only two sets, Dennis takes a deep breath and relaxes.

"The topic of the talk show is OK"	*Strong test*
"We can stop at this point."	*Strong test*

As a safeguard, a counter-confirmation is yet to come:

"We must continue to work on the issue."	*Weak test*

Now the best possible emotional stability seems to have been achieved for the upcoming event. Finally, Dennis once again thinks about the upcoming appearance. He seems quite calm and says: "Now, I am already looking forward to it; one doesn't appear on television very often. I see my mother proudly sitting in front of the TV and it feels good in some way. By the way, I can visualize that studio ground and it is much smaller and clearer now. It is as if I am seeing that place from high above."

That good feeling continues. Dennis sleeps well the night before the talk show and is confident, quick-witted, and humorous during the live appearance.

Note for coaches: Your own basic attitude is important

For a successful coaching process, the basic attitude of the coach is important in every coaching scenario. When you apply a muscle test during a process, you could communicate information pertaining to your own emotional state to your fellow human beings in direct physical contact. Naturally, this happens in a non-verbal manner, for example, by means of physiological information, such as electrical skin resistance. And even in the absence of direct physical contact, you can send indirect messages to your counterpart by means of the elements of expression, such as tension or facial expressions. We have already mentioned a little bit about the topic of mirror neurons. Naturally, the phenomenon of empathy also takes place in your coaching customers.

For goal-oriented communication, it is not optimal under any circumstances to always "purely" perceive what is going on within your client. As always, it is about the healthy dosage and the ecological use of this human ability. Above all, the professional communicator should be able to react to the reflection of his client's feelings with a resourceful emotional response. "Experienced therapists have clarified their own personal issues to such an extent that they can perceive the description of their clients' problems with emotional stability", explains Joachim Bauer, Professor of Medicine, psychotherapist and author of the well-known book "Warum ich fühle, was du fühlst [Why I Feel What You Feel]".

In our opinion, this requirement applies not only to the therapists, but also to the coaches because they are continuously exposed to their client's problematic physiologies. In confidential coaching sessions, coachees exhibit disappointment, anger, helplessness, insecurity, or even physical exhaustion. Naturally, the coachee expects understanding for his issues and feelings and he does not intend to energetically drag his coach down, but wishes that his issues trigger confidence and, above all, creativity during the coaching. It would be little help if the coach were to stare at the coachee with his eyes wide open in apparent shock when the coachee tells him about his personal disasters. The subconscious of this person will say, "oh no, I have overburdened the poor coach, and I should spare him." That would be the end of the collaborative problem-solving session. The belief in the positive possibilities of change in the coachee–especially in their most complex situation—is one of the most important displays of any coach.

When you are coaching and particularly when you are testing, use a couple of simple self-management techniques for your own equilibrium. Make sure that you have consumed sufficient food and water. During your work breaks, stimulate your thymus gland time and again, move your body after prolonged sitting and listen to the wingwave music every now and again. During direct testing, simply take a couple of deep breaths consciously. The exhalation ensures the balance of the parasympathetic physical response in a matter of seconds, which spreads positively.

When communicating with the coachee, in every process, consciously think of the following sentence every now and then: "This person is full of abilities, he can achieve anything." If you react to human emotions, such as crying or anger outbursts in an uncertain manner, allow yourself to undergo a waving session, as a client would during supervision or in coaching. Coaching clients understandably want emotionally stable and balanced coaches.

3.6 The Statement Tree: How Can the Accuracy of the Myostatic Test be Explained?

Wingwave coaches often hear questions such as, "how did you come up with the idea of testing the relationship with my aunt? That was brilliant." However, the varying, baffling test results are less likely to arise on the basis of intuition or inspiration, but are often the result of a carefully followed statement pattern according to the statement tree in wingwave coaching. Tests and fine tests help in filtering the smallest possible trigger of stress and wisdom and in the world of experience of the coaching client, not of the coach. Given the requirements, wingwave coaching is client-centerd because the path to the solution always runs with the personality system of the coaching client. Just think of the example with Eva's laptop keyboard–even the most professional coach could not have uncovered the stressor merely on the basis of experience or his intuition.

The statement tree predominantly works with the presentation of words and/or sentences, and is oriented toward the imaging brain research. There are many studies which show how specifically, quickly, and selectively our brain responds to words. We have already discussed the crocodile effect, which has been well documented by the brain researchers. The reaction of the cerebrum to words is extremely interesting. For example, we offered to the English-speaking test subjects three audibly similar words: lick, pick and kick. Thus, to lick with the lips, to pick up with the hands, and to kick with the feet. These three words triggered neural activities in different regions in the cerebrum and interestingly, in the areas of the tongue, hands, and feet. Thus, the term neurolinguistic expresses precisely different brain activities which we achieve using words.

Why does the myostatic test, combined with the coaching statement tree and words, enable such precise insights into the structure of our stress pattern? It is a fact that all external stimuli are controlled by the limbic system. Words and sentences are stimuli, which often reach the nervous system via the auditory canal within a fraction of a second. Our brain stores words according to their spelling or their semantic meaning and with the aid of the limbic system, it registers all the emotional experiences we have experienced in connection with specific words. It has also become apparent that words related to stress have a different effect in the limbic system than favourable words. The hippocampus is an area in the limbic system which appears to play an important role in this memory process.

"The nerves in the hippocampus can be directly observed as to how they learn new content" as the well-known brain researcher Manfred Spitzer writes in his book "Lernen – Gehirnforschung und die Schule des Lebens [Learning – Brain research and the school of life]." He impressively describes that by observing the hippocampus activities on a computer screen, one can predict the location of rats in specific corners of a cage without seeing the animals and the cage. Ten minutes after a rat had become familiar with the cage, one could recognize the learning outcomes in their hippocampus because "each neuron had a preference for a certain location in the cage." For example, certain neurons always fired rapidly whenever the animal was in the rear left-hand corner. The researchers did not have to see the rat, since by looking at the neuron activity reflected on the monitor, they were able to determine where exactly the animal was located in the cage.

This associative ability of the hippocampus relates not only to places, but to words as well: "In the case of human beings, one was able to demonstrate that learning vocabulary, just like the rodents learn places, depends on the formation of representation in the hippocampus. Just as in the case of the rodents, one could predict on the basis of the activation of cells in the hippocampus, where exactly the animal was located, and one could also predict on the basis of the discharge of individual neurons in case of a human being, whether he has noticed a word or not."

All these results arising from the brain research suggest that each word, as well as all other information, such as images, odours, etc., is allocated contextually and emotionally within fractions of a second. Therefore, one can explain why human beings also react to the presentation of the years of their life in a test, and we can thus find out at what age a biographical stress occurred. For example, a significant stress response could arise from the combination of the words "16 years." Such a statement is under no circumstances purely factual information outside the world of individual experience. After all, every human being has perceived the implied year of his life as a part of his identity: "My name is Reinhard and I am 16 years old." As a result, the limbic system with its associative abilities knows very well that an issue-related stress is present here: "The hippocampus is capable of supplementing the incomplete information because it is, amongst other things, very strongly interconnected to itself. Such networks finish off the incomplete input by using the stored information", Manfred Spitzer writes further on this topic. Then by means of these associative correlations, the corresponding limbic signals enter the body almost simultaneously with the word and all other external stimulus: heart rate, blood vessels, metabolism etc., even our muscle tone is activated to be consistent with the experience of the stored word or stimulus. This word-stimulus reaction principle uses the statement tree for the identification of stress imprintings.

3.7 The Schematic Representation of the Statement Tree

Statement Tree I: Test the cause of stress

Determination of the stress disorder:

☺ Emotion, such as fear" etc.

☺ Physical stress, such as "pain" etc.

☺ "Destiny stress" / "higher powers" (It was probably meant to happen!) / "Systemic stress" (Affiliation to a group, for example: "Women do not do that!")

Further testing with Statement Tree Part II

Classification based on the timeline:
The stress is from the

☺ Past
☺ Present
☺ Future

Testing of the stage of life:
☺ Adult life
☺ Childhood
☺ Youth

Testing of the years of life:
☺ Testing over intervals of decades (intervals of ten years, for example, "20th to 30th year" etc.)
☺ Five years segments
☺ Test of individual years of life

Testing of age, life and family history before birth

☺ Ideas about the narrated life and family history

☺ Emotional restrictions, which are not one's own

☺ Client's own birth

☺ Pregnancy of the mother (Fine testing of individual months)

☺ The procreation

☺ The relationship history of the parents

☺ Life history of the father / mother / grandparents etc.

Fine testing context
☺ Family
☺ Relationship
☺ Profession / school / education
☺ Leisure time / hobbies / studies / personal commitments (for example, church)

Testing of persons / things / topics

☺ Man / Woman

☺ Within the family: Individual family members

☺ At school: Teacher, subject, way to school, classmates, school building

☺ A particular test

☺ School leaving examination, year of observation etc.

☺ Fine testing also in the case of hobbies / profession

☺ Studies (for example, in the case of medical studies, subjects, such as pathology)

in the case of the persons tested

☺ These are your own feelings.

☺ These are the feelings of someone else.

Testing experience character

☺ A single event

☺ A pattern (for example, "The same unfair teacher, every day for over four years")

<table>
<tr><td colspan="2">

Statement Tree II: Determine emotions and soma stress

</td></tr>
<tr><td>

The pleasant emotions / suitable resources for interweaving

</td><td>

The unpleasant emotions

</td></tr>
<tr><td>

- Pleasure
- Joy, Fun
- Love
- Power
- Abundant freedom ("Born to be wild")
- Satisfaction, inner peace, serenity, patience
- Hope, confidence
- Pride, self-esteem
- Security, contentment
- Desire / perseverance

</td><td>

- Rage, anger, indignation, being irritated
- Fear, anxiety, panic
- Grief, loss of pain
- Helplessness, powerlessness, feeling of being at someone's mercy
- Shock
- Lack of feelings
- Surprise, confusion, "feeling of being in the wrong film"
- Guilt, responsibility
- Shame, hurt, insult, humiliation, sense of being dirty
- Disgust, hatred, revulsion, antipathy, creepy

</td></tr>
<tr><td>

Emotions on the topic of overindulgence

</td><td>

Physical stress

</td></tr>
<tr><td>

- Pleasure
- Freedom
- Security, belonging ("Your friends are here")
- Pride, recognition, self-esteem ("I deserve it")
- Justice (compensation)
- Satisfaction, peace, relaxation
- Power, control ("Itching to fight", "everything is mine")
- Somatic strengthening

</td><td>

- Intoxication (narcosis, alcohol etc.)
- Shortness of breath
- Vertigo
- Fatigue
- Pain
- Overexertion, exhaustion
- Hunger
- Thirst
- Temperature (warm / cold)
- The "head is not functioning": Blackout, Lack of concentration
- Death and dying

</td></tr>
</table>

3.8 Examples of Stress Trigger Lists: "Wave Away" the Fear of Flying and Preparation for a Sports Competition

We will now present two lists of examples for the systematic working with the statement tree in the case of specific issues. Of course, these schedules can be expanded. They should be understood as the fine filters for locating possible stress triggers. Since they are based on practical experience, they are not exhaustive and are being continually expanded. There are similar collections for conflict moderation, eating disorder management, fear of dental treatment, self-confidence, appearance etc.

If the coachee weakens at one of the points, the wingwave coach proceeds as follows: Determine the locations of the emotion, body scan, sometimes identify biographical stress as well, wave the coachee back into stability and perhaps "interweave" resources as well. This is, of course, a brief description. We will introduce the exact process along with the individual steps in Chapter 4: "The Processing Steps of Wingwave Intervention".

Example 1: Identify the stress trigger for the fear of flying

- Test out the entire process from leaving the house until the flight:
- Journey by taxi, bus, or train
- Entering the terminal building
- Check-in luggage and security check
- Find the gate / the flight is called
- Standing in the queue, walking through the gangway, finding the seat
- The stewardess gives flight safety instructions
- Fastening seat belts
- The aircraft starts rolling, then stops
- The speedy start, the take-off
- The altitude is reached, the aircraft is flying straight, there are bell signals
- Turbulence, the aircraft is jolted

- Test of height, speed: What is actually the stressor?
- Going to the toilet
- Travel time in the case of a long flight (the coachee cannot wait, is bored etc.)

Example 2: Preparation for a Sports Competition

- The opponent in the competition / "fear of the opponent"
- The venue (for example, home game, away game, other country)
- Nature of the activity area: for example, artificial turf, bunkers (in Golf)
- Competition uniform
- Equipment (racket, ball, dental protector)
- Fans, audience / hostile or opposing audience
- Battle cries, background noises
- Press, cameras etc.
- In the case of squads and teams: the teammates
- Own trainer
- The referees (for instance, the referee decides unfairly), yellow and red cards, whistles and words such as "out" etc.
- **Sponsors**
- Travel conditions: flight, hotel, different climate etc.

3.9 List of Stress Triggers and the Self-Coaching Compass: "Magic Words"

We have already mentioned that we do not recommend a self-test using the muscle feedback system. We recommend professional execution by a trained coach or working with the wingwave music; for the latter, you will find some instructions in this book. However, there is an excellent self-coaching opportunity for dealing with stress words. It is not an equivalent alternative to the myostatic test, but presents a perceptible aid in regulating stress.

If you are, for example, preparing for an important situation–perhaps a speech or a sports competition—make a list, as described in the previous chapter, of the possible stress triggers. Then read through this list loudly and slowly and notice which of these listed words you feel a sense of discomfort, for example, with the name of the "feared opponent" or with a term, such as "cold-calling." With the aid of the "magic words" method, you could change these keywords in such a manner that they become the key to a resourceful attitude: for serenity, humour or even courage and determination. This approach is an independent method and is described in the book, "Magic Words – der minutenschnelle Abbau von Blockaden [Magic Words – Removal of Blockages within Minutes]." Moreover, you can use the wingwave application to combine the magic words and the wingwave method for your personal self-coaching. In this chapter, you will be provided with a brief introduction to the topic.

Maybe you know the saying: "the moment I hear that word, I become completely different!" We are talking about stress words, such as "dentist," "tax declarations," "key figures," "root canal treatment," or "eleven metre shooting." Naturally, every human being has an entirely individual reaction to words. Many people can experience a physical sensation such as a chill going down their spine when they hear the word "shark" but alternatively, scuba divers experience a thrill of joy, when a dive with a "shark guarantee" is offered to them. It has recently been shown that most people can imagine their stress words right in front of their mind's eye in thick black block letters. Sometimes the words seem like the famous "sword of Damocles" hanging above their head. Other people hear the word in their mind's ear spoken by a creepy voice with an eerie reverberation: "Economic crisis."

The approach of magic words is extremely simple: We change the inner representation of the word by means of sensory-specific mediums, also known as submodalities in NLP. For instance, we could write something like "economic crisis" in a floral font, or as an illuminated sign of a cocktail bar or in teeny-weeny writing right in the bottom corner. One can change what they hear internally perhaps by changing it to the voice of Mickey Mouse or imagining it coming from a ball of cotton wool. There are infinite variations, but we need to find a style which facilitates and neutralizes the mere thought of the word and links it to a good or strong feeling within the meaning: "I can manage it!" Using this measure, we do not change the world around us, but the way we react to the world. The 'Magic Words' method is well-suited for fast emotions' coaching or particularly effective with children: A school subject, the name of the teacher, the different grades, the word "report card" and "class work" etc. become quasi magical. The method is purely neurolinguistic since it transforms the function of the word as a key to individual experience.

Illustration 16: "Fear" – Magic Words (Drawing: Lola Siegmund)

Self-coaching tip: Words enchant – "Magic Words"

Think of a specific stress word, which appropriately reflects your discomfort with a stress situation. Now present that word to your inner sight, hearing or feeling with the following sensory elements. Feel it within yourself and discover which measure of this sensory coaching lessens the discomfort or even triggers positive qualities of emotions.

1. *Visual possibilities*
   - Colour of the letters – monochrome or really colourful
   - Format of letters, for example, curved or script
   - Size of the word, for example, very small writing
   - Spatial position: Lying on the floor, in the left or right corner, far away on the horizon
   - Decoration of the word: The letters have faces, are decorated with little flowers or colourful sweets

2. *Auditory possibilities*
   - Change the voice of the word for example: "Speedy Gonzales – the fastest mouse in all of Mexico"
   - Hear a children's choir sings the words.
   - Simply hear it very softly spoken inside you, as if one has turned the volume to its lowest setting

3. *Feeling qualities*
   - The word appears in different materials: As a cloud, on top of a cake, carved in wood, as a mountain stream in the meadow etc.

Let yourself be inspired and develop further sensory-specific representations of your keywords, which transform a stress word into a magic word. When you transform only 2 to 3 centrally important words from the list of your stress triggers into magic words using this method, you will experience distinct emotional relief when dealing with the overall issue because the magic words' effect rapidly generalizes itself to the overall thematic experience. When you combine the effect by listening to the wingwave music, the effect is enhanced.

4

THE PROCESS STAGE OF THE WINGWAVE INTERVENTION

4.1 Introduction to the Process Stage

In this chapter, we will summarize the most important steps of the wingwave intervention. The presentation contains the original EMDR format, enhanced by the wingwave method, particularly by the myostatic test. You can use it to further enhance your expectation from a wingwave session and, at the same time, experience a good introduction to self-coaching using this method.

You have already learned several finer points pertaining to the implementation of the method in the first two chapters, in which we presented the wingwave coaching process with our clients Karsten, Eva, and Dennis. Therefore, if you are interested in the specific details concerning the implementation, read through these next paragraphs.

With regard to the frequency and duration of the sessions, it can be said: "as a rule, the coach and the coachee meet for approximately two to five coaching hours for each topic. Within this time frame, the coachee may expect the coaching to have a significant effect. If this is not the case, coaching should not be continued using wingwave."

4.2 The Twelve Phases of the wingwave Intervention

1st Phase: Preparation of the content

The coachee is extensively prepared for the wingwave intervention. During preparation, he also learns a little bit about the basic assumption of the method that the unpleasant emotions could wind up unprocessed in the nervous system as resistant stress imprinting. Wingwave gets a natural, endogenous processing operation up and running, which helps in overcoming the issue not only cognitively, but also with regard to the quality of perceived emotions. We will explain which phenomenon—such as the "kitchen boy effect"—can occur during processing. For the course of the inner experiences, we will search for a metaphor together, for example: "everything is happening like in the movies, but you are safely sitting in your chair."

Above all, we would like to mention the tunnel metaphor: "If a person is afraid of tunnels, his wish would be that the train driver accelerates in order to come out of the tunnel and into the light once again as quickly as possible. He would not pull the emergency handle in the middle of the tunnel." Thus, we make it clear that the coach will continue to wave especially when an unpleasant feeling is building up like a wave before it can flow away. In this context, we mention the "kitchen boy effect" at the same time: When the evil spell is lifted, the kitchen boy still gets the slap on his face. In resource coaching, we say that with the aid of wingwave, even positive emotions and general emotional states can be further strengthened and stabilized.

At this juncture, it can be tested as to how exactly the intervention should be performed: how far from the eye the waving is performed and which surrounding circumstances are pleasant? Would the coachee, for instance, prefer to take off his glasses or keep them on? As already mentioned, even bilateral stimulations, such as auditory stimuli or alternating tapping on the hand, shoulders, or knees can be agreed upon or tried out. Furthermore, the positioning of both of the chairs is part of the practical set-up, thus the setting. The coach and the client sit opposite each other with their chairs arranged as though the they are two ships on a river just on the brink of passing each other by.

2nd *Phase: The myostatic test*

The coach and the coachee now adjust themselves for the muscle test. If necessary, the basic strength level of the coachee is further increased by tapping on the thymus gland or by drinking water. If the coachee tests strong and does not react to the artificial stress stimulus, such as the wrong name, irritation of the vagus nerve by pressing the navel, wearing a battery-powered watch or by saying a contextually absurd sentence, the coachee still needs to be unblocked. This is accomplished by means of slow opening waving: top, middle and with a downcast look. Subsequently, as a result, the coachee responds to the test in an emotionally responsive manner.

The coachee now thinks of something beautiful or uplifting: for example, a place, an activity or someone dear to him. With the aid of the muscle test, he finds out how strong he is evaluated in the test in the case of positive imagination. In this manner, the myostatic test also becomes a positive anchor for the stable emotional state of the coachee. The coach notes down an anchor word for the resource belief, for example, "beach," "painting," "granddaughter" etc. For the coachee, these are emotionally, positively charged vita words.

3rd *Phase: The establishment of non-verbal signs*

The coach and the client agree on two non-verbal signals. It may happen during the process that the coachee is, in his state of emotional involvement, "at a loss for words" and finger and hand signals come more easily than speaking. The stop signal indicates that the client wants a break from the intervention; with the continue signal, he is giving permission for the continuation of the waving to move the emotion on. Incidentally, well-prepared clients rarely use the stop signal within the meaning of the tunnel metaphor. The coach does not provoke problems, rather he works with phrases such as: "It could be possible that you want to sneeze or want to have a sip of water suddenly. Then signal me to 'stop'." We do not say: "Use the stop signal, when the experience is really, really bad for you, and you are unable to endure it." Thus, we only take care of unnecessary reservations.

4th Phase: Specify the issue and focus

Now the memory or the imagination is precisely determined on which the coachee should focus his inner perception during the waving. When remembering a stressful experience, it is either the most unpleasant image, the most unpleasant sentence that he has heard or a disconcerting imagination of a future event.

In resource coaching, the client may think of a project for which he or she needs good ideas. In sports coaching, the client puts himself, for example, into a motion sequence, which he wishes to perfect or accelerate. You will find some examples for resource coaching in Chapter 8.

Using the myostatic test, we then determine whether the said imagined scene actually triggers stress. If this not be the case, testing is continued. For example, a coachee with work challenges says: "I think of my choleric boss"–and the test turns out to be strong. Although the boss is an unpleasant person, however, he is not the trigger for the work challenge. The search for a stress trigger is then continued: "It is the sight of the piles of paperwork on your desk." When, in this case, the myostatic test is weak, the coach and the coachee have found the precise emotional entry into the issue. In case of a pattern–"this happens over and over again"–one determines a single situation that is characteristic of that pattern. One always starts with scenes arising from the present or with the initially described experience of the coachee.

Finally, we test the resource arising from Phase 2 once again, so that the coachee can consciously and sensitively feel the difference in strength between stress activation and resource activation.

5th Phase: Find an obstructive self-cognition

In this case, the client searches for a so-called I-sentence, which reflects his emotional experience with regard to the issue, such as "I am devastated," "I am helpless," or even "I am an idiot" etc. Often the targeted assistance of the coach is important in order to precisely find the sentence that gets straight to the point of the emotional quality of the chosen issue. However, the sentence should not be a factual description, such as: "I was deceived," when one falls for a conman, as here the statement describes only facts, not the emotional interpretation. In this case, one such statement would be: "I am naive and stupid," which corresponds to a subjective self-assessment, which stresses, tortures or depresses.

6ᵗʰ *Phase: Determine a positive self-cognition*

At this point, the question is asked: "What would you rather prefer to believe about yourself with regard to this issue and/or when dealing with this issue internally?" One tries to find a sentence, which represents a good counterbalance to the obstructive sentence such as "I have power," "I can do it," or "I am competent." It is naturally clear that before the intervention, the client feels far away internally from the quality of feelings, which correspond to the positive sentence. True to the motto: "Beautiful sentence! It would be nice if I could believe it." Thus, the sentence is tested as well: "Think of the imagined scene and say: 'I can do it.'" As a rule, the test turns out to be weak.

The test is further complimented by adding a cognitive assessment: "Let us assume that one could measure the subjective credibility of the sentences on a scale of 1 to 7. Whereby 7 means: 100 percent correct, exactly true, while 1 means: completely implausible. Now, in view of the focused issue, what rating would you give to the positive statement on the scale?" In this case, most of the clients give ratings between 1 and 3 because the belief is still a long way away from the content of the emotional experience.

Illustration 17: Credibility Scale

7th Phase: Name the emotion or the physical stress

This refers to the feeling or emotion which the overall psycho-physiological condition of the client reflects when he is thinking about his issue. If the coachee names an emotion, we verify it by means of the test: "It is anxiety." If the test is strong, we must continue our search: "It is shame." Maybe the muscle test is weak at this point, so one knows that the process should work with the feeling of "shame." This is once again followed by the emotions, which were subjectively perceived as negative, from our statement tree:

List of the unpleasant qualities of emotions:

- Rage, anger, indignation, irritation, annoyance
- Fear, anxiety, concern, panic
- Grief, loss of pain
- Helplessness, powerlessness, feeling of being at someone's mercy
- Shock
- Lack of feelings
- Surprise, confusion, "being in the wrong film"
- Guilt, responsibility
- Shame, hurt, insult, humiliation, sense of being dirty
- Disgust, hatred, revulsion, antipathy, creepy

Sometimes, all the negative emotions test strong. We then test another statement: "It is emotional stress." If the test sustains, the process continues as follows: "It is physical stress." In the case of a weak test, we focus on the list of "soma stress" in the statement tree: pain, fatigue, etc.

In resource coaching, emotions or overall psycho-physiological conditions as perceived by the client and which they want to strengthen as their objective are identified. Since, at this point, we are on the positive side of the scale, a strong test represents our muscle feedback compass: "I need serenity." In the case of a strong test, it identifies a large degree of serenity.

List of pleasant qualities of emotions:

- Pleasure
- Joy, fun

- Love
- Power
- Unlimited freedom ("born to be wild")
- Satisfaction, inner peace, serenity, patience
- Hope, confidence
- Pride, self-esteem
- Security, "endearing habit"
- Desire / perseverance

8th Phase: In case of interpersonal issues: "Who is stressed?"

In this phase, we also test, within the sense of the phenomenon of mirror neurons, the perceptual position using the following statements: "It is my anger" or "It is the anger of someone else."

9th Phase: Rating of subjective touch and body scan

In this phase, we work in the coaching with a bipolar scale. It ranges from -10 through 0 to +10. The value 0 means: "I feel neutral." The rating -10 means: "This is the worst conceivable feeling of discomfort." Naturally, the minus side of the scale is required to illustrate subjective unease. A +10 rating accordingly means: "It is nicer, better or more pleasant." This scale does not measure how strong the feelings were when the event was recalled. Rather, the coaching clients state how intensively they feel at this very moment, by the memory.

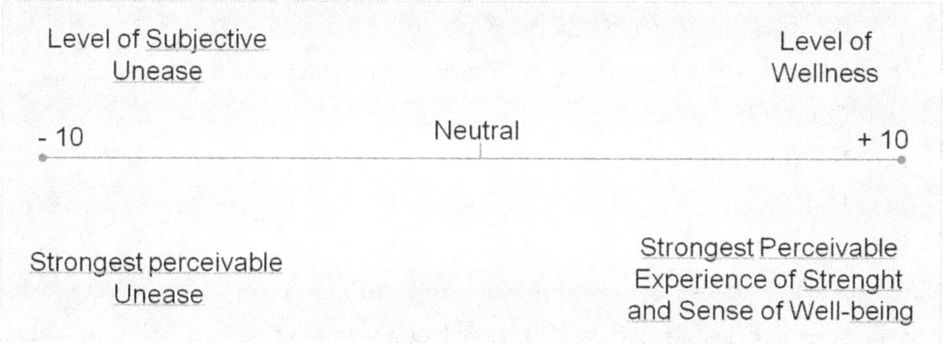

Illustration 18: Scale of Subjective Experience

The positive side of the scale—the wellness scale—is often used in resource coaching. However, it is also used by the clients within the course of the processing of performance stress imprintings. This is because after a successful wingwave intervention, a lot of clients feel relieved, liberated, "just like new". These pleasant effects are then rated on the wellness scale.

The rating is then subsequently integrated with the body scan, which is also important for successful self-coaching. In the body scan, the body searches from cell to cell to find out: "Where exactly do you feel the uneasiness in the physical experience?" The answers could be: A tension in the neck, a constricted feeling in the throat, heart palpitations, pressure on the chest, or in the stomach. Similarly, in the case of positive emotions or feelings, one can determine the focus of the body. If the client indicates several areas, the coach asks further: "Which area is responding most intensively?" Or even: "From which area is this feeling emanating?" With the aid of the myostatic test, the weak test helps us figure out the most sensitive area. Sometimes, during the testing, the client even places his hand on the mentioned body parts. Within the meaning of an NLP filter–the submodalities, we can differentiate more precisely: Is that body echo:

- Mild or intensive?
- Cool or warm?
- Is the feeling centerd, for example, like a knot and/or does one feel clenched? Or is the area more expansive?
- Does the feeling have movement or is it completely calm?
- If it has a movement: is it flowing or radiating?
- Are the waves, rhythmic or uniform?
- What is the direction of this movement: forward, backward?
- Going up or coming down, circling?
- If circling: which direction?
- Does it have any other specific quality, for example, tingling or prickling?

These precise findings concerning the body echo are important because during the intervention and above all in self-coaching, they prove to be a quick success barometer. After each set of waving, one can say and perceive in a targeted manner: "The feeling is becoming slower, milder and is clearing away" etc. In the case of a positive feeling, the perception can also be: "The feeling is stronger, more intensive etc."

10th Phase: The intervention

In this phase, the client focuses on the image and/or the voices or sounds of the inner representation of his issue that was determined in Phase 2. He once again thinks of the negative cognition arising from Phase 4. Now, the waving starts: a set may comprise of 20 back and forth movements; one back and forth movement per second. In a set, we usually wave for as long as it takes for the client to show a shift has taken place: a deep breath, a cough, a relaxation of muscles and a distinct swallowing reflex are signs of physiological and emotional shift. Overall, as many sets are performed as are necessary until the initial topic indicated in Phase 4 is tested strong using the myostatic test. On the plus side of the scale, in subjective wellbeing, no limits are set for the intervention. At this juncture, the coachees often give the signal to continue because they feel the intervention to be particularly pleasant.

It is important to wave alternately at all different eye levels (auditory, kinaesthetic, visual) to involve as many neurons and sensory channels as possible into wingwave. NLP has taught us that the eye level of a person also indicates whether he is thinking in terms of images, sounds, words, or emotionally. Illustration 19 shows the well-known NLP eye movement pattern and instructions to access it. The eyes directed upward are searching for inner images; those directed horizontally, between the ears are auditory inner.

During this sequence, the process can sometimes change its direction and quality in a matter of seconds. In wingwave, time and again, we closely test the current state of events.

The stuck emotion is continually noticed, immediately waved away, and then tested for stability. In between, the coach leads back to the issue arising from Phase 4 which was originally focused on, and tests the subjectively experienced change: "What is happening now?" The coach should avoid

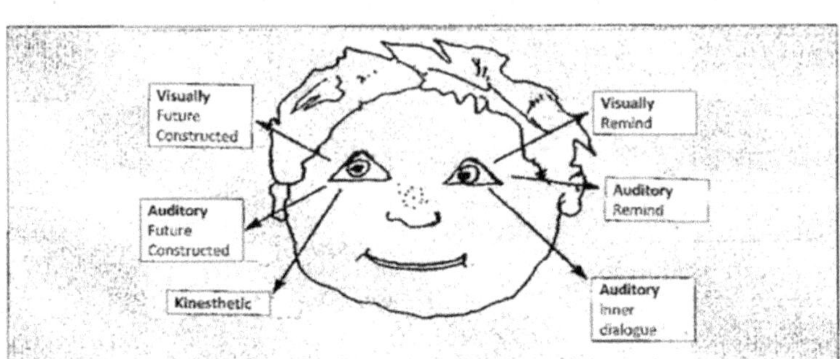

Illustration 19: Eye Movement Pattern

saying things like: "Do you still feel the constriction in your throat?" As this could point to a recall of something, that has now passed in the process. We constantly formulate the monitoring of the mental state in an open-ended and neutral manner. This phase is concluded when the initial situation arising from Phase 4 tests strong.

11th Phase: Statement test: "The initial situation is OK" and "the entire issue is OK"

If the test of the second sentence turns out to be weak, one must, in each test, move within the statement tree to find out the stress behind the stress. One of our clients always felt insecure when he had to make a presentation in a meeting in front of his superiors and colleagues. In Phase 4, he focused on an issue that was characteristic of a situation, which then tested strong after a couple of sets. However, the sentence: "The entire issue is OK" tested weak. During further testing, we ended up at the emotion of "shame" at the age of eight years in the context of school. It was "stress with the teacher" of mathematics.

Thus, an adult's problem with a presentation led us to the coachee's school experience, and, in fact, to a mathematics game. In this game, all the students stand up in the beginning and the teacher presents mathematical problems. If a student knows the answer, he can sit down. This is great for those who sit down right away and bad for those students who must remain standing until the end.

This game left a performance stress imprinting in our coaching client. Whenever he stood up and the others remained seated—just as in a meeting—his subconscious spoke: "This is the worst thing that can happen!" Naturally, in business, it is often the successful people that remain standing, while others remain seated. This was the biographical stress problem, which had to be waved away.

Physiological and cognitive change during the intervention within 6 minutes: „The Maths Game"

Shame	Feeling of guilt	Anger	Release, Relief
„It's embarassing".	„I'm a failure."	„The teacher is crazy."	„It was a long time ago!"
Test emotion	Test emotion	Test emotion	Test emotion
	2 sets	2 sets	3 sets	
Test body scan "weak knees"	Test body scan „heavy shoulders"	Test body scan "power in arms and legs"	„Everything flows and is light." Final test: „It's ok now."

One „Set" means about 20 „waving movements". The sets are always conducted until the next physiological change, and then the emotional status is tested again.

Illustration 20: Mathematics Game

In illustration 20, you will recognize the rapidly changing qualities of emotions "sweeping through" the process within a matter of seconds. In the end, even the following sentence sustains: "The entire issue is OK." If the test result of this sentence is still weak, another stress imprinting must be searched for with the aid of the statement tree to stabilize it as well. The eleventh phase ends when the sentence "The entire issue is OK" is finally tested strong.

12th Phase: Cognition check, body scan and positive anchoring

If the client now feels free, relieved, or mentally strengthened, we once again return to the initial topic. We would then test how much the client believes he can now move forward from the original stress which was determined in Phase 5, when thinking about the initial situation. Most of the time, a higher rating is assigned on the belief scale, 6 or even the maximum rating of 7. The coachee now thinks of the starting scene and states a positive cognition in that issue in conjunction with the test. As a rule, he can cope with the experience or the imagined scene, and, at the same time, firmly believes in the positive sentence. It is then once again followed by the body scan: "Where do you notice the good result of the intervention arising as a positive resonance in your body?" The coachee names the area of the body and thinks of the starting situation, and the coach speaks the positive cognition aloud. Slow waving is performed once again to firmly anchor the resources into the initial topic. Finally, the coachee is asked to imagine a future event—one that resembles the starting situation—along with the positive body scan and the positive cognition. In this manner, we can anticipate that now he can be in his power, and can now cope with and absorb such experiences.

The coachee is further informed about the after-effects of the intervention:

- One could feel tired and pleasantly exhausted so should then follow his need for a quiet environment if necessary.
- Daydreaming could occur because the new information is now "spreading around" in the nervous system. This daydreaming or wandering of thoughts is a good sign of a successful integration of the processed issue. Everyday trances are healthy for the mind. They ensure that the "batteries" of our brain are recharged during the day.
- Sometimes, even further memories or intensive dreams may surface, which are associatively connected with the processed issue. These could also be associated, in turn, with corresponding emotions and

consequently, and can even lead to the "kitchen-boy phenomenon". Well-informed coachees could always confidently deal with these mental phenomena. The newly surfaced memories or even dreams are noted down and are then processed during the next session in a well-proven method.

Note for coaches: Summary of the 12 phases

1. Preparation of the content
2. Set-up the myostatic test, including a resource test
3. Establish "Stop" and "Go" signals
4. Specify the issue and determine the focus
5. Find the obstructive Self-cognition (limiting belief)
6. Determine and test a positive self-cognition (what would the client like instead?)
7. Specify and test the quality of the emotion or physical block
8. In the case of systemic issues: "I have stress" – "Someone else has stress"
9. Rate subjective discomfort and body scan
10. The intervention
11. Statement test: "This situation is OK now" and "The *entire* topic is OK now." Go through the statement tree until the test result of the second sentence is also strong
12. Cognition check, body scan, and positive anchoring

Some coaching clients will be unable to easily determine some issues, such as their "inner dialogue" and "feelings, sounds, visuals". The "feeling", "seeing", or "hearing" may be a challenge. So, play around with this part of the intervention and perhaps, go through sentences and language to meet the "auditory channel". In addition, clients with a strength or preference for the visual process may have some difficulty with any auditory focus; therefore, one should not insist on using auditory cognition in this case, as this could distract from the outcome. In such cases, testing, focused perception, and actual intervention lead to equally good results.

5

CHANGE THROUGH UNDERSTANDING: KNOW-HOW COACHING

In this chapter, we will provide further background knowledge about the effectiveness of wingwave coaching. This information is useful for understanding yourself and the method. Often, people stand in the way of their positive transformations because they lack the valuable information concerning their mental situation and the path to achieve their objective. And we have already demonstrated in Chapter 2 by means of the helicopter example that, in most of the cases, the achievement of the objectives has not so much to do with the desire, but with the knowledge, and thus, the know-how.

Know-how is extremely important to understand and categorize one's own reactions. In the absence of know-how, the lack of knowledge is superseded by belief. Here, we are talking of "beliefs" to distinguish the concept from the religious faith. Beliefs are fixed, mostly subconscious presuppositions about the functioning of the world and, consequently, about one's self. They are reviewed very rarely or even never because subjectively, they are true. Significant mental power is unfolded by beliefs. For that matter, there are success-boosting beliefs, as well as restrictive beliefs, but often beliefs can cause limitations of the mind.

The following section deals with such beliefs, which are significant for the framework of resource-boosting coaching. Beliefs are very important for people in peak performance. The transfer of resource-boosting know-how is an important component of belief coaching, which is presented in Chapter 8. Belief coaching is for people who want to be and remain highly productive in their fields of activity not just for the short-term, but for the long-term as well.

Incidentally, the following information is also important for the maintenance of resources, irrespective of the wingwave and other coaching methods. The topics in this chapter should be understood as a collection; they are not always directly related to each other.

5.1 Should the Positive Changes Be so Fast?

Many of our clients often experience the relieving effect of wingwave coaching with an incredulous headshake: "Does it work that fast? I simply cannot believe that."

Thus, the belief contradicts the 'just lived' positive experience. Without ever thinking about it, many people have the belief that one can influence something big, only with something great. One virtually assumes a one-to-one relationship: "My problem is so big, so surely a bit of waving is too small to be able to help." Something bad can only be fought with something unpleasant. Thus, people believe impulsively that a bitter and green medicine is particularly effective. Many patients suffering from back pain are often disappointed when the physician prescribes physiotherapy instead of "proper" surgery: "It is so painful; surely it cannot go away by just simply 'exercising'."

Above everything else, there is an archetypal belief that happiness, success and health always require sacrifice. The more painful and onerous the sacrifice—one believes this subconsciously—the greater the guarantee of reward or salvation. The question is not relevant as to whether it is about the victim and/or the use of a meaningful measure to achieve the goal, but whether it is a "great" sacrifice. And great means strenuous, painful, and as complicated and as tedious as possible. In many companies, a subconscious belief exists that the longer a meeting takes, the better the results. Although the facts speak quite the opposite, one, at least, has that feeling of having performed something great because one has eventually persevered late into the night.

This belief is archetypal because it comes from Stone Age times. No sooner had human beings started using their brains, they started making sacrifices. Here, we are talking about meaningless sacrifices as opposed to the spiritual gratitude for the gifts of life. The motive for the sacrifice is obvious. Naturally, our thinking ancestors suffered from the unpredictability of nature, on which they were so dependant. And nothing is more repugnant to human nature than dependency and helplessness. They quickly conceived the idea that striking a deal with a higher, invisible authority who was responsible for the weather, would gain influence and control over nature. "If I give up my most beautiful sheep, it will rain." Perhaps this was their belief. Maybe it worked once or twice coincidentally. However, the third time, the rain maybe didn't come despite the sacrifice of the sheep.

Now, a human being tends to remain faithful to his beliefs. Eventually, at this juncture, one might have the freedom to say: "What an absurd idea I had! What has the killing of a sheep got to do with the weather?" But on the contrary, he would rather say: "Maybe, I should have sacrificed two sheep!" The main point is that the belief remains intact. And thus, within some tribes, it even meant human sacrifices. The currency in these dealings is called loss and pain. One believes that a supreme being duly records this "payment" into a little booklet and then returns the "profits" in the form of good weather, health, happiness, or success.

For this reason, even today, many people still do not like to say out loud that they are doing well or that, finally, they are happy. They simply have an archetypal fear that some supreme being will quickly look at the "ledger of fate" to check whether a payment was made for this positive experience. Our proverbs speak volumes in this regard: "Don't start celebrating just yet—the worst is yet to come." Or: "Don't count your chickens before they hatch." These beliefs packed in the proverbs often obstruct a person from seeing the functioning and most obvious solutions, and prevent their implementation.

Against the backdrop of these beliefs, many good solutions appear to be "too simple" or "too easy". One does not think objectively or in a result-oriented manner, but superstitiously. By identifying this, we are not meaning to say that one should not work for success in life. The only important thing is to focus your energy on the functioning and not on the "particularly amazing" measures. That is why, in wingwave coaching, we focus on the systemic butterfly metaphor mentioned in the introduction: "The wing beat of a butterfly is enough to change the weather on the other side of the world." This means: Short waving and/or minimal input, and maximum effect. With these thoughts, we open the possibilities for our clients to not only experience this simple-working method, but also believe in it. Even without a belief in "one-to-one solutions", the wingwave experience often contradicts the experiences gained in life up to now with regards to the transformations. "It is just not possible that I have been trying for weeks to come to terms with this issue, and, now, this little bit of waving might actually work and change everything!" At this point, the butterfly metaphor is helpful in integrating the transformation phenomenon not only at the level of experience, but also at the level of belief within the meaning of the know-how.

5.2 How Does "Peak Performance Stress" Affect Perceptual Processing?

Many of our coaching clients have another belief problem. They are often unable to understand why they react so sensitively to seemingly trivial things, and do not harmonize this self-awareness with their self-perception as a strong performer. Do you remember? One of the problems with our client Karsten was that he considered himself to be a "Mimosa". We must explain, in detail, to many of our clients why they react in a certain manner and so sensitively to their surroundings. With unfavourable beliefs, you can be standing in your own way and unable to correctly assess your stress situation.

The *first restrictive belief* is often formulated as: "My work cannot stress me out. It gives me so much pleasure because I have such great responsibility (or enjoy it and find it interesting)." This assumption is further nourished because the stress theories differentiate between distress and positive stress. In the case of distress, the activity is associated with unpleasant emotions, such as anxiety or fear, while alternatively, positive stress is characterized by enthusiastic, joyful, or even euphoric actions. For a long time, it was the general opinion that only distress brought harm to the body, and not positive stress. However, stress science has shown that both forms of stress drain our "batteries" equally, as, for example, was explicitly emphasized by the brain researcher, Gerhard Hüther.

Even in the case of positive stress, every healthy person must regenerate. In addition to regular eating and drinking, physical and psychological relaxation, as well as sufficient sleep are part of regeneration. We assess that overstraining in the case of positive stress can be an even higher risk than in the case of distress. The explanation for this is simple. For everyone, it is difficult to sensibly measure out enthusiasm, excitement, or even passion. In such a case, there exists a much greater danger that one may "lose inner control over oneself" when compared with the case of an activity, which one finds boring or stressful.

In addition to this first mistake, there is still a *second unfavourable belief* in the case of peak performers: "Peak performance makes you tough in the long run." However, our coaching clients explain frequently that, "For years, I have been getting five hours of sleep every night which I have become used to." Human beings can get used to a lot of things, for example, even a prison cell. However, that does not necessarily mean that the habit has a positive effect on the body, mind, and soul. Our body can tolerate any form of stress as long as it is released regularly, ideally on a daily basis, by means of regeneration, and the body finds its way back into balance. If this "replenishment" is avoided on a regular basis or is refrained from, the stress metabolism can derail. The stress hormones are no longer produced on demand or for some reason, lead to a continuous production that are detached from external events. Things may come to such a point that one can no longer relax and may feel constantly "wound up internally". This permanent stress activation leads to one always searching for tasks and jobs time and again to discharge their inner "high speed energy". Thus, the vicious circle of stress is perfected. The body can no longer switch back to its normal functions.

In line with this is a *third problematic belief*: "I can catch up with everything during my next vacation." Or even: "When I retire..." The human body consists of biological living material; each cell must replenish every day. For a moment, imagine the following situation: On your birthday, you receive a potted plant as a gift with instructions that it needs some water every day. Consequently, you secretly think to yourself, *Such a waste of time! I will give ten litres of water to that plant once a month; it really amounts to the same thing!* This example makes each of our coachees smile instantly. "It is indeed remarkable that we expect our body to come up with a strategy, which the potted plant would not survive." Most people express their views in this way or in a similar manner when they consider this metaphor.

The *fourth irrational stress belief* is the belief in sacrifice that is described in the previous section. It is believed that health and personal sacrifices are automatically rewarded, not only in the form of money, but also in the form of success and recognition. And since everything is for a "good cause", the subconscious belief in sacrifice leads to the irrational conviction: "Nothing bad will happen to me." Or even: "The end justifies the means." One can mistakenly assume themselve to be protected or safe, although, seen from the viewpoint of stress-related medical care, one is constantly dealing with this sensitive area. Specifically, chronically high arousal is subtle, and creeps up over the months and years in the case of many high performers, especially due to positive stress.

The terms "arousal" refers to the general level of activation in the nervous system. Colloquially, it is also said that someone is "under pressure". If this "pressure" has a medium, balanced level, we feel a pleasant mixture of wakefulness and serenity. However, if this arousal is too low, a person appears depressive and lackadaisical. Think of a toy train: If the amps are too low, the trains run too slowly; if the amps are too high, the trains fly off the track. Accordingly, the general arousal of a person can be chronically too low or too high. In the case of excessively high arousal, a person appears to be "tense", "like at 180", "under pressure", or even "irritable", which, in management circles, is often confused with being "dynamic". This arousal emanates from the limbic system, and thus, that part of our brain, which is responsible for the formation of our emotions. The respective arousal of a human being decides how stimuli and experiences are received from the environment. Now, visualize this reaction phenomenon using the following example.

Example:

Situation 1: As a guest, a man strolls through a house, which he likes very much. He looks at the pictures, the furniture, and the view from the window. Suddenly, a small cat scurries past his feet. He is slightly startled, but then, with a brief chuckle thinks, *Oh! That was just a cat,* and he feels immediately balanced again, and continues his tour.

Situation 2: A couple of hours later, a man goes through the same house. He looks at the pictures and the furniture. However, this man

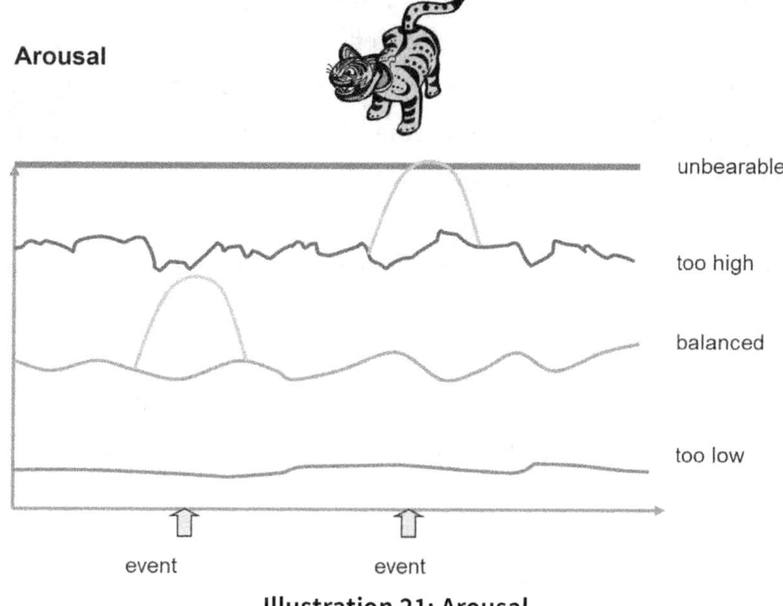

Illustration 21: Arousal

is a burglar. His nerves are "stretched to breaking point", he is highly aroused. Suddenly, the small cat scurries past his feet. He screams, drops everything, and runs out of the house and tells his counterparts that he has seen a huge tiger.

At this point, remember Karsten's descriptions once again. Before he experienced the disappointment with his young colleague Sönke, the agency had just won a huge presentation. It was preceded by a very laborious and "stressful" time with a lot of overtime. Karsten's arousal was still correspondingly high when Sönke confronted him with the resignation. This is one of the reasons that Karsten felt so sensitively affected by it. Resistant stress imprinting can be formed during an important peak performance time and is not only due to the event itself, but is also caused by the respective disposition in which we are confronted by it. High arousal acts like a magnifying glass on the events and the stimuli around us. However, Karsten felt it as a kind of contradiction that with so much success, he suddenly felt like he was being thrown off track by a somewhat everyday event, such as the resignation. This misjudgement is, in turn, justified by the mistaken belief that positive stress does not have a negative effect.

Therefore, in our coaching sessions, we work with clients on two levels. On the one hand, we focus on the actual event or the issue, which they have brought into the session. We then work indirectly on the perceptual processing if it emerges that our client has been performing during a chronically high arousal time, which may have created an unfavourable beliefs structure. We will describe this special approach in Chapter 8 on the topic of "Belief Coaching".

It's important to note that adequate and recuperative sleep, along with a good dose of self-coaching, is sufficient to resolve the development of high arousal. Above all, the dream sleep ensures that our emotional memory is recharged and the limbic system is calmed in a pleasant manner. It is not without reason that we say: "Just sleep on it for a night; tomorrow everything will look completely different." Of course, there are people who manage with very little sleep. However, over 90 percent of the human population require an average of seven or eight hours of sleep every night to regenerate completely. The first three to four hours of sleep is used for purely physical recovery, the last three to four hours is when the body reaches deep, restorative sleep. At this point, it then moves to the "shallow" REM sleep, including lots of dream phases. If this phase does not happen very often or is reduced, it results in an insufficient emotional processing of everyday events and consequently, remains in high arousal. If you often wake up after three to four hours of sleep and are unable to go back to sleep thereafter, it can be an indication of being in a too highly elevated chronic arousal. However, in this case, a corresponding self-coaching method can help in going back to sleep, and thus, help in overcoming the sleep maintenance insomnia. We will describe it in detail in Chapter 7.

5.3 Social Pain and Social Indifference: The Trauma With Fellow Human Beings:

The most common types of stress imprintings, which become the topics for coaching, are often interpersonal disappointments. Whether they are with superior officers, colleagues, clients, friends or one's life partner, one's audience, or with a trainer. For example, we were once working with Benno, a young top athlete, whose world fell apart when his trainer suddenly "left him completely on the sidelines" because he had performed poorly in a competition. "Previously, he had taken care of me quite intensively for weeks, and now, he acts as if I am no longer there." The young man looked like someone who "no longer understood his world". His actual problem was reflected in the sentence: "I thought he liked me."

This sentence again conceals a comprehensive belief system concerning the topic of "interpersonal relationships". Such a belief system forms a kind of foundation for every human being, on which his relationships with other people are built. If this belief system is damaged, his once solid foundation has a shock, and the world "comes crashing down".

Time and again, the question has been asked, why some people can overcome a severe trauma, such as an act of violence or an accident, without post-traumatic stress disorder. Although they are shocked, this shock dissipates gradually over the course of weeks and months.

Only ten years ago, it was thought that traumatized people were psychologically unstable before the trauma. But today, it is known that a trauma can "devastate" even a psychologically stable person. An unfavourable prerequisite is—as already described—an excessively high arousal, which a person brings along into the situation. For example: "One had far too little sleep the day before." Another unfavourable condition is the reaction of fellow human beings involved in the situation of the person being hurt: "Do you console and support him or do you give him another kick when he is already down on the ground?"

There is the example of the young girl who was raped. The parents said, "Well, it is not surprising given the outrageously tight skirts you are always wearing." The onset of chronic traumatization was unfortunately guaranteed. People who are acutely shattered and shocked need the emotional support of the people they trust, almost as desperately as the air we breathe. This applies not only to closely related people, such as parents, a life partner, or friends, but we even place our subconscious trust in those people who become a person of trust by virtue of their role, such as a doctor, policeman, nurse and, of course, the executive. Since people in these professions are often not aware of how meaningful their choice of words can be in the presence of an acutely traumatized person, there is a great need for training in these circumstances.

We have already mentioned that during a brain scan, social traumas of this kind are clearly indicated in the pain center. Accordingly, ostracism, rejection and ignorance by fellow human beings cause a lot of physical pain because the brain is the most vital element of the body. Today, these traumas caused by fellow human beings are also called "social pain".

Over the last few years, Benno had invested all his spare time in his sporting career. He had this feeling that somewhere along the way, it would all "pay off". Above all, he believed that those around him would keep score of his commitment according to the motto: "After all that I have done." Subconsciously, solidarity in the team was a fundamental prerequisite for him to get involved in the game thus far. The implication was that the others, for example, the trainer, would support him even if he was experiencing "bad luck". However, he was dropped like a hot potato. What was deeply damaging for Benno was the fact that he had never expected such a reaction from this trainer. "I perceived him to be almost like a father figure."

Social pain sets in especially when one is confronted with the fact that the inner "values and belief model", thus their inner world, is apparently incompatible with the values and belief model of a person in their support network. An inner model of the world gives you the security to find your way in the world "out there". One lives with the belief that this model is sufficient to anticipate the reactions of fellow human beings, and, therefore, to be able to rely on this promise. If this is not the case, one can then feel as though they have been "caught off guard" or deeply unsettled. "But he simply cannot do that." "This cannot be for real!" "Why doesn't he understand my situation..."

The model of the world turns out to be an insecure illusion and leads to disillusionment. If you had a perpetually envious competitor, would it not shock you at all to be treated unfairly by him? You would surely be very angry, but your inner world would remain intact because you did not expect anything different from him. Karsten was "shocked" by Sönke's resignation because he did not expect such a move from him. In such a case, there was an absence of the proverbial "internal fortification", the missing chance to be able to "adjust" himself appropriately in a timely manner.

The actual injury is not only the anger or the pain of what has been done to a person. The traumatic insecurity arises from the fact that one never assumed that such a thing would happen, and thus, vulnerability sets in. The well-known saying fits this case: "I feel like I am in the wrong movie." For these reasons, in our coaching sessions, we also test beliefs, which our clients bring along concerning the interpersonal relationships in performance-related areas, such as: "I will get thanks for this." Or: "If I play fair, others will too." Or even: "That won't happen to me." If these subconscious assumptions hold high potential for disappointments, we can expand these subconscious assumptions by means of coaching to be better prepared and thereby, become more serene for the broad spectrum of human reactions in the field of peak performance.

In this context, we also impart knowledge about human nature: How can you consciously establish a positive vibe with different people? How do misunderstandings occur? What is a transfer of emotion? Why is envy a natural phenomenon that a top performer must face? This know-how then becomes a protective emotional state, which helps a person flow smoothly. For there is nothing worse that can happen to a top performer than to "become easily offended" and "blocked internally". Therefore, later in this chapter, we will present the topic of "insults and feelings of revenge" as the performance inhibitors.

But before that, we will provide information about yet another source of stress: Not only we, but our fellow human beings can be angry, offended, exhausted, and sad—and that can rub off on our emotional state. Therefore, in the next section, we discuss interesting information on the phenomenon of mirror neurons.

Note for coaches: Just listen and be there

Many coaching training programmes offer professionals an abundance of interventions and possible applications of psychological formats, such as a list of statements, working with the internal team, of course, wingwave coaching, and much more.

As always, time and again, even the coaching clients ask for understanding and human solidarity, especially in communication with the coach. It is well-known that executives often have too few competent dialogue partners. This is not because they do not want to exchange opinions, but because there are too few suitable persons. "Discussions about problems", and the family, of course, should not alarm employees. Nothing can be confided with friends because executives are often persons entrusted with confidential information.

Many good coaching hours still result from active listening: The coachee speaks out, the coach tries to understand, questions, and helps in unscrambling the thoughts. As a coach, you also often perform valuable work when you listen to the coachee. This results in a positive connection, which is perceived as social warmth, in which the coachee can "come out of his shell". It is only then that the active interventions are meaningful.

5.4 The Effect of Mirror Neurons: Your Stress is My Stress

The topic of mirror neurons is of importance because many coachees report not only about the blockages of their own emotions, but also give an account of their difficulties with the emotions of people they are close to or have relationships with, be it work or personal. For this reason, under the wingwave statement tree, the following note can be found for a communication situation: "These are your own feelings" / "These are the feelings of the others". "I cannot criticize my employee because it makes me uncomfortable to hurt him", expressed a department head of an automobile company. "Thereby, I can withstand an argument and I am not afraid of not being liked. My mind tells me that I must imperatively point out his mistake to him. But I feel that it will hurt him. That is my blockage."

Warum ich fühle, was du fühlst [Why I Feel What You Feel] is the title of the book written by the Professor of Medicine and Psychotherapist, Joachim Bauer, which is mentioned further with regards to the topic of "mirror neurons". We can sense what another other person feels by way of empathy. A coachee may be receptive to the emotions of their mirrored partner and anticipate the hurt emotion in his own body before saying anything. In addition, we can sense the emotions of other people around us and take those emotions on too. This other person could, perhaps, react insultingly, dismissively, or reproachfully. He could deal with that, but not with the "mirror of feelings" in his own neurology, which now becomes the topic of his coaching. At times, a lot of children do not approach their parents with their problems because they sense that their parents would either be upset or worried. This is not about a lack of trust but about whether the other person will be supportive.

An Italian group of researchers discovered that while sensing the feelings of our counterparts, we, as human beings, exhibit brain activities, which allow us to experience these feelings in reality. As described in the chapter above, the pain center reacts in us when we feel rejected or unloved. This finding makes it clear why the coachee in question felt inhibited at the thought of a confrontation with the employee. This is because it could realistically happen at a neurological level that his counterpart tangibly senses some emotion. As is generally known, "anguish" is a synonym for the word "pain", which once again, gives a neurolinguistic reference to the emotions associated to words.

These findings make it clear how important empathy, rapport, and the proverbial positive wavelengths are for therapy, coaching, and counselling. Although for all professional coaches, this does not need to be said in the sense of occupational routine, it is still fascinating to receive scientific confirmation from the point of view of brain research. Furthermore, one also understands the importance of the "mirror of emotions" for corporate communication. According to Bauer, it is a part of the tasks of an executive to sensitively perceive the reactions amongst employees and to draw conclusions out of them about the quality of cooperation. "A happy face in the company is often interpreted as: "He is probably doing very well", or: "He is not busy enough; we need to give him even more work." It is rare that anyone would think: "How wonderful that he is enjoying the work!"", Bauer observed. He pointed out that the stressed-out facial expressions of too many colleagues can provoke a new employee to develop a subjective discomfort at the workplace solely because of the mirror phenomenon and, therefore, he gradually loses his original motivation and performance capacity one after the other. In 2006, at the annual international wingwave conference, Joachim Bauer called for "senior management to recognize it and learn to change it".

With the aid of supervized meetings amongst colleagues, wingwave coaches decided to test their own reactions to the subjectively unpleasant or stressful emotional photographs of people in problematic situations. The desired strong test result in view of the emotional stress of another person means the coach can cope with what they see. The strong test means the coach remains in contact with his sources of strengths and abilities, even though someone else is looking stressed. One would expect this same reaction from a doctor, a lifeguard, or a successful detective, for example, "Miss Marple".

However, if the test was weak, the respective emotions are again diagnosed using a systematic fine test. For your own experience, you may test sentences, such as: "When I perceive this person, am I sad, anxious, or helpless etc.?" In doing so, each emotion is tested individually. To experience the feelings of the counterpart, use the test statements: "This person is angry, he is in pain, is offended, etc." The sentences are spoken by the coachee or by the tester. In doing so, the linguistic accuracy is important; thus, the predicate should be in the first or third person.

In the testing of this wingwave mirror, many people are tested weak either in their own area of concern or only in the mirror experience. However, some people are tested with a stress reaction on both sides of the mirror. Interestingly, in the case of one's own or mirrored concern in a weak test result, the emotions and feelings are never the same. For example, Sabine, a handball player, when looking at an injured player, tested weak with the sentence: "This person is in pain." Her own weak reaction on the mirror of emotions was not pain, rather initially, the sentence: "The sight makes me helpless." After the first set of intervention, the reaction of helplessness was overcome. Then we tested the sentence: "This sportsman is in pain." Sabine grabbed her knee when we waved on this sentence. Then, she suddenly laughed and exclaimed, "He is just taking a dive!" This means that athletes often "click on" the mirror neuron's stress of their opponents by means of exaggerated pain behavior to weaken their fighting spirit.

Consequently, the wingwave mirror also opens new perspectives for successful sports coaching. In the case of many coachees, further testing revealed a "sore point" in the story of their lives. For example, in former times, one had to take care of younger siblings, who used to have stomach aches and cried all the time, or parents were unable to deal with their emotions, such as fear or grief, and, therefore, did not impart any coping strategies on their children. Thus, they tend to believe that people—above all, adults—quickly break down, and, therefore, they should not "annoy them". These stress memories are then additionally processed with wingwave. However, in the case of Sabine, this processing of hidden biographical stress was not required according to the test.

Therefore, the phenomenon of mirror neurons and the intervention of the wingwave mirror, play an important role in all forms of systemic coaching. Quite often, we have managed to test that people walking around in states of exhaustion, with a sense of shame or anxiety, are not necessarily caused by experiences that they have personally undergone, but by the emotional connection with important fellow human beings, who have expressed these somatic and emotional states of stress.

Often, people react correspondingly to stories of their family history before their birth. It has nothing to do with reincarnation, rather the emotions used, which the family members transfer to their children during the storytelling. In such a case, we "wave off" even the notions, which our coachees have developed with regards to these narrated stories, which, likewise, can lead to liberating positive results. We have elaborated on this approach in our book, *Imaginative Familienaufstellung [Imaginative Family Constellation]*. In this book, we have combined wingwave with the systemic family and even organizational constellation. These formats can be conducted both imaginatively, as well as in group constellations, depending on whether the groups are available and whether there us enough time.

Naturally, the positive effects of the mirror neurons' phenomenon could also be used in coaching. NLP has taught us the resource-activating formats of modelling and strategic learning. "It is one of the few possibilities of stealing another person's resources without harming them", a colleague of ours once said. When we use positive modelling in the wingwave mirror, we are proceeding in the format similar to the stress topics described above. The coachee is again presented with twelve photographs, which show people in different positive expressions. Again, by means of a body scan and the myostatic test, we determine the positive reflection of the emotional resource in the bodily experience, while the coachee looks at these photographs. Even here, the emotion is precisely defined and using slow waving movements, the coach "weaves" the emotional resource into the perception of the client.

Self-coaching tip: Modeling of emotions

Collect images of people, actors, or even figures that express positive or resourceful emotions from magazines, books, or the Internet: Happiness, peace, courage, success, etc. Follow role models such as Pippi Langstrumpf, Buddha, or Einstein.

Now, work with the wingwave music or the butterfly method. Observe your "emotional model", feel the positive resonance in yourself, and, in doing so, perform the self-intervention. Experience how your mirror neurons receive the resourceful emotions of your "model" and spread a correspondingly positive, serene, or energetic feeling within you.

5.5 Why Are Insults and Feelings of Revenge the Biggest Performance Blocks?

After the systemic excursion into the world of emotions of other people—in the emotions of a counterpart—we return to the emotions perceived by our coachee, and, once again, link our story of western heroes to the topic of "being let down by fellow human beings". Most of the classic western movies are based on the same plot: A lonely, serious or gloomy-looking hero rides restlessly through the region to find someone to take revenge upon. As long as the issue is still on his mind, he cannot do anything useful with his life—he cannot fall in love, cannot settle down, cannot build a house, let alone plant a tree. Time and again, this eternal story is watched by a spellbound audience of millions, who can understand this hero from the depths of their hearts. Within each of us, there is a restless hero who still wants to settle scores.

There was a teacher who prophesied that a person would live a life as a failure; the arrogant cliques, which one ostracized; the ex-lover with his condescending remarks. And now, there is the challenging superior, who, in human terms, is a catastrophe. The motto is: "You will still be surprised."

This can mean two things:

1. "You will get nothing more from me."
2. "I will show you—now, more than ever."

This blocked inner attitude has been documented over recent years, and has been given the technical term: post-traumatic embitterment disorder. A few years ago, Evelin Kroschel wrote a book on this subject with the title *Die Weisheit des Erfolgs [The Wisdom of Success]*. She clearly demonstrated how insults give rise to feelings of revenge and thus, how much valuable performance capacity is lost in companies. At this point, we would just like to mention that a person in peak performance does not "get back at someone" with insults and feelings of revenge, as this, above all, blocks his own resources. Unfortunately, this "activity of settling scores" is at the expense of personal charisma. The cowboy in the previous scenario shows his gloomy face to everyone, and lets his trauma be known everywhere, even to those who have done nothing to him. At this point, think of Karsten once again, who after his disappointment with Sönke, began to respond dismissively to other young colleagues. The risk of hurting innocent persons is particularly high in the case of a chronic state of being insulted.

The entire energy of an offended person is directed toward a form of compensation. Thereby, the disappointing thing is that in these forms of trauma, one can only hit back at the perpetrator satisfactorily in a few very rare cases. Unfortunately, these costs do not only take up a lot of time, but with the reparation put on hold, even personal development is put on the backburner, as the example of the cowboy shows. However, long-term peak performance is always concerned with personality development, and it has nothing to do with personality coagulation until the clarification of the case. However, the most unfavourable aspect of the feelings of revenge is the willingness, if need be, to go over "one's own dead body". In civil times, it means willingly jeopardizing one's quality of life and health in favour of reparation. In such a case, wingwave coaching can be of valuable help in overcoming the inner insult, releasing oneself from the state of being hurt so that the restless rider can become a sedentary farmer with rich yields of harvest. For even if life rages around you, the inner world can remain in balance.

5.6 Threat to Life by the Rustling of the Leaves

These statements show that performance stress imprinting in visual terms is often not comprehensible for any person. A person can feel hurt, injured, or wounded without ever being or having been, in physical danger. This is just because another person made a casual remark, or an article was printed in the newspaper, and due to all of this, emotions start running high as though one's life was in danger. Sometimes, one may wish that, at least, something "real" would happen, for example, an accident. In the case of non-evident injuries, many people start to mistrust their emotions and consequently, even themselves. The emotion is apparently not justified by the situation, and one thinks of making a fuss, as the following examples shows.

Example:

Let us imagine that it is springtime in Stone Age times. An ancestor is sitting at the campfire in the evening and looking forward to his dinner. He then hears a rustling sound behind him. He turns around but sees nothing. Suddenly, he is bitten by a poisonous snake, which he did not see because of its grey colour. Fortunately, he survived the bite. However, now whenever he sees a snake, he is gripped by panic attacks—and this not only happens at the sight of grey snakes, but in the case of green, orange, or dotted snakes. A garden hose—had such a thing been invented at that time—would have become critical. This phenomenon is called generalization.

It is now autumn, and our ancestor goes into the forest to catch his evening meal. Suddenly, three leaves fall and rustle down from the tree right in front of him. Our hunter suffers a severe panic attack. However, he does not know why and does not relate it to the mishap with the snake, which similarly had appeared at the same time as a rustling sound. However, this no longer comes to his mind after so many months. He is perturbed by his exaggerated reaction, and now must also deal with his self-worth problem:

"How embarrassing! I am known as a brave hunter. What are the others going to think when they learn of my autumn phobia?"

A shaman wants to help him by means of a breathing therapy, whereby he cautiously confronts him with rustling leaves. Unfortunately, it does not help because this approach misses the actual issue. Our statement for this is: "The rustling of the leaves is treated all too often in coaching or in therapy." Using wingwave, we navigate right into the source of stress and consequently, to its resolution. The coachee feels rehabilitated and relieved when he can understand the "psycho-logic" of his issue.

Self-coaching tip: a minicheck for performance stress imprinting (PSI)

The factors promoting the formation of PSI are summarized below. This list can help you assess whether you are at a possible risk of PSI. Should this—as we hope—not be the case, this small list will serve as a valuable preventive option of not giving PSI a chance at all.

1. Over the last few months, due to distress or positive stress, you have gradually developed a too high chronic arousal, and, therefore, are easily offended at any "jibes" coming from others through a mental magnifying glass. Suddenly, trivial things are having a strong emotional impact on you.

2. Any component of a current situation—and that can only be a particular tone in the voice of a dialogue partner—subconsciously reminds you of a biographical stress related to your life story, and, accordingly, leads to an emotional flashback phenomenon.

3. A person or a group of people have disappointed you, although you had never expected such actions or reactions from these people. Thus, your inner image of the world is shaken. You think that you are in the wrong movie and maybe think: "This cannot be for real!"

4. In your life, everything is fine thus far, but many or important fellow human beings around you are under constant stress, are suffering, exhausted, or even irritated. You feel that you are at risk of getting infected by the "mirror neurons", and do not feel strong enough to protect yourself or to reach or criticize other people or to encourage them.

5. You are suffering from PSI because of a stressful experience and you are surprised that the effects are not calming down on their own as they used to. Once again, you think: "This cannot be for real" because you have known, up until now, that "time heals all wounds". You are not aware that your mental self-healing powers are blocked because the event has overstrained your stimuli-processing mechanism on a purely physical level, and now your sense of time with regards to this event is no longer functioning as it used to. But this does not mean that you are a Mimosa, because something like that can happen even to the most physically stable human beings. Just stick to your positive self-image, do not allow yourself to be pressured, and quite simply, get "that thorn removed" by a wingwave coach. This is healthier than ending up with a mental unbalance, as we are going to describe in the next section.

6. You have high expectations—euphoric beliefs—from yourself and from the world around you, which do not take into consideration the limitations and weaknesses of human beings in their earthly existence. Therefore, you are particularly vulnerable to experiencing insulting or painful disappointment time and again. The consequence can be an "embitterment syndrome", as we presented in Chapter 8 with regards to the topic of "Belief Coaching".

5.7 Why is Compensation an Energy Guzzler?

Imagine that someone has pain in his hips, but instead of of seeking treatment for the pain, he has become accustomed to taking on a pain-relieving posture: He now moves in such a manner that the painful hip is no longer burdened. Thus, he compensates for the painful area with the muscle groups from the healthy areas of his body. For a while, it works perfectly well. However, after a while, even the healthy area of the body reacts to the constant overload and starts giving him problems.

Even in a psychological experience, every person tries to keep himself in balance. If, consciously or subconsciously, he is suffering from resistant stress imprinting, he tries—and this is a completely healthy impulse—to find a counter-balance to this latent impairment. Picture the post-traumatic stress as tinnitus on an emotional level: An emotion, which is subjectively classified as unpleasant, such as fear, anger, grief, shame, or disgust manifests as a "constant noise" in the world of emotions. A continuous tone cannot be rendered ineffective by silence and tranquillity, and the best remedy is to drown it out with even louder sounds, and thus, to subjectively eliminate it.

Performance stress imprintings take place as continuous activation at a subconscious level. One feels virtually "buried" uncomfortably, without ever having to think of a triggering event. Images and memories can sometimes fade out, but the emotional pressure or prickles remain. This naturally feels unpleasant. Then, suddenly, one makes the discovery that the intensive work is "louder" than the unpleasant discordant note. Initially, this comes as a relief and the psyche now experiences work as good medicine against the unpleasant permanent impairment—the "buried stress" as a coaching client called it once. Thus, the work numbs the psychological paraesthesia and compensates in this manner. Its actual function no longer exists in the attainment of success, happiness, and personality development, but primarily in its therapeutic effect. If the work becomes "quieter", tranquillity sets in and unfortunately, one hears and feels the emotional discordant note once again. Thus, the person becomes "hyper" again very quickly.

People compensate for it not only with work, but also with excessive eating, drinking, smoking, exercising, and partying. No limits are set to "drown it out". The compensatory action is often selected on a random basis. Any random activity, which "drowns out" the chronically tumultuous stress, is registered as a medicine by the nervous system and used accordingly. This is the reason why it is futile to discuss with people why it is detrimental to be a workaholic or to eat too much; their subconscious is already aware of it. The detriments are simply accepted as they are in the case of an excellent and effective medicine. Much more important is understanding what are the positive effects of the behavior. This compensates for and ensures that the pain or the stress apparently diminishes. It ensures the equilibrium.

Although compensation has a positive intention, the consequences are a high depletion of energy. The nervous system suffers from the inner "Sleeping Beauty's castle" with the unpleasant prickly, thorny hedge and must endure the continuous stress emanating from there. It mjust then organize a complex behavioral system to avoid contact with the inner thorny hedge and not get stuck in there. It is as though a car is permanently driven at full speed with its handbrake on.

Using this metaphor, we motivate clients to bring their "sore points" to be healed. Many of them say, "Had I not experienced this catastrophe at that time, I would not have been so successful today." Naturally, with compensation, enormous success can often materialize. However, we can assure you that after wingwave coaching, all our coaching clients have been able to maintain both the level of performance, as well as their motivation. Though, in all the cases, the compensatory "away-from-motivation" transformed into a "toward-motivation", which was perceived by everyone as the great gain for a positive quality of life. For example, Karsten summarized this effect in one sentence, "It just feels healthier!" The nervous system does not need to activate and apply brakes at the same time; it can provide energy to everyday functions in a pleasantly smooth manner instead. This results in a pleasant flow-experience in the performance-related context, which can also be established as a positive trend in the initial scientific studies on wingwave coaching.

6

WINGWAVE PUT TO SCIENTIFIC TESTING

6.1 Introduction

As already mentioned, wingwave has been researched in several university programs. The work conducted at the University of Hamburg by Nadia Fritsche on the topic of "test and performance anxiety" has been presented in this book. This chapter deals with further results of the research. Marie Luise Dierks, the Professor of Public Health, writes on a wingwave study on the topic of "speech anxiety", which we conducted in collaboration with the Hannover Medical School.

It further delves into a research contract, which the society "Bahnungsmomente e.V.", now renamed as "Gesellschaft für Neurolinguistisches Coaching – NLC", assigned to the Deutschen Sporthochschule Köln [German Sport University Cologne] in 2010 for two main topics:

1. First, to investigate the neurobiological basic assumptions of the wingwave method, and specifically to examine the usefulness of the myostatic test as a "compass" in the process of intervention.
2. Second, to investigate the effectiveness and sustainability of wingwave as a coaching method.

Within the framework of his doctoral thesis, the graduate psychologist Marco Rathschlag researched the effectiveness of wingwave and supervized a series of bachelor theses on the topic of wingwave. The research focused on overcoming stress caused by sports injuries, on the effectiveness of the wingwave music to lower the heart pulse rate, on the performance-enhancing effect in a 5000-meter running event and on coping with arachnophobia, to name just a few examples.

In this chapter, we present the results of the "Study on Sports Injuries" in detail. It is about athletes who cannot find their way back to their usual performance level, although the injury was healed from the medical point of view. Wingwave helped them to find their way back to their full performance capacity.

At present, further research projects are being planned in collaboration with the medical faculty of the University of Lübeck on the topic of "student's health" and "fear of flying". These projects are still in the very early stages, but we are very pleased that they will further build on research works that have already been carried out.

In 2019, a wingwave research project about coaching of pupils was carried out under the leadership of Junior Professor Stefanie Hüttermann at the German Sport University Cologne. The 100 children aged between 11 and 12 were assigned to either a control group or experimental group. The sports psychologist and psychologist (M. sc.) Frank Weiland was writing

T=0: before coaching, T=1: immediately after coaching,
T=2: 6-8 weeks after coaching

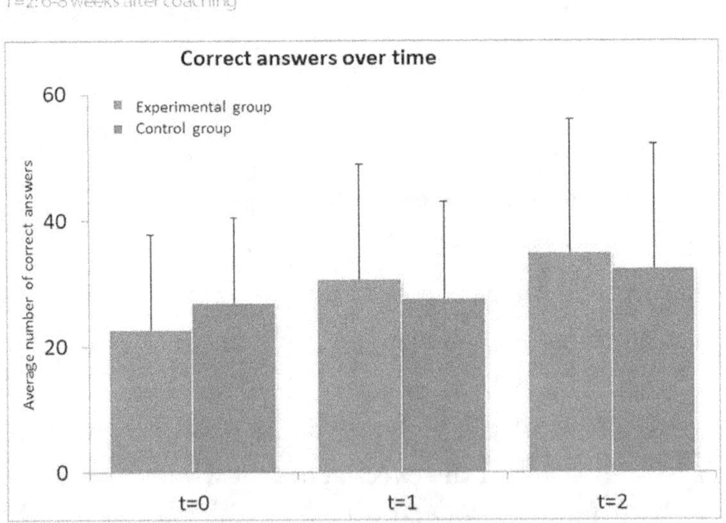

Average values of correct answers in the KLT-R of the experimental and control group over time
(t=0 to t=2). The maximum possible number of correct answers is 180.
The error bars indicate the standard deviation.

his doctorate about this subject and was able to present really good results from the study in 2019: only after three hours of wingwave-coaching, the children are having fun at school again, they are able to concentrate better in exams and make significantly less mistakes in them. The complete presentation can be read in the book "wingwave coaching for children and youth" from Cora Besser-Siegmund and Lola A. Siegmund.

6.2 Transform Performance Stress Into the Joy of Performance? By Marie Luise Dierks[5]

For many people, speaking in front of small or large groups is associated with high stress and unpleasant feelings. The stresses manifest themselves in diverse forms, such as minor anxieties, slight heart palpitations, sleepless nights before the presentation, stomach and intestinal problems, breaking into sweats, jitters, and restlessness. To a lesser extent, probably every person, who is about to give an important speech, is aware of this. Yes, these symptoms, commonly referred to as stage fright, also help to mobilize all energy reserves to give the perfect public performance. However, in some human beings, the fears assume such severe proportions that they become ill or evade the situation completely, frequently with negative consequences for their professional development.

In these cases, both behavioral training, as well as psychological-therapeutic measures will help. In behavioral training, the frightening situations are performed repeatedly, with the aim of bringing about familiarization and thus, more certainty for subsequent performances. For that purpose, there are helpful tips to deal with the symptoms; often the presentation techniques are imparted and video analysis is used.

An alternative way of dealing with stage fright and fears of public appearances is to address the (minor) traumas and anxieties, which underlie the fears of performance, and manage these fears and anxieties with the aid of interventions used in psychology, psychotherapy, or coaching.

The subject matter of the research project was on whether the wingwave method, with its focus on quick identification of the stress-causing triggers in the past, present, or future expectations, and the rapid processing of anxieties and fears on the basis of bilateral hemispheric stimulation, is suitable in reducing the stress of performance.

---

[5] Professor at the Hannover Medical School in the area of "Public Health"

The Study

From 2006 to 2008, we conducted investigations in collaboration with the Besser-Siegmund-Institut. The aim was to investigate the significance of the wingwave method compared to other interventions in the case of fears of performance. The individual assessment of the anxiety symptoms immediately before the presentation and in the course of time, as well as physiological parameters, such as blood pressure and heart rate, were defined as the extent of effect.

All the participants in the study suffered from performance anxiety and registered for intervention based on newspaper advertisements without being informed about the nature of this intervention. The intervention differed, although the basic framework was similar for all the groups: After a brief preparation, all the study participants had to deliver, initially without being "coached", a five-minute speech on a general topic assigned to them in front of an audience of strangers (approximately twelve people). They were then given a coaching and/or a training session, and a day later, they presented a speech on the same pattern as on the day before in front of an audience of strangers.

The Design and the Participants

Three groups were compared with each other:

1. **Group "wingwave +":** The participants of this group (n=11) were given one-hour wingwave intervention within the course of a one-day behavioral training session (video recordings and analysis, tutorials, presentation rules).

2. **Group "Pure wingwave":** The participants of this group (n=10) were given two hours of wingwave coaching as a measure and no additional behavioral training.

3. **Control group:** The participants of this group (n=10) were given a one-day behavioral training session on the topic of performance and presentation confidence (video recordings and analysis, tutorials, presentation rules).

The study participants included 22 women and nine men between the ages of 21 and 56 years, predominantly with a high educational qualification. They were not informed about the nature of training and/or the measures before the beginning of the intervention. The participants were assigned to the control group and to the "wingwave +" group on a random basis. After evaluating the results of both the initial groups, the "pure wingwave" group was established with the hypothesis that the structure and contents of the behavioral training, such as video feedback and tips on body language, could represent stress-triggering parameters themselves—at least, shortly before the performance.

At the beginning of the study, with the aid of a standardized survey instrument, the participants gave information pertaining to their general fears and anxieties before the presentation (stage fright rating scale). The current physical and psychological states of each participant (scale of performance stress) were recorded immediately before the short presentation. In this process, the presenters assessed, for example, the extent of their excitement, their heartbeats, their anxiety, their restlessness, and even their joyful expectations or their confidence on a scale of 0 = Not present at all to 6 = Very strong presence. Both the questionnaires were specifically developed for the study. In addition, the blood pressure and heart rate of all the participants were measured before, during, and after each presentation using a special technique, which allowed for continuous measurement over a longer period of time.

Results

With regards to blood pressure and heart rate, the three study groups exhibited virtually no difference at all in the before and after comparison. In both the first, as well as the second speech, most of the subjects from all the groups had a distinct increase in blood pressure and heart rate. This phenomenon is also manifested in people who, on a subjective level, feel better psychologically during the second round of their speech. Presumably, even a "positive state of excitement" can also be accompanied by increased blood pressure. A further aspect is the physical, as well as mental exertion, which can be held accountable for an increase in the physiological function, which needs to be investigated further.

In all three study groups, the negative feelings and physical symptoms, such as palpitations, sweating, or jitters, declined immediately before the second round of the presentation, thus after the intervention. The trend of this reduction was higher in the participants of both the groups with wingwave than in the participants of the "classic presentation training". Statistically, significant differences were evident between the "pure wingwave group" and the control group—in this case, the reduction of excitement before the presentation and fewer heart palpitations.

When comparing the three groups, the differences in the positive emotions are especially interesting. At the beginning of the intervention, the control group was more positive than both the other groups However, they lost the "joyful expectation" and "fun" during the behavioral training, whereas an increase of positive emotions was registered in both the other intervention groups. Above all, the group "pure wingwave" experienced increased positive emotions, such as determination, joyful expectation, and fun in the context of speech. The differences between these groups and control group are statistically significant.

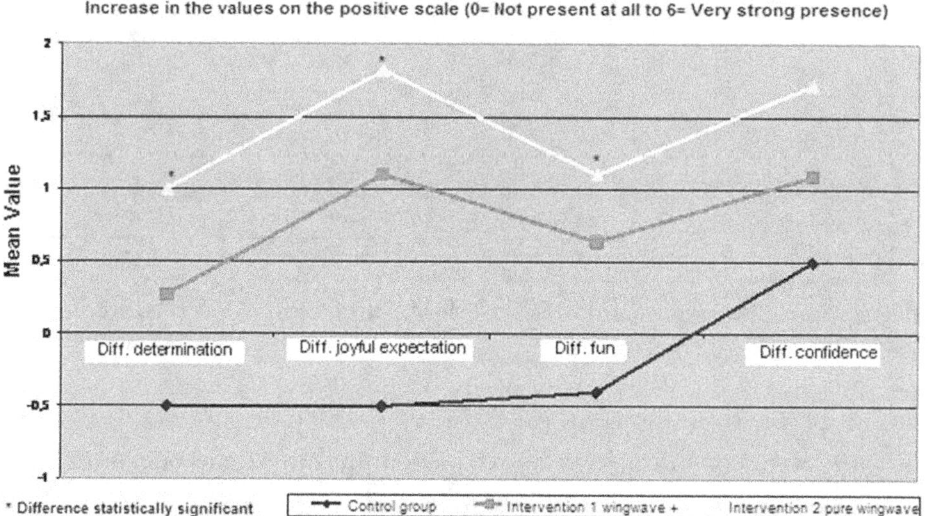

Illustration 22: Values Before and After the Intervention

The positive effects were maintained even after the immediate coaching and/or behavioral training. The survey conducted four months after the intervention shows that the general anxiety of people to deliver a speech in front of a certain audience had reduced in all three groups. When looking at the everyday professional life of the relevant target groups, colleagues, superiors, business partners, and strangers, the level of stage fright before the intervention—observed across all the three groups—was on an average rating of 4.6 on a scale of 0 (= no stage fright) to 6 (= very severe stage fright), and after the intervention, on an average rating of 3.5. The "pure wingwave" group benefitted with a reduction of stage fright by almost 2 points. Considering the audiences comprised of "business partners" and "strangers", the difference between these groups and the control group is statistically significant.

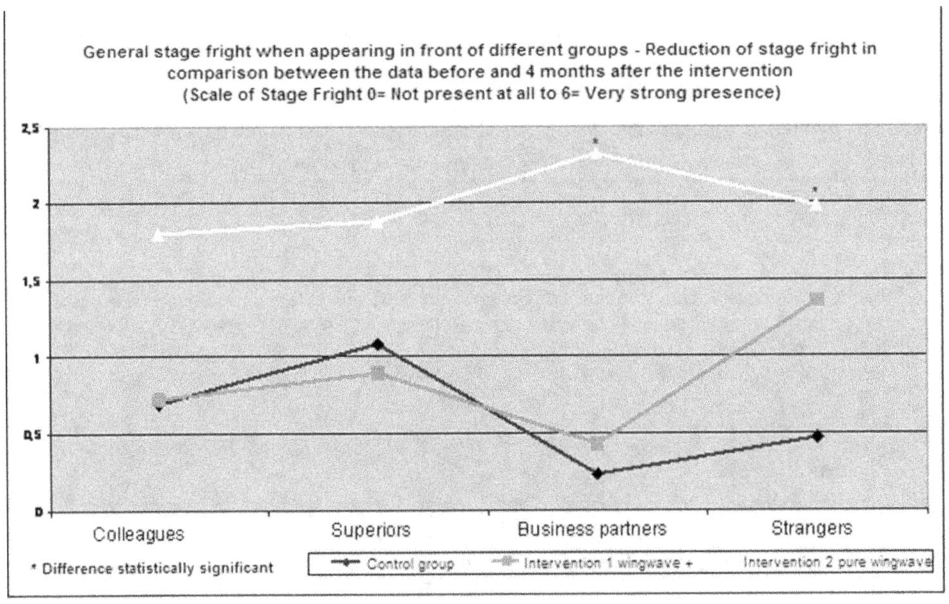

Illustration 23: Development of Stage Fright Four Months After the Intervention

It is an interesting question to ask as to whether the greater intensity of the wingwave coaching (two hours), as compared to the one-hour intervention of the "wingwave +" group, influenced the trend of the "pure wingwave" group in performing better. Or, whether the elements of the behavioral training, although helpful, became stress triggers of a different kind themselves.

These questions and a generalization of the results cannot be answered conclusively against the background of the small number of cases and the factors, which were not monitored any further and which influenced the assessments (for example, social desirability and familiarization effects), and against the background of the exploratory character of the study. Further investigations are necessary to strengthen the results.

Nevertheless, the results are rather encouraging for the further application of the wingwave method to reduce stress during public appearances, specifically, the fact that personal confidence in a presentation and the joy in the challenge can be significantly increased.

6.3 Doctoral Thesis of Marco Rathschlag on the Topic of the "Effectiveness of the wingwave Method"

Marco Rathschlag, graduate psychologist and professor at the Deutschen Sporthochschule Köln [German Sport University Cologne], wrote his doctoral thesis on the topic of "Self-Generated Emotions and Their Influence on Physical Performance". In the winter of 2013, he completed his doctorate.

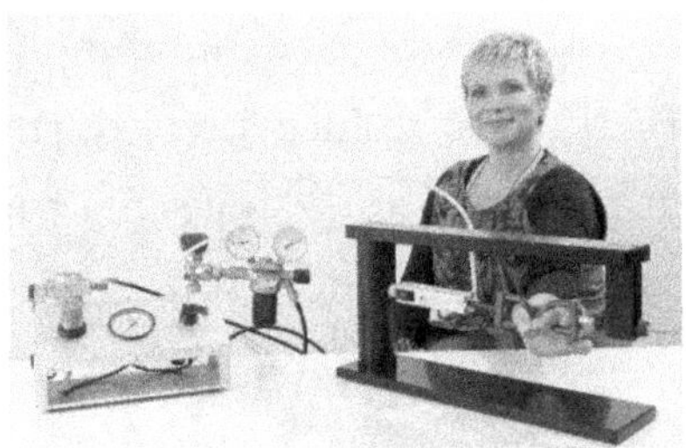

Illustration 24: Measuring Machine for the Myostatic Test

In cooperation with the Department of Biomechanics and Orthopaedics of the Deutschen Sporthochschule in Köln [German Sport University Cologne], a machine was developed, which objectified the myostatic test. Amongst other things, it could be demonstrated significantly that no fatigue effect occurs in the individual finger strength of the subjects when the myostatic test is conducted repeatedly. For this dissertation, the influence of various emotions on muscle strength applied during the myostatic test was researched.

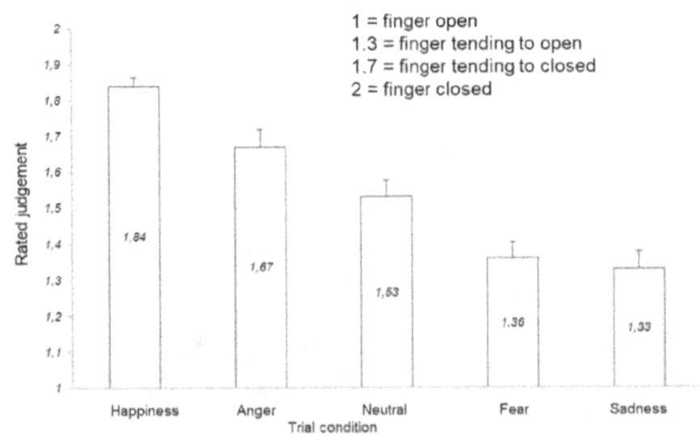

Illustration 25: Influence of Various Emotions on Muscle Strength

Instead of a person, an objective machine was used to generate a pulling force to separate the fingers. First, it was investigated under which emotion the subjects exerted maximal strength. The participants in the study were asked to think of a situation in their life, with which different emotions were associated. The results were clear: The subjects could exert maximal strength in their hand and finger muscles when associated with the emotion of happiness or joy.

Thus, the strength results were significant with the emotion of happiness in the first place and in the second place, with the emotion of anger. The weakest strength result was demonstrated with the emotions of grief and anxiety. In this respect, it makes sense to interpret the increase of strength during the myostatic test as a positive coaching effect.

In a follow-up project, it was investigated which de-stressing effect a one-hour wingwave intervention can exert on the topic of fear. 50 students with "a mixture" of topics relating to fear registered for the study. These fears included fear of examination and performance, fear of certain conflicts, and everyday fears, such as being in an elevator. All these cases involved "isolated" fears, which only impair people in specific situations. Otherwise, the subjects felt healthy, able to work, and cope with all life situations.

25 participants were coached using the wingwave method; the other 25 formed a control group without intervention. At the beginning of the test, the finger strength of all participants was measured using the myostatic test machine, whereby the participants were asked to think of the topic of fear or anxiety. It showed similar weak values as it had in the preliminary study. Furthermore, all the study participants were subjected to two written psychological tests in which values not only related to the specific topic of fear or anxiety, but also related to the general level of anxiety.

Illustration 27 shows that two weeks after the one-hour intervention, there was a clear increase in the finger strength reaction of the wingwave group during the myostatic test when the subjects thought about the coached topic of fear or anxiety. The control group, which was not coached, still tested weak.

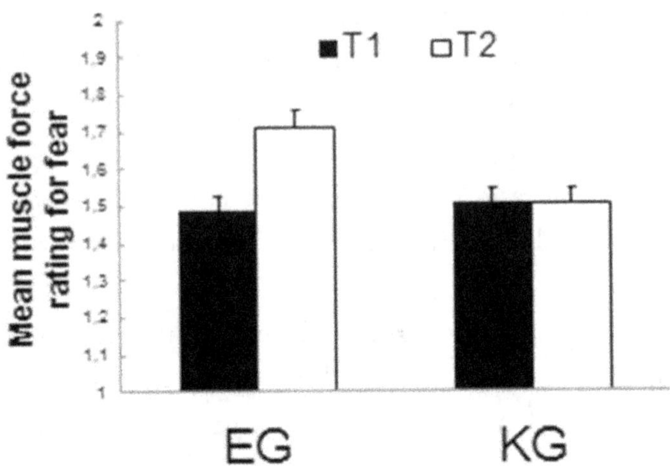

Illustration 26: Finger Strength Reaction After Two Weeks: EG = Intervention Group, KG = Control Group

Even in the psychological tests, there was a distinct improvement in the wingwave group: The values of anxiety decreased both with regards to the specific topic of anxiety, as well as general anxiousness.

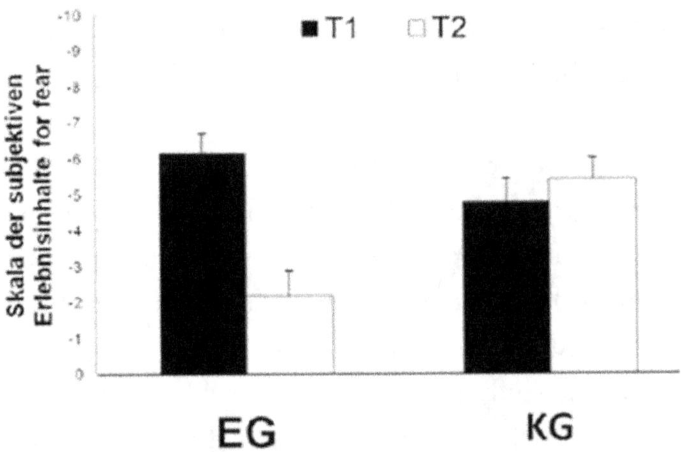

Illustration 27: Results on the Scale of Subjective Experience

The overall results were once again reflected in the "scale of subjective experience", which is used as a measuring tool for an emotional state in wingwave coaching. Once again, there was clear positive development of the wingwave group as compared to the control group.

Thus, wingwave coaching causes a significant decline in anxiety, which is perceived as a physically negative emotion, reduces general anxiousness, and strengthens the effect of positive emotions.

Furthermore, irrespective of the observation of the method, it can be said that stress relief and positive emotions can cause measurably increased strength in the hands and probably in the musculature of the entire body. Therefore, it would be extremely meaningful to organize each coaching or therapy process in consideration of individual physical strength responses of the coachees. From 2015 onward, the methodological society, "Gesellschaft für Neurolinguistisches Coaching – NLC", will be devoted to this topic. All the information is available at https://nlc-info.org.

In February 2014, the results of Marco Rathschlag's research were published as an article, "Reducing Anxiety and Enhancing Physical Performance by Using an Advanced Version of EMDR: A Pilot Study" in the renowned scientific journal *Brain and Behavior,* and were, therewith, presented to an international professional audience.

Altogether, five interesting theses have been produced at the Deutschen Sporthochschule Köln [German Sport University Cologne] on the topic of wingwave, for example, and on the de-stressing effect of the wingwave music.

Marco Ratschlag has presented the results of various studies on "Freudeforschung und wingwave-Grundlagen-Forschung [Research on joy and fundamental research on wingwave]" in the book, "*Mit Freude läuft's besser [With Joy, the Going Gets Better]*" (page 39-81). The book was a collaboration with Cora Besser-Siegmund, and was published in 2013.

6.4 Results of a Study on Sports Injuries[6]

The work focuses on the wingwave method and its effect in the psychological rehabilitation after sport-related injuries. The basis of the investigation is the assumption that a severe sports injury not only causes physical damages, but also affects the psychological state of mind of the persons concerned. It has often been observed that despite being healed from a medical perspective, the athletes still complain about mental problems. An exploratory approach exists in experiencing the stress condition, which can have an inhibiting effect due to the formation of a blockage. The use of a short-term wingwave coaching method should help in clearing this blockage and in restoring the performance capability of the injured person at the mental level.

To investigate the possible effect of the coaching method, a test design with a comparison of two times of measurements was selected. Between these two points of measurement, each of the twelve participants was given one-hour of wingwave coaching. Four selected coaches supervised the subjects who had suffered injuries of different types and severity. The measuring instruments were the scale of subjective contents of experiences according to Besser-Siegmund, as well as a questionnaire to gather the subjective evaluation. They were used once before the coaching and once immediately afterward. The scale demonstrated the momentary perception of stress when the subjects were asked to recall the situation of injury. The questionnaire recorded the influence of the performance-inhibiting and performance-enhancing factors.

The most important results showed a statistically higher significant change between the two points of measurement. This confirmed the four established hypotheses. The stressful effect of the memory of the injury-causing situation decreased after the provision of coaching. The results of the subjects were compared based on the type of injury. In this case, the

___

[6] Summary of a bachelor thesis of Vera Schellewald, Deutsche Sporthochschule Köln [German Sport University, Cologne], 2010.

results confirmed that the wingwave method was effective irrespective of the type of injury. Moreover, the comparison of the results of different coaches showed that the positive effect is not to be attributed to the person undergoing the coaching, but to the characteristics of the method itself.

In conclusion, it can be established that the method of wingwave coaching has a positive influence on the mental state of the subjects. Consequently, its use can support the psychological rehabilitation of an athlete after an injury and contribute to enhance the subjective wellbeing.

6.5 Studies on the Sustainability of the Positive Effects of Wingwave Coaching

Three months after the performance measurement undertaken by Vera Schellewald and Dominik Kutscha, the athletes who participated in the study were examined at the *Deutschen Sporthochschule Köln* (the German Sport University in Cologne) for a second time, which established the consistency of the results. Kutscha's thesis on this sustainability study has also been published as a book[7].

A further sustainability test to examine the effects of wingwave in the fight against arachnophobia was conducted under the guidance of Marco Rathschlag nine months after the interventions, and was likewise able to confirm the evidence of the positive effects of interventions.

In 2004, the Besser-Siegmund-Institut conducted the evaluation of 871 results of the clients using the documentation files of 23 coaches. Accordingly, 70% of the coachees achieved their initially defined goals after an average of 4 hours of wingwave coaching. In over 70% of the tested clients, this effect lasted for more than one year.

---

[7] D. Kutscha (2012): Der Einsatz der wingwave-Methode nach Sportverletzungen – eine Nachfolgeuntersuchung [The use of wingwave method after sports injuries. A follow-up study]. Saarbrücken: Akademiker-Verlag.

7

SELF-COACHING OF RESOURCES WITH OR WITHOUT WINGWAVE MUSIC

A study in collaboration with the *Medizinischen Hochschule Hannover* (Hanover Medical School) shows the special value of the wingwave coaching for a sustainable access to positive emotions. In this chapter, we present formats for which coaches can use the wingwave process, both as described thus far, and as a method for targeted resource coaching. Resource coaching is also perfectly suitable for self-management. So you can try out the methods described here, we begin with the self-coaching approach as an entry point.

Resource coaching refers to the sources of mental strength that each person already possesses. Resource coaching does not, however, replace the training of skills. Athletes, for example, train their general fitness on a regular basis and above all, focus on the special techniques and skills involved in their individual types of sport. Resource coaching, however, can influence which mental activity occurs during trainings. It can ensure that these athletes remain motivated even during a "dry spell" and that they can withstand difficult situations by remaining strong instead of submitting to fear. It can help them maintain speed and creativity at a peak level and retain the curiosity and willingness to learn what is necessary to succeed.

After presenting several coaching techniques, we will summarize the most important steps once again for self-coaching. Sometimes, these summaries are brief. Here, we will concentrate on the essential strategy, which gives intervention its special profile. This chapter will very briefly introduce the numerous possible combinations of wingwave as well as a few selected NLP elements. There are many more types of interventions, for example, working with the timeline or imaginative constellation work, such as the one described in our book, *Imaginative Familienaufstellung (Imaginative Family Constellations)*. The following pages should thus be regarded as the "appetizer".

7.1 Three Self-Coaching Techniques

From the outset, we would like to mention where self-coaching with the methods presented here should *not* be used under any circumstances: When processing the resistant stress imprinting and in belief coaching, which are presented in this chapter. In PSI, it is rare that any person can dissociate themselves to such an extent that they can be a coach and the person affected at the same time. Unfortunately, the result of such a self-experiment could be that one gets tangled up in the thorny hedge of his inner Sleeping Beauty's Castle, and thus, instead of being able to calm and integrate the inner stress, it becomes further aggravated. Therefore, we would like to explicitly warn against a self-coaching attempt and highly recommend always entrusting such issues to a professional coach.

Although belief coaching is not as delicate as self-coaching, it is, however, often ineffective. It is not at all easy to find the subconscious sources of our belief systems because, well, it is indeed subconscious. An outsider is much more likely than you to get an overview of your unfavourable thought patterns with which you unintentionally complicate your life or make your life more difficult. Here, too, cooperation with a coach leads to faster and better results. We also recommend a practical introduction to self-coaching topics by an appropriately trained wingwave coach.

In the following, you will learn three options of self-intervention. Please experiment and find out which of these techniques is most effective for you. All three of these options involve the activation of a so-called bilateral hemispheric stimulation, or to put it more simply, you can motivate both the cerebral hemispheres of your brain to work optimally on the subject at hand.

Intervention Option No. 1: Self-Initiated Eye Movements

Some of our clients manage well to initiate the eye movements themselves. During this process, one looks for the fixed visual points on the left and right of the respective field of vision, for example, a window or a vase, and then one lets the eyes move back and forth between these points like a windscreen wiper.

Intervention Option No. 2: Wingwave Music

During self-coaching, most of our clients prefer to use wingwave music specially developed by us, which can be listened to through headphones for a bilateral stimulating effect.

Under this link, you will find a song for you to download free of charge:

https://wingwave-shop.com/book/strandspaziergang.mp3

If you want to further work with wingwave music in your self-coaching, you can buy MP3 downloads of the albums and individual tracks in the Wingwave online shop. You can also download the wingwave music using the wingwave app.

As you know, the wingwave music consists of a rhythmic tone which alternates from left to right while background music is playing. While listening to this music with headphones, concentrate on the issues you would like to self-coach. Even the musician, Leo, who we mentioned at the beginning of the book, activated his creative writing ability using this technique. It is extremely suitable for finding your way back into your inner equilibrium. Furthermore, you can also listen to the music while doing physical activity, for example, while jogging.

Intervention Option No. 3: Butterfly Technique

As a third method, we recommend the "Butterfly Technique", which we mentioned earlier. You can make good use of this technique by lying down or sitting in a comfortable position. To use this technique, cross your forearms above your shoulders so that your fingertips are touching both your shoulders. In this position, touch your shoulders with the palms of your hands and alternate gently tapping your shoulders from left to right, synchronized with the waving rhythm. This helps you achieve the desired neural stimulation effect.

We would like to make an agreement with you to use the term "processing" as a generic term for all "back and forth techniques" from now on. "Bilateral Hemispheric Stimulation" is simply too uncomfortable for general use. In practical application, for example, it says: "Now the processing is carried out." It is up to you whether it is eye movements, auditory stimulation, or the butterfly technique. The term represents the information that the respective bilateral stimulations cause an accelerated processing and integration of a mental topic or memory. The term "set" then means—as already described—a group of several movement passes.

7.2 Activating Power Sources Consciously

Every person has experienced powerful, happy, or contented moments in life. These positive moments and the feelings they generate, however, do not have their origins solely in external situations. In fact, it is a certain ability within us that transforms perceptions into positive feelings and emotions. At times, we may think that these positive emotions are not present in certain situations, but this is not true. The difference between the situations in which we feel good and those in which we don't simply has to do with our ability to access the positive feelings and emotions. Understanding this makes all the difference. Sources of strength can be recalled by anyone; nobody needs to wait passively for an external situation to trigger them, as the following example shows.

Our client, Peter, is interested in getting a new job, and he has finally been invited to the assessment center for an interview. Peter expressed his fears by saying, "I feel somewhat queasy because I really do not know what is going to happen to me." We asked him to think of a similar situation in his life in which he did not know what was going to happen to him, but he did not feel queasy in view of that uncertainty. We found the information quickly. Peter is an enthusiastic football player. Before every football game, he is also not able to prepare specifically for every move because every match is different. Nevertheless, he looks forward to the many surprises and unknown factors. "Somehow, I know for sure that I can handle all the unpredictable factors."

In working with Peter, we first asked him to select a finger or a toe, which he can wiggle easily. This wiggle will later become the motorized "success switch" for voluntary retrieval of overall positive feelings. Peter decides to select his right little finger. Then, we ask him to think about an exceptionally exciting game, which was fun for him and which involved quick and flexible responsiveness.

From this point forward, you can easily recognize the phases of wingwave intervention. "In your thoughts, please select an intensive moment in the game, of which you have a particularly good memory, and in which you knew that you were in perfect harmony." Peter nods. "Now, look for a positive

I-sentence, which aptly expresses your self-perception." The answer comes spontaneously: "I can do it." Peter then mentions the term "power" as the emotion. Although it is not a classic emotion, for Peter, it's the word which best describes his overall psycho-physiological state. "Now, perceive the feeling of power, which this memory triggers in you. How intense is it now, at this very moment, when you think of the game?" Peter gives it a rating of +5 points on the wellness scale. We test the sentence further. "This power is the right emotion needed for the assessment center." The test result is strong. In the case of a weak test result, we would have looked for and tested additional resources, but in this case, we spontaneously find the "perfect ingredient".

Please not that we did not ask, "How strongly did you feel this situation at that time?" Instead, we asked, "How strongly has the positive state of mind been evoked by the pure memory of it right here and now?" This is followed by the intensive body scan in search of the body echo. "Where exactly in your body is the memory of this power experience located?" Sometimes, we support the body scan with the following question: "Just imagine, I am a Martian or Mr. Spock and I am not familiar with any emotions at all. How would I describe this feeling in detail? How ddoes the body perceives a feeling of enthusiasm or power? Is there a tingling in the ears or does one get a hot big toe?"

This questioning helps the clients sharpen their perception and to 'feel' very precisely during the body scan. "My chest feels light, as though it is flowing with energy. In addition, I have a particularly good and pleasant cool feeling all around my eyes, like you feel when you are wide awake and aware." After the body scan, we perform the processing. In the case of Peter, it is the classic slow pleasure waving. After the first set, the feeling of power is perceptibly strengthened. We continue until the overall positive experiences needs no further enhancement. At the end, when thinking about scenes from the game, Peter's subjective power level increases to +8. He undergoes the body scan once again, but now, while feeling the positive body echo, he wiggles his right little finger. At the same time, he thinks of the sentence, "I can do it!" Thus, the overall positive inner state is anchored to the movement of the "success switch".

After this preparation, we ask Peter to think about the upcoming assessment center interview and at the same time, wiggle the little finger when thinking about this imagined scene. "I immediately feel this pleasant surge in my chest," he says spontaneously. "That uneasy feeling is completely gone." We anchor in this positive development with several sets of slow REM phases. With the help of this intervention, Peter's good feeling developed to the point of +5 on the wellness scale.

In the real situation, a couple of days later, Peter uses his success switch time and again, thus inconspicuously wiggling his little finger every now and then. During his entire time in the assessment center, he taps into his strength resources and can immediately adapt to any surprising situation. As a result, he got the position he wanted. "It is interesting that on that morning, I even looked forward to the selection procedure," he said later. This statement clearly reflects the results of all the research on the topic of positive emotions through wingwave coaching.

This form of emotion management is a proactive, preparatory approach. You decide with what state of mind you wish to step into a specific situation and trigger a positive state of mind before the beginning of your performance. You do not wait and see what the situation does to you; you do something with the situation. Above all, in interpersonal communication, within the first few seconds of an encounter, you achieve positive personal charisma about your environment with the help of this method.

You can "collect" several states of resources within your personal success switch. Your subconscious is smart enough to activate the exact matching resource in the appropriate context.

Self-coaching tip: Consciously activate the sources of strength

Preparation: Decide in favour of your self-coaching technique—eye movements, butterfly technique, or wingwave music. You can listen to the wingwave music from Point 1 onward.

1. Think of a future situation in which you need your positive resources.
2. Determine a "success switch": finger, thumbs, big toe, etc.

3. Now, think of a situation in the past in which you had the exact resources, which you want for the future situation: happiness, enthusiasm, courage, alertness, responsiveness, humour, detachment, etc. Thereby, it does not make any difference in which specific situation it happened. It is not decisive what you did, but *how*, thus using the inner activation you mastered or experienced in that situation.

4. Pick out the best moments, which you are going to focus on going forward.

5. Determine a positive I-statement, which correctly describes your perception of yourself today.

6. Name the emotion, which applies to the overall condition: happiness, satisfaction, enthusiasm, etc.

7. Assign a value between 0 and +10 to this overall positive wellbeing on the wellness scale.

8. Perform a body scan to focus the positive body echo on the pleasant memory.

9. Carry out the processing until the wellness experience cannot be increased any more.

10. Feel the good emotion, think of the positive I-sentence, and wiggle the success switch to anchor the feeling.

11. Think of the future situation and, in doing so, use your success switch. In this manner, your subconscious has already linked the future event with an inner source of strength.

12. Anchor the positive experience by means of a few more sets and, in doing so, continue to wiggle the success switch.

13. When you experience the situation live, use your success switch in a targeted manner.

7.3 Positive Self-Motivation

Experienced readers of NLP have probably missed the fact that the interventions of the auditory sensory channel—the hearing—presented here is somewhat underrepresented regarding the range of experiences. Thereby, consideration of all the sensory channels in internal and external perceptual processing is part of a successful coaching process, because with the help of this method, you can, of course, change not only visual representations, such as the recalled images, but also auditory inner perceptions. This includes, for instance, the intra-personal dialogue, which every one of us constantly holds with ourselves. Often, this communication with one's self creates the "mood" in which a person finds himself.

Envision for a moment that just a few minutes after you wake up, you use your language in your thoughts: "Oh, what time is it? Have I woken up on time? Can I stay in bed for a few more minutes?" After a few more minutes, the inner voice then becomes somewhat stricter: "Go on, get up now!" In this manner, we internally moderate our experiences and deeds all day long.

This self-communication is indispensable self-management, which every human being uses. Above all, even self-motivation takes place using this principle. It is not only images and visions that inspire us to perform, but also our inner voice. These must work especially hard when a person, for example, must overcome a strenuous phase on the way to achieving a goal.

In the phases of perseverance, one should be one's own optimal coach to mobilize the required energies. However, this is exactly the weak point in most of our coaching clients. Naturally, they sometimes try using power statements, such as "you can do it" or "I am successful", but the sentence does not contribute to any 'rousing' effect. If these sentences are screamed internally in a panic, they have a frightening effect rather than a motivating one. The same applies to a threatening commanding tone or reproachful lamenting. To make matters worse, the unpleasant tone of the inner voice intensifies in hectic moments and continues to escalate the stress arousal further along the line.

The tone of your inner voice has the same effect on you as though someone from the outside is speaking to you. Hectic, scolding, or panic-stricken voices may pull a person down, regardless of how uplifting the intention of the sentence may be. Thus, they have a demotivating effect. Therefore, it is extremely important to transform the inner tone into the right "music", according to the saying: "The tone makes the music, meaning it's not what you say, but how you say it." It is particularly during strenuous times that a positive inner voice can have an uplifting or even electrifying effect.

When you perceive that your inner thoughts are racing, pounding, or whining through your head in the form of sentences and your inner voice, use your processing method. You will notice that the auditory thoughts rapidly become more pleasant. The inner voice starts to become calmer, sober, or pleasantly powerful, depending on what has a particularly motivating effect on you. The amazing aspect of the wingwave effects is—as we have already described—that during the processing, subconsciously and automatically, it is precisely when a solution is found that there is the most positive effect on you personally. In NLP, we have always said: "Please describe how a voice should talk to you so that you feel optimally motivated." This step is superfluous in wingwave coaching because mostly, the best results emerge naturally during the processing without being asked for or suggested by the coach.

The more often you use this self-coaching, the more often you will use a positive self-motivation in stressful situations. Use this method when you experience unpleasant surprises and you think of sentences such as: "Oh, how terrible!" Or when you are in a panic, "What should I do, what should I do?" By using this method, transform your inner voice into a powerful energizer and you will feel motivated very quickly to find a creative solution for the respective situation.

You can also embed this form of positive self-motivation in yourself. Whenever you succeed in making the inner voice sound especially congenial and motivating, simply grab one of your earlobes. Once you have done this more often, the brief grasping of your earlobe will trigger the motivating voice at lightning speed, promoting a good constructive sentiment.

Self-coaching tip: Positive self-talk

Preparation: Choose your processing technique. If you have decided in favor of the music, please leave it switched off for the time being.

1. Consciously check for a moment: What is the quality of your inner voice when you think of your thoughts in a peak performance situation or in a moment of stress? Recall such a situation or wait until you shortly remember it, and then perform a live "technical inspection of the voices".

2. If you are not sure whether these inner voices in their special tonality are bestowing you optimal strength, then determine what is having a somewhat demotivating effect on you:
   - Is it loud and hectic?
   - Is it too fast?
   - Is it scolding or threatening?
   - Is it mocking or condescending?
   - Is it urgently whispering?
   - Is it lamenting?

3. If you are working with the music, put on your headphones now. For readers using other techniques, prepare for the beats of the butterfly or the eye movements. Now, let this voice resound in the inner ear. Perform your processing until the inner voice transforms and has a congenial and motivating effect. Find out what bestows you with the best-possible inner strength. It could be:
   - Calm and composed
   - Playful and humorous
   - Dynamic and captivating
   - Friendly and empathic
   - Powerful and convincing

4. Anchor this effect to your earlobe and use this anchor whenever you need a powerful motivational boost.

7.4 Self-Image Coaching: Let Your Personal Charisma Shine

Of course, the personal charisma of a human being depends on all kinds of factors. One of the most important is self-image, which a person has developed about themselves. It is widely known that that the greater the positive effect we have on our fellow human beings, the greater we agree with our self-image. A lot of people have an ambivalent relationship with their own appearance. Often, a person finds flaws in himself or herself, which are not obvious to other people. One may have a pimple, but others may not see it so vividly.

You do not pay attention to the small details in another person. Instead, you pay attention to the overall impression a person leaves on you. Alternatively, it consists of static pieces of a puzzle, such as clothing, height, or hairstyle. However, the magic of personal charisma emerges from moveable elements, including facial expression, muscle tone, blood circulation, size of the pupils, breathing, voice, way of laughing, gestures, and attitude. One cannot buy these personal characteristics from any shop in the world because they originate in the brain. Your inner state is the conductor of these movable non-verbal expressions.

If you find your self-image to be personable, express this attitude precisely to yourself as well as through your non-verbal signals. You radiate self-confidence, and thus, automatically act in a self-assured manner. This takes place in the first few seconds of an interpersonal encounter and sets the signals for the future atmosphere of making contact.

But what exactly is self-image? It is a picture you have of yourself in your mind – in the same way that you create an image of another person. However, for that purpose, you do not create just any kind of picture. There are people, such as partners or colleagues, who you have seen a thousand times and you have collected hundreds of memories in your head of them. However, you only search through a very few for the "image of the person" from this mental archive. If I appreciate someone specific, I look at them as an attitude, which expresses their competence. Maybe I saw this person stuffed-up and with a red nose once, but I store this picture somewhere else because it is not representative of my assessment.

Likewise, when "creating an image" of your personality, your environment does not focus on a pimple, which you had terrifyingly discovered in the morning while looking in your bathroom mirror. Rather, one will notice an image of you, which reflects the overall impression that you have made on your fellow human beings. For your own self-image, you should search for an image of yourself, which in your opinion, excellently reflects your abilities and likeable qualities. For this purpose, if you are unable to retrieve such a positive image of your personality on the spur of the moment, look at several photographs. Pick one image you can confirm using an I-sentence: "I like myself in this photograph" or "I look good in this photograph." If you do not have any such photographs, search for an extremely good portrait photographer to create several "positive self-images". This investment is just as important for your mental "success outfit" as business attire or a tailor-made suit.

Exercise: Enhance Your Positive Charisma

Very consciously, perceive the above described positive image of yourself or the good photographs. Now, close your eyes and observe your self-image on a "mental canvas". Now, notice which emotion that image triggers in you when combined with the sentence: "I like myself." Is it pride, happiness, or satisfaction? Give a rating to this emotion on the "Wellness Scale".

Continue with the body scan: "Where in my body do I feel the positive body echo with this image and this sentence?"

Start with the processing. Experience how the positive feelings become increasingly more intense. Perform as many sets until the good feeling cannot be enhanced any more.

Now, place the palm of your hand on the top of your chest. By doing so, you have anchored the positive self-image, along with the pleasant body echo. Just by briefly touching this spot, the associated non-verbal pattern is retrieved in your expression within a matter of seconds, and, consequently, immediately affects your environment.

This exercise can have good effects for the enhancement of your non-verbal positive charisma. However, sometimes, it may also be important to work with images of yourself, which are not very pleasing. In such a case, of course, the subjective discomfort is "waved away" or neutralized using your personal technique. However, you should only proceed in such a manner if you do not have any serious problems with your self-image. If the latter is the case, a coach or a therapist should handle this issue. In self-coaching, you should prefer to work with the positive images in a targeted manner. The images do not always have to be razor-sharp, full-body photographs. Successful portraits will fulfil the purpose of the exercise.

We had a client called Klaus who wanted to feel good in a suit, so he wanted to work with a problematic self-image topic. "I think these clothes are terrible; I always feel like a puppet in them." Even in his job, he used every opportunity to wear something colourful or casual. "This is simply who I am—not that other person." Naturally, this denial of a certain image for one's self was extremely problematic because, above all, he always had to endure important professional situations in a suit. He realized that this "suit allergy" could be thoroughly damaging to his charisma at any decisive moment. Therefore, we worked with him on this issue.

With respect to his self-image in the suit, he described a feeling of immobility and stiffness in the neck and shoulders during the body scan. During processing, this feeling rapidly transformed into a pleasant bodily sensation, which was immediately apparent and positively reflected in his facial expressions. "Now, I feel pleasantly self-confident in the suit; it is indeed a relief and an enhancement," he said a few weeks after this intervention.

Self-coaching tip: My positive self-image

Since we have extensively described the exercise in the text, we are only presenting a summary here.

1. Pick one or two positive photographs of yourself.
2. Put on the headphones and start the wingwave music or prepare yourself for another type of processing.
3. Perform the body scan: Where do you feel the most pleasant resonance of these self-images? Place your hand on your chest once you have focused on the pleasant body echo.
4. Continue with the processing until you have achieved the most pleasant effect.
5. In subsequent situations, just place your hand on your chest for a moment as an anchor to retrieve the positive self-image experience.

7.5 Visualising Goals and Objectives

Many of our clients want to work successfully toward their specific goals. They wish to exhibit at an important event, place a product or even successfully place their own personality in the market or in public, attain a specific position, or gain a victory in some sporting event. Based on several mental training approaches, it is already well-known that one should, as far as possible, visualize one's goals and paint them in the most beautiful colours. This allows future perspectives to develop strength like a mental magnet to which one feels drawn. It gives birth to a longing to achieve the goal, which justifies every endeavor. The effect is a self-fulfilling prophecy. Many studies have shown that people with positive objectives are more likely to achieve their goals than people who either do not have or have only worked out weak future scenarios. Thereby, from the perspective of NLP, it is important to not only visualize your goals three-dimensionally, but also to hear, feel, smell, and taste them.

Similarly, Sabine had also established a goal in her inner experience. As a journalist, it was her dream to become the head of the department one day—if possible, in the field of fashion. "In front of my mind's eye, I always see my own office, which I will have all to myself." We asked her how she visualizes this image of her goal. It soon became apparent that she only saw the office in front of her mind's eye; her own personality was not part of it.

When visualizing, very often, people only see the trophy in front of them without ever holding it. However, when coaching for objectives, it is extremely important to visualize your individual self having achieved the goal. Therefore, we ask our clients to always create a lively image of a successful future individual-self, who, in a mentally visualized future image, is tremendously delighted to have reached the goal, and, in doing so, also appears happy and healthy.

This is not the case with Sabine in the first place. When we asked her to see herself in her own office as the head of the department, she said, "I look rather harassed in there." She then focused on this image before the processing. We wave until the future Sabine looks really happy, relaxed, and thereby, upright and exuding authority. In this case, we chose the emotional state of the present-self when perceiving the future-self as the "barometer of success. When Sabine was satisfied with this vision of herself, she achieved seven points on the "Wellness Scale". It is only at this point that we askedd her to merge with her future-self in her thoughts and to experience, with this association, how the future feels. After this future-test, she returned to the present and looked at her future-self once again from the outside, whereby, we asked her to raise her right hand and look at the successful head of the department.

Your own hand is an excellent anchor for the "memory of the future". Whenever one invests in the future, it is always associated with an activity in which the hand is in focus. The hand is holding the telephone, the computer mouse, or a pen. It is holding the hand of another person, or raises the glass during a business meal. "This actually works," Sabine said later. "I was sitting with my Editor-in-Chief and coincidentally, looked at my right hand, and immediately, saw my future-self in front of my mind's eye. I immediately straightened up and had a completely different voice." Whether it was solely because of that, we do not know. In any case, Sabine has her dream job today. During her promotion, her Editor-in-Chief said that she had gained a great deal of "grit" over the past few months.

Self-coaching tip: My successful future-self

Listen to the wingwave music or prepare yourself for your processing method.

1. Think about an important professional goal.
2. Visualize a successful target situation in which your future-self plays the leading role.
3. Perform the processing until the future-self feels really good.
4. Now, go for a "future test drive". In your visualization, merge with your successful future-self. Thereafter, detach yourself once again, and return to the present.

5. Raise your right hand and simultaneously look at your future-self and at this hand. From now on, whenever you look at your hand, you will know in the present what you are striving for and feel positive target energy.

6. In later exercises, anchor several future-selves in your hand. For example, the visualization of a happy retirement.

7.6 Coaching of the Objectives "In Vivo"

The term "in vivo" originated from behavioral therapy. In this form of coaching, a great deal of importance is placed on the processing and training of a desired behavior or feeling, not only in the mind but also in transporting the results arising from the mental training to the corresponding live-situation. This procedure ensures that later, in a corresponding situation, the brain receives as many "sensory keywords" as possible for the priming of the resourceful experience and behavior.

In Sabine's case, we could, of course, not go into the editorial department or the offices of the head of the department to conduct our coaching intervention. Nevertheless, there was a good solution. One evening, Sabine worked longer than all her colleagues, so she simply sat down in the empty office of a head of the department. She felt the chair, looked at the desk and the room, and held the telephone for a moment. She brought this experience into the next coaching session. She focused on the experience, felt the pleasant body echo, and we performed the processing until she had collected +8 on the wellness scale with this recalled memory.

If our clients have an important meeting ahead of them, we ask them to appear in the next coaching session in the clothes they are going to wear on that occasion. Some bring files of their "stressful project" or a photograph of a superior officer or colleague they dislike. If the opportunity arises, we go along as far as possible into the in vivo training. As happened once, we managed to go to a large banquet hall with one of our clients where he had to give a speech in front of a large audience a few days later. Then, while looking at the many chairs, we performed the processing at that place, which, of course, very closely resembled the live situation. Thus, during in vivo coaching, there are no limits to creativity.

Self-coaching tip: success through live-moments

You have already familiarized yourself with the wingwave coaching of resources. Simply combine this approach with in vivo self-coaching by seeking out, gathering, or re-enacting as many sensory-specific experiences as possible for "interweaving" the resourceful state into a significant experience. For this purpose, here are a few examples:

- Get photographs of the important conversation partners.
- Put on the clothes you will wear in your important moments of performance.
- Take hold of the important items that are associated with the performance-related context: telephone, golf club, microphone, etc.
- Assume the posture that is in context with the moment of the performance.
- If possible, seek out the rooms or buildings where you are going to "perform" or obtain good photographs of the "places of performance".

7.7 Experience Creativity Enhancement

For people in the field of peak performance, creative ideas and innovative thinking are especially important. New products and marketing strategies must be developed on a constant basis as the environment can be changeable depending on where the performance or job takes place. Moreover, this requires great flexibility in thinking. The ingenious solutions are in demand, especially in difficult and deadlocked situations, and the competition does not sleep either. That is why it is important to have a brilliant idea or decisive invention first.

Even if successful, most of our coaching clients are still not able to rest on their laurels. This is specifically true for artists, people in the media or the fashion industry, and even many athletes. Just think of the designs of fashion collections or the development of sporting events—they all must draw from their creative sources daily to stay on top of developments.

Speaking of "creative sources", this term is, of course, a metaphor, and we prefer to work with metaphors if our coaching clients want to enhance or restore their general creativity. This is because, interestingly, every human being describes a creativity blockage with a metaphor. It is simply a matter of paying attention to the client's choice of words. Here, we not only experience the metaphor very quickly, but also learn which sensory channel it is represented by internally, as the following example shows.

Visual Metaphors

"Somehow, all this has not fully come to fruition."
For this purpose, the association of immature fruits is practical.

"My ideas have dried up."
In this case, one visualizes a source, which is not bursting any more.

"I have no more ideas."
In this image, the ideas fall from above, such as blossoms, colourful rain, or balls. In this process, we always step into the metaphor with the client in the form of a sentence, and paint it together with him.

Auditory Metaphors

"I have no brilliant ideas."

Or

"Somehow, this is not brilliant enough."

Even in this case, the coachee develops specific references based on precise enquiries: Does he visualize the "brilliant idea" like an auditory backdrop of a firework display or like a start-up sound of a sports car?

Emotions and Motor-Skills-Related Metaphors

"Otherwise, I am always bursting with ideas."

"I cannot go any further."

"I am blocked."

"I feel stuck."

In these descriptions, it is, for example, important to discuss the localization of the obstacles: In a blocked-state, there could be a hurdle in the way, and possibly, outside the physical body; in case of a stuck-state, there is an absence of the necessary inner muscle movement.

Olfactory and Gustatory Metaphors

Even though these are not used often, when they do appear, it is extremely effective to process them.

"This is all too bland."

"There is no salt in the soup."

Of course, some of these examples could also be mixed forms of senses. Thus, one person could imagine the "brilliant spark" to be audible, the other visual. Similarly, one person may experience an "effervescent idea" as warmth flowing through the body, whereas another may look at it as a fountain in front of the mind's eye. It is important to coach the client in his power of imagination to such an extent that he can describe his metaphors in specific details with regards to sensory perceptions and contents.

Once the metaphor has been described, the coachee focuses on his respective problem in his inner visualization: One looks at the dried-up source or the arid riverbed, listens to the grinding noise of the engine that refuses to start, feels stuck in the muscle and/or the obstacle blocking from the outside, or thinks of a dull taste in the mouth. At the same time, with regards to his contributed metaphor sentence, the coaching client thinks something like: "I cannot go on any further." For this purpose, processing is then performed. Almost always the metaphors rapidly evolve toward a positive direction. All of a sudden, one sees a fireworks display in front of the mind's eye or feels the revitalized muscles so that one can "continue further on".

Self-coaching tip: Creativity enhancement

Prepare your processing method. If you are working with the wingwave music, put on your headphones now and start listening to the music.

1. Describe your creativity problem internally in words. Determine which sensory channel, or sensory channels you prefer to use linguistically.
2. Develop metaphors using your own sentences.
3. Focus on the "present-state" of your metaphor, for example, "unripe fruits".
4. Perform your processing until the "fruits are ripe" and into "fruition", thus until the selected creativity metaphor has evolved into a "happy ending".

Note: This exercise is intended for general creativity enhancement. However, you can, of course, think about a specific task, for which you need good ideas. For example, an article, which you need to write. Focus on your issue, and when searching for ideas, perform your processing method repeatedly. By the way, Leo, the musician who has already been mentioned several times, uses this strategy when he is writing and composing.

7.8 Overcome Inner Limits

There is a very interesting goldfish experiment. If you put a goldfish in an aquarium, it freely swims around in its terrain. If you separate this aquarium with a transparent pane, the goldfish naturally only has half as much of the original area and it will swim in a circular movement in that area. Now, if the tank is divided into four parts using a partition wall, the goldfish will have very little space to swim. You might think that our goldfish will be very happy when the partition walls are removed again and it has the whole aquarium to swim around in. However, it does not do that. It simply continues to swim in its one-quarter space and never again tries to expand its sphere of activity. The partition wall has now become a part of its brain.

Naturally, we cannot compare the brain of a goldfish with that of a human being. However, they do have one thing in common: Neural pathways. These are formed in the brain when an activity or a thought pattern is regularly carried out or used over a long period. These are the neural interconnections between the brain cells with which our habits are represented in our head.

In his book *Die Biologie der Angst [The Biology of Fear]*, the brain researcher, Gerhard Hüther, works with a plausible image: Imagine you are standing on a mound in a landscape and are observing the connections between the houses, villages, and cities. There are narrow trails, somewhat wider dirt roads, asphalted village streets, comfortable country roads, and the multi-lane motorways. Naturally, the wide motorways offer the greatest driving comfort for the motorists: One drives fast and always straight ahead.

Invitation to an Experiment

For this purpose, take part in an experiment for a moment. Just join your hands for a few seconds. Then consciously, join your hands the other way around, so that the thumb, which is always at the bottom, is now at the top.

> Now, examine your holistic physical sensation—your body echo—with this unusual way of joining your hands. Most people describe this body echo as "funny" to the point of unpleasant. This unpleasant feeling arises because one is creating a new or different neural pathway when joining hands in this unusual manner. Alternatively, when one joins the hands correctly, one drives on a familiar neural pathway (familiar road). Although one feels more comfortable when joining hands in a normal manner, it does not mean, however, that joining hands in an unusual manner is a worse method of joining hands. To be precise: It is equally good.

It is quite natural that dealing with a new unfamiliar area feels "funny" because our brain has not yet created any neural pathways for this purpose. The development of new connections costs the brain more energy than the utilization of already established connections. One can measure the calorie consumption of the brain with the imaging procedures. Here, it becomes apparent, for example, that many calories are used in the case of pure learning and exercising when compared with retrieving already developed abilities. The acts and thought patterns that have been experienced hundreds of times before, simply become "second nature to you" –no matter how complicated they might have been in the beginning. Therefore, as opposed to us, the acrobat in a circus can carry out his somersault quite easily because he retrieves it from the perfectly developed neural pathway.

Transfer this experience to each new path, which is open to you throughout your life. Have you ever approached a topic hesitantly because you had a "funny" feeling about doing it? Unfortunately, many people assess it as a "bad premonition" and believe a funny feeling is reason enough not to have a go and try something new. Therefore, one tries to replace the familiar experience with as much theoretical information as possible. But, however good the collection of theories may be, they do not save the venture into the other part of the aquarium, and consequently, the confrontation with an unfamiliar experience, which evokes that "funny feeling".

Surprisingly, 30-year-old Wolfgang was offered a job in Mexico by his company. Despite gathering intensive information, he still had that "funny feeling" in his thoughts about living and working in a foreign country for two years. During the coaching, we asked him to focus on any imagined—designed—image of his future in Mexico. "I do not see the work, rather my apartment over there in the front of my mind's eye," he said. He then described his body echo as "diagonal": "It is as though something in my stomach does not fit, like two pieces of a puzzle that do not belong together. "And in my mental ear, I imagine the unpleasant notes of a violin, which is just being tuned up."

Only after two sets of waving, the earlier diagonal feeling changed on the wellness scale to anticipation. "Before Christmas, I did not know what presents I would have—and I was still happy", he said.

The partition wall in the head is breaking. Nevertheless, this intervention changes nothing in Wolfgang's careful preparation for his stay in Mexico. This method does not make him unhesitant or daring. However, it opens the sensory and emotional susceptibility for the positive possibilities of new situations and prevents that one possibility of only driving on the same familiar motorway. Because many country roads also lead to a hidden castle, which one would never find staying on a motorway. In such a case, wingwave coaching means entering a wing of a building and opening the internal and external possibilities, which had seemed closed until now.

Self-coaching tip: Overcome inner limits

Now, listen to the wingwave music or prepare for your personal processing method.

1. Think—in a playful way—about a situation that you have not yet conquered: A new position, a new procedure, a new professional or private partner, relocation, starting a family, a new hobby, etc.

2. Focus on the imagined inner image of this theoretical possibility of life.

3. Check: What are your present objections against this possible future perspective?

4. If, apart from the factual arguments, you still perceive a "funny feeling", investigate its body echo. Perhaps you react to the thoughts, such as "I don't know", "it's unfamiliar", or "I have never done it"?

5. If this happens to be the case, perform a processing with regards to the "funny feeling", and allow yourself to be surprised by how your inner experience develops in anticipation of new impulses.

Note:

- During the processing, join your hands in an "incorrect" manner, thus the other way around. If you are using the butterfly technique, cross your arms in the opposite manner. This is an anchor to the experience that unfamiliar possibilities could be just as good or even better than the familiar ones.

- Sometimes, when doing something innovative, you can stand in your own way with the belief that it is always imperative to do the same thing. The flip side of the coin is the fear of making the "wrong" decision. However, it is only a belief that directions in life should always be stamped "right" or "wrong". Sometimes, there are ten "right ways", which one can develop, and not even one of them is "wrong". Read more about this aspect in Chapter 8 - "Belief Coaching".

7.9 Personality Coaching With Imagination Strategy

There are limitless possibilities on the topic of imagination because *"to imagine"* means nothing other than "visualizing something". It's about imagining inner mages and representations of things, which one has not experienced so far. The spectrum ranges from envisioning a future event through to symbolic fantasies and daydreams. Using these fantasies, people like to reflect on the world through their thought patterns, emotions, and personality traits. These psychical structures are experienced every day, although one cannot see them. Therefore, one must imagine them instead.

One of these possibilities of imagination is quite prevalent and is the so-called embodiment of the parts of personality. Here, we would like to dwell upon one of these possibilities of imagination. The very concept that part of our personality is already an embodiment is because realistic little men or beings can neither be found in our heads nor in other parts of the body. Nevertheless, this image has continually been dealt with linguistically: "He is standing in his own way," or "I must overcome my inner demons." These phrases imply the idea that, internally, we are a small society once again. Most of the psychotherapy approaches operate on this model. One need only think of the classic Freudian trio "Id [in German "Es"], Ego [in German "Ich"] and Super-ego [in German "Über-Ich"]". Even in NLP, there are detailed, system-oriented interventions when working with the parts of the personality. It is always the objective to transform these parts into an internal team, based loosely on the motto: "Together, I am strong."

One imagines the embodiment of the parts of our personality not only in psychotherapy, but also in arts and culture. There are plays in which the actors not only play the external human roles, but also psychic phenomena, such as, "the guilty conscience", "joy", "bravery", or the "inner scaredy-cat". Speaking of cat, even in fairy tales, most of the animals symbolize human characteristics. Think of the "clever fox", the "silly goose", or the "wise owl".

If our clients complain about undesirable behavior or an annoying characteristic within themselves, then, most of the time, we work with the imagination of the parts of our personality. Once we have explained this model of perception, we ask them to visualize an image of this characteristic or behavior. In such a case, the possibilities are endless: Jack Nicholson, Cleopatra, a witch, an elephant, and even a skunk have been in the "mental cinema" of our clients.

Daniel is a trainee in a publishing house and suffers from the fact that he always gets annoyed with a certain colleague. "He gets on my nerves all the time with his cynical remarks. I then become bright red with anger and that is exactly what he wants to achieve. Unfortunately, I allow myself to get provoked far too quickly." We ask him to embody this rage into a fictitious figure. "I do not have to think long at all about it", he said. "I see a real Rumplestiltskin in front of me, who is jumping around with rage."

First, with the aid of the body scan technique, Daniel perceives his anger as a body echo. Above all, he feels the tension in the muscles of his jawbone. In doing so, once again, he thinks of his obnoxious colleague as he expresses himself. Then, he imagines Rumplestiltskin as a visual embodiment of his anger. As the processing begins, Rumplestiltskin becomes increasingly calm. In the end, he suddenly sits on a branch of a tree, contentedly eats an apple, and lets his legs dangle. In this image, Daniel's shoulders feel relaxed and pleasantly warm.

The next time his colleague comes to tease him, he had to laugh. "It was not artificial, I found the situation really funny", he told us later.

One can use this technique of imagination in certain situations. Many people experience a "top side and a flip side" and neither of these sides wins. "It feels like an inner conflict," described one of our clients. In this case, the conflicting emotions or thoughts are also imagined as parts of the personality, which one visualizes at the same time. Most of the time, even this simultaneous imagination reveals something about the problematic inner situation: Either the parts look contemptuously at each other or they clearly want to have nothing to do with each other. If processing is performed now, the parts of the personality can reconcile or merge: They change their appearance, become friendly, approach one another, or assimilate. Thus, this technique also strengthens the inner team spirit.

Neurolinguistic Coaching (NLC) works a great deal and extensively with the imagination of the parts of the personality and the strength of the "inner team". It is always concerned with the integration of these inner strengths and not with an inner struggle. This is because every triumph over a part would be a loss at the same time because the "loser" continues to remain a part of us. You can read more about this so-called systemic personality model, for instance, in our book, *Coach Yourself – Persönlichkeitskultur für Führungskräfte [Coach Yourself – Personality Culture for Executives].*

Self-coaching tip: Emotions management - Working with different parts of the personality

Prepare for your processing. Then go through the following steps:

1. Think about a situation in which you were dissatisfied with your emotional reaction—too anxious, too angry, too tense, too frustrated, etc.
2. Give this feeling a character or personality. It must be fictitious, such as an animal, a cartoon character, a character in a novel, or an actor that you only know from a distance.
3. Visualize how this character descriptively embodies your emotional state. Feel the body echo of the stressful emotion.
4. Now, perform your processing, and in your imagination, observe the part of your personality moving into this character,and see how it behaves, speaks ,and moves.

7.10 Find Restful Sleep and Switch Your Brain Off

During periods with a lot of responsibilities and challenges, thoughts do not often stop flowing through the mind. At some point, everyone has experienced it where they have not been able to sleep a wink or sleep was disturbed. Many people are not able to sleep at all in the first place; others wake up during the night and then unintentionally deal with their daily issues. Thereby, the especially unpleasant aspect is quietly lying down when faced with a lot of things, which still need to be done and thought about. Passive lying and resting still strengthen the feeling of being at someone's mercy in view of the thoughts, which revolve around, approach, or even overwhelm a person.

In this respect, NLP offers several possibilities of thought modification. A simple mental technique is the reverse motion in the so-called mental cinema: One makes clockwise circling thoughts to rotate in an anticlockwise direction, and the approaching thoughts are led into a roundabout. Or one looks at the thought-images through an imaginary lilac-colored filter. Slow motion or time-lapse often prove to be of help.

Many of our coachees regain their peace by means of such simple strategies. Thereby, it is extremely important not to "get rid" of the thoughts, but instead, do something with them. An effective strategy is taking over an active experience of thoughts, whereby not the thoughts, but you are in motion. The contents become static, and you take on an active role by means of an imaginative rotation of thoughts. In this process, our coachees choose a "thought-mobile" where no limits are set to the imagination. It could be:

- A dream car
- A dream sleigh, like the one ridden by Santa Claus
- A dream ship
- A mental flying carpet
- Any favourite animal, like a magic elephant or a unicorn
- A pink cloud

Our coachee, Nico, decides on a dream powerboat with which he wants to cross his conceptual world with a corresponding engine sound. We ask him, "Now, think of your new project for a moment, as you always do at night while falling asleep. Now, enter your powerboat. Perceive this place with all your senses: How does the steering wheel feel in your hands? Perceive the typical noises; look at the bow in front of you. Let me know when the boat starts to move." Nico nods. For this driving experience, we also initiate the body scan. "This is a pleasant forward movement, as though I have received a gentle push in the back," he explained in his body echo.

When thinking about one's "thought-mobile", if one senses even the slightest whiff of an imaginary movement, one focuses on thoughts once again. Even Nico's thoughts returned to the project. "Visit the world of your thoughts with your powerboat. Sail for all the aspects of your project mentally," we tell him. At the same time, we perform the processing. Nico chooses the butterfly technique.

During the subsequent "boat ride", Nico's facial expressions are completely relaxed. During the process, he sits calmly and relaxed in his chair. After a short time, he has to yawn suddenly. "I believe, I must dock right away", he comments. "I will wrap it up now. I am no longer interested in these thoughts."

Interestingly, all our clients who have tried the "thought-mobile", report a similar calming effect. There are probably three reasons for this:

1. One does not have to fight against the thoughts anymore.
2. That unpleasant feeling of being at someone's mercy disappears.
3. Quite often, most people associate the pleasant sleeping and dream experiences with movements, such as floating, flying, or driving. It is even said that they "glide across the world of dreams."

Self-coaching tip: Drift into sleep with your "thought-mobile"

If you wish to use eye movements as the processing method, perform the movements with your eyes closed. After all, we are dealing with the sleeping aid. In this case, most people prefer the butterfly technique. If you are working with the wingwave music, place the player within reach near your bed. Thus, you can make use of the calming effect of the wingwave music if you wake up during the night.

1. Design a "thought-mobile" for yourself.
2. Enter or get onto your thought-mobile and set it in motion in your mind.
3. As soon as you perceive the slightest imaginary movement as the body echo in response to the imagined scene, start performing the butterfly technique.
4. Begin a journey of your world of dreams in your "thought-mobile". Do not suppress the thoughts, but drive or fly around them more often. It is important that your thought-mobile keeps moving.
5. After a short period, you will feel a calming effect. You will glide into a world of dreams or a pleasant tranquil experience.

Tips:

- This mental technique is, of course, also suitable during the day as a way of getting away from it all or as an evening ritual.
- Naturally, you can also choose the direct variant: Focus the body echo on unpleasant thoughts and perform the processing. However, the thought-mobile is more fun to work with.

8

BELIEF COACHING: THE CONSTRUCTIVE HANDLING OF BELIEFS

In Chapter 5, "Change Through Understanding: Know-How Coaching", you read about how to replace restrictive beliefs through know-how. However, often, pure know-how is not sufficient for overcoming the limiting beliefs because it typically only reaches the grey cells and not the emotional center of the brain.

Even the most obvious evidence has only a weak effect, as can be seen in the example of spinach. Many people now know that spinach is not as healthy as was asserted in former times. In this regard, the magazine, *Medikament und Meinung (Medicine and Opinion),* reports that a typing error is the cause of the belief that spinach has a particularly high iron content and is, therefore, healthier than other vegetables. In fact, the leafy vegetable contains considerably less iron than several legumes. The overestimation of spinach goes back to an error made by a secretary, who, at the turn of the century, while writing a research report on the amount of iron in spinach, misplaced the decimal point by one position to the right. Therefore, spinach was awarded 16.0 (instead of 1.6 milligrams) per hundred grams. Although, the error was discovered and published by one sceptical German chemist in 1930, this finding gained less publicity than the initial error and, therefore, did not stop the triumphant progress of spinach, especially as a children's meal.

Today, we know even more. We know that if spinach is heated more than once, which was and is done quite frequently with infants' meals, it develops extremely intolerable, even slightly harmful substances for an infant. In this respect, generations of children followed their instincts when they spat out spinach, instead of forcing it down their throats. Nevertheless, millions of parents and grandparents continued giving spinach to their children and grandchildren despite their apparent loathing of it because **spinach is healthy**!

If, during coaching, we transform the negative, debilitating beliefs into positive beliefs, we are, in the case of most of our peak performing clients, pushing an open door. Who would not like to think, "I can do it!" with the deepest emotional conviction instead of. "I have been defeated." However, many people, even in the peak performance area, have their own "spinach beliefs". They believe in mental success recipes, which "power up" only for a short time, but on a long-term basis are not as "iron-rich" and as "easily digestible" as assumed.

Just consider how enthusiastic parents continued to believe in the health value of spinach even after their children complained and spit it out. You can now imagine how important it is to take a constructive approach for the modification of these irrational beliefs, called "euphoric traps," to transform them. Because in coaching, it is often a question of letting go of the belief in miracles to maintain peak performance over the long-term and to make your inner world "unshakeable." It is about setting the transformer at such a speed at which the train can successfully keep going without being derailed.

8.1 The Belief Mirror: The Disillusion of the Delusion

The physician Johann schedules a coaching session to prepare for an important lecture at an international conference in Berlin. "Although I have delivered many speeches in front of many people, this international congress is something else. Moreover, there is bound to be a discussion after the lecture, which I must be able to respond to as well." We respond, "But you come across as very eloquent." He replies, "Nevertheless, I am having sleepless nights because of this lecture." We ask, "What do you fear?" He says, "That I might say something, which the assembled experts find stupid, and then I will no longer be able to straighten things out." We ask, "And how would that be for you?" He responds, "Almost unbearable, everything just constricts inside me when I think about it."

At this point, one could apply the classic wingwave intervention: Johann thinks of a listener who is disparagingly shaking his head, and the processing is performed for that purpose. In belief coaching, we go one step further. In such a case, we use a provocative questioning technique, which is called: "The coach acts dumb." The aim is to force the innermost fears so far that they surface and are exposed. Here we often find a subconscious irrational euphoric belief as the causative stress trigger. We always prepare our clients for this situation by saying, "Now, I will ask you a series of funny questions and while doing so, I will pretend as though I do not understand you at all." We do this because we have found that the effect of a provocative technique is just as effective when we are transparent about our methodology as when we simply surprise the coachees by being provocative. The only difference is that in the case of transparency, the relationship of trust remains intact.

Coach: "You say that the audience of specialists could find your contributions stupid. Of course, it could happen. What is so dreadful about that?"

Johann (looks aghast): "In such a case, I would not want to be seen by my colleagues anymore!"

Coach: "Why not? I do not know of any such law prohibiting this. All convention speakers are allowed to roam freely in Germany, even in front of their colleagues."

Johann (grins slightly): "Yes, but then everyone thinks, 'He is the one who spoke such nonsense at the congress'."

Coach: "And what's wrong with that?"

Johann: "I do not want people to think of me like that!"

Coach: "What or how should they think about you then?"

Johann: "Think good things, of course!"

Coach: "And do you think good things about every other person?"

Johann: "Of course not."

Coach: "But all your colleagues all over the world should think well of you, right?"

At this point, we discontinue the game because in the discussion, something has now developed which we call a "belief mirror". Due to the exaggerated enquiries, we have come across a potential "point of collapse" in Johann's belief system because, up until now, he has been latently living according to the motto: "I have to be well regarded and respected by everyone." Of course, everyone is pleased when they are shown appreciation and receive recognition, but the problem with these subconscious beliefs is the "HAVE TO". This "HAVE TO" allows no kind of criticism or rejection by fellow human beings at all. If that happens, a world can come crashing down. Johann can save himself from this "problem", and even from the greatest fear of it, if he can trick his belief. Incidentally, we call this type of belief, a belief which can neither be fulfilled by people nor by fate, a "euphoric belief".

Johann's belief feigns a goal, which no human being has ever achieved. It is not "humanly possible" to be always well received by everyone because we each have a personal life story, a personal model of the world, and individual prejudices. It is possible that you turn your nose up at someone and, naturally, it is possible that someone may be looking for a person to whom they can vent their anger and they discover you, a completely innocent person, to be an ideal target for their aggression. You, as a successful human being, may naturally trigger envy in those less successful. One subconsciously thinks that all that Johann must go through should not have to happen. He is suffering from the notion that he will no longer be able to correct a possible impression that he might create on a large audience simply because he is not perceiving the described possible hostile reaction as a normal occurrence in life but as something that is uniquely directed at him.

It is humanly possible to make a good impression on a lot of people—just not on everyone. A healthy ability to express changes in emotions arises, especially when this "HAVE TO" becomes a wish: "I wish that as many people as possible would like and appreciate me." Such a sentence leaves enough space for self-initiative. It also, however, offers a sufficiently high tolerance level for frustration in the case that the wish never comes true. Therefore, this deception leads to the best possible stability because the world can no longer come crashing down so quickly. Inexplicable and undesired rejection by others is eventually a part of life, like the rain or wind is part of the weather.

8.2 Become an Optimist

Johann has the same objections against these statements as many other coaching clients: "Do you want to turn me into a pessimist? Only pessimists attune their thoughts to negative events." Johann has also heard of mental training, in which one should internalize the sentences: "You can do whatever you want" or "My power is limitless." "Such sentences surely give you the strength to achieve even the impossible," he says. Our response is, "From time to time, we have experienced that. Although the irrational euphoric beliefs allow you to dream and visualize that the goal is possible, they can, however, obstruct their realization in life rather than encourage it." This statement can be illustrated with a simple example. Let's assume that you need three people for the realization of a new project. The project manager, however, is someone—to put it in exaggerated terms—who likes to think, "I can do anything because I have unlimited powers." This irrational euphoric belief will most likely lead to bad planning and consequently, become the stumbling block for the entire project.

"Anything is possible—you only need good ideas!" This is the belief of a successful entrepreneur with whom we worked in Hamburg. On the one hand, this belief comprises limitless possibilities, while on the other hand, it includes a realistic embodiment of "feasibility", the realization of visions. It permits sensible planning and imagination. For what's the use of "unlimited power" if the tact and flair to find a simple solution is missing? The sentence of this entrepreneur is not pessimistic at all. What is important is that it remains sufficiently realistic for the manifestation of the ideas.

In rational emotive therapy, according to Ellis, these inner sentences—also referred to as cognitions—are examined to assess whether they are functional or dysfunctional. These somewhat dry concepts put the requirement from the success belief in a nutshell: Beliefs are useful when they are functional, thus making the realization of our plans possible. They should be realistic in the truest sense and entirely in keeping with the motto: "Do not dream your life; rather live your dreams." You should always verify the compliance of their beliefs with the criteria of the so-called SMART principle: **S**pecific, **M**easureable, **A**chievable, **R**ealistic, **T**imely. If you do this, they will become effective motivational and priming factors for defining—and accomplishing—the target.

In this context, remmeber the famous example of how a person describes a half-filled glass of water. The pessimist looks at this glass and says with disappointment, "Oh, the glass is half empty." Alternatively, the optimist is pleased, "Great, the glass in indeed half full!" But even the greatest optimist would never say, "Great, the glass is indeed filled to the brim!" because it does not correspond to reality. An optimist can be a realist as well, who estimates his resources in an appropriate manner. He is not one who fantasizes and deludes himself.

In contrast to the optimist, an idealist may see that the fuel gauge is indicating a half-full tank and says, "Great, the tank is full!" and drives into a desert and gets stranded ten kilometres before the desired oasis. The optimist would accept the half-full tank, drive to the gas station once again, fill up the tank, and probably carry an additional spare can with him to be sure of reaching the much-desired oasis. This is exactly the difference between dysfunctional and functional success beliefs. Thus, it is better to be an optimist instead of an idealist.

8.3 "We are invincible" - The Typical Belief-Trap of Peak Performers

Of course, until now, none of our clients has claimed to be invincible. Nevertheless, this beautiful word aptly describes the mental state of irrational, and, therefore, even dysfunctional euphoric beliefs a lot of people in performance situations have. In the following, we will once again introduce you to four of these predominantly subconscious beliefs, which harbour the danger that the respective person may sabotage his own success. We will briefly describe why this sentence could be a belief-trap, and we will present possible beliefs as an alternative.

"Anything is possible!"

Apart from the risks of bad planning, this belief also harbours the danger of failing to recognize when a project is going downhill, and, therefore, being able to recognizze when to divest or simply get out and cut your losses. If you hit the limits of possibility, this belief can make you depressed. If anything were possible, then this situation obviously reflects nothing other than personal weaknesses. The euphoric effect of this belief often causes people to feel comfortable or "get a kick" only in risky borderline situations so that they can experience how their beliefs come true. This may even subconsciously lead to provoking a risk situation or not to prevent such a situation in time. Used in conjunction with extreme sports, we often speak of "adrenaline junkies."

Functional Beliefs:

"If there is a solution, I will find it, or I will find the person who will find it."

"I will do all that is humanly possible."

"I will do my best."

These beliefs make sure that the person feels valuable, even if he/she—for a change—does not work wonders.

"It won't work without me!"

Such a belief obstructs both constructive teamwork, as well as a successful delegation, which is often of great value for the maintenance of peak performance. In many companies, such an attitude prevents experienced employees from developing young talent at the right time.

Functional beliefs:

"I can give valuable impulses."

"I am a good leader."

These beliefs preserve self-awareness, even if one does not play any decisive role. For example, you can think beyond the last sentence as follows: "I am a good leader and need an environment, which appreciates this ability." Maybe this seems to be a bit presumptuous; however, it ensures that the inner world remains intact even when you are not involved—for whatever reasons. Of course, this belief works only if leadership qualities exist. The glass must be half full.

"You will thank me for it!"

Beliefs of this kind virtually program a possible collapse of the inner stability. As a rule, people with such an attitude have a very ethical value system as a firm foundation of their personality. However, it becomes problematic when one assumes that all fellow human beings share the same value system. "Of course, I would be grateful if another person would stand up for me in the same manner." Therefore, one automatically starts judging others by one's own standards. For this reason, many highly committed people suffer a real social trauma when, for example, a company for which they have given years of dedicated work, quite unexpectedly, appears disappointed instead of thankful. Of course, there will always be ungrateful, callous, egomaniac, psychopathic, cowardly, or unscrupulous people. The glass is just half full and not filled to the brim with good people.

Just envision this topic with a metaphor from the realm of great marine life. Dolphins, for example, are very highly socially developed, intelligent, playful, and friendly sea mammals. With all their friendliness, a dolphin would never think that all the visually similar large sea dwellers are also dolphins. The dolphin knows very well that there are sharks, and it is optimally attuned to that fact. Dolphins do not faint with horror when a shark shows up. They do not try to discover the good aspects of a shark and play with it. Instead, they very vigorously and successfully drive it out of their territory because they know that the shark does not have the best interest of the dolphins at heart. Now, on the flip side, if the dolphin has successfully defended itself against the shark, it would not suddenly think after this experience that every large being with a similar figure—even other dolphins— are sharks. It can still differentiate between the species, and it continues to desire to be with like-minded beings.

Thus, we do not wish to make our coaching clients distrustful, but rather—as already described—we wish to take care of their "functional beliefs" with regards to the issue of "fellow human beings" as well. If it fails to happen, the original problem can become exacerbated. One starts to quarrel and wants to show the other that they "cannot always take the easy way out" or "they should just comprehend what they had done wrong". This is as though the dolphin would swim behind the shark, push it into an underwater cave, and talk to it until it apologizes for being a shark. Please refer to Chapter 2 on the topic of revenge, in which we discussed the energy wasted by the desire to make amends.

Functional Beliefs

"Everyone is different."

"I cannot change people; I can only get along with them."

"I can change a person only if he wants it as well."

"There are dolphins and sharks, and I am prepared for both."

"Likeminded people are a gift, but I do not have any cosmic right to that gift."

"I must always find the right solution!"

This belief subconsciously insinuates that life is a quandary of wrong solutions, and the right solutions stand out like a safe island. One false step, and you are swallowed up by the swamp. It is only when people are confronted with two possibilities that they think quickly: "And if I make a wrong decision now?" Our learning imprinting in digital thoughts leads to a very simplified perspective: Yes or no, right or wrong, black or white, 1 or 0. But, for a moment, think about the saying: "All roads lead to Rome." Therefore, there can be ten possibilities, all of them on safe ground, and all of them may be the "right" solutions, if you can make the most of them.

Of course, each of these ten ways comes with its own difficulties. In the digital right and wrong thinking, every experiment leads, in novel ways, to the fact that even in moments of the smallest difficulties or breakdowns, one says: "Well, I made the wrong choice. That would not have happened with the other solution because apparently, that was the right option." Thus, creativity and energy of any kind are still obstructed by strife. If, in the end, it turns out that another approach would be more ideal, many people still hold this fatal belief, on top of it all, that one may decide only once and then never again. "In for a penny, in for a pound." Therefore, one should no longer leer at the other nine solutions. Thus, solutions become knots that bind us.

Functional Beliefs:

"All roads lead to Rome."

"Even for the greatest inventions, there were many series of experiments."

"I will make the most of it."

"Setting forth is my objective."

"The proof is in the pudding."

"There are no mistakes, only results which one must utilize."

"One who starts something is also allowed to establish, while trying that, it was not optimal to have started at all."

When we ask our coachees to express these functional sentences in the context of a myostatic test, often the test does not turn out to be strong. In such cases, emotions trick the mind once again. The euphoric sentences simply feel way too good! As in the case of chocolate or an apparently lucrative investment, an excessively good feeling becomes a problem in such a case!

8.4 Say Goodbye to the Trap of Euphoria

Belief coaching requires the coach to have considerable know-how about the psychological effects of sentence structures. Overall, there are three types of dysfunctional sentence patterns: Deletion, distortion, and generalization. You can find an exceptionally precise representation of this topic in the first NLP books by Richard Bandler and John Grinder, *The Structure of Magic, Volumes I* and *II*. However, for most readers, the foregoing observations may be sufficient to get an intuitive feel of the consequences of the dysfunctional beliefs.

The joint examination of beliefs with regards to their success and self-worth functionality is also called "disputation." After we identify the dysfunctional euphoric beliefs in the belief mirror, another series of conversations takes place before the actual intervention in which we jointly dispute with our clients the beliefs that have been found. During disputation, the contents of the discussion are somewhat like those which we have just presented in Chapter 8.3. The functional beliefs are developed together. Of course, initially, this part is predominantly controlled by the mind. Then ,an emotional departure from the dysfunctional belief takes place with the aid of bilateral hemispheric stimulation.

In this case, we work backward with wingwave: "Although we have now discovered the dysfunctional beliefs, they also somehow make you feel good. And of course, the statement 'I can do everything' generates a very positive body echo."

Often, during the processing, clients focus on this euphoric body echo. Then, something extremely interesting happens. Normally, the processes go into the sense of well-being. Subjective discomfort breaks down; pleasant feelings become more intense. However, when we must deal with dysfunctional euphoric beliefs, the opposite happens during processing. The euphoric feeling disappears. "It's as though I had been high before, and now I'm getting more sober from second to second," is how one client described this effect. Others use terms such as "grounded", "landed again", "no longer under power", or "as if woken up", which is also reflected in the myostatic test. Suddenly, the SMART Beliefs have a strong effect.

It is precisely this effect, which has, in turn, activated our respect for the individual wisdom of every human being. By means of bilateral hemispheric stimulation, people find their way back, entirely on their own, from being a sensitive and charged-up person to one having a stable and supporting equilibrium. Using their own mental integrative capacity, they get over their euphoric traps during the process.

8.5 The Internalization of Ego-Strengthening and Health-Preserving Beliefs

As already mentioned, a new belief or several new beliefs are developed together with the client, and these test strong after the "disillusionment intervention." We often intensify this positive effect using the Magic Words method, which we have developed for the rapid reduction of mental blockages, and for the establishment of positive keywords and sentences.

In the process, we ask our clients to visualize new and functional beliefs written in front of their mind's eye. Thereafter, once again, we intensify the representation of beliefs on the "mental screen" with the sensory-specific methods based on NLP:

- Size of the letters
- Font, printed or handwritten
- Color or colors of letters
- Background color
- Three-dimensional material, such as neon script, script carved out of wood or written in clouds in the sky, etc.
- The sentence is put together with a corresponding sound quality: A certain voice or voices speaking or singing the text
- Additional auditory support, such as a drum roll, a gentle twittering of birds, or roaring sounds of organs

These sensory impressions are worked on until the sentence gives the client a good, stable feeling. The client then focuses on the sensory developed positive beliefs, perceives the stabilizing body echo with this sentence, and processing is performed until the client feels the result to be optimal. In a similar manner, one proceeds with other beliefs, which the client still wants to internalize to strengthen his inner balance.

9

OTHER COACHING AREAS

Until now, we have presented the most important examples with regards to the application of EMDR and/or wingwave method in coaching. In this chapter, we would like share some of our thoughts on other areas in which wingwave coaching may be very helpful.

9.1 Sports Coaching

Top athletes are subject to considerable performance stress, especially in tournaments. After each loss in a tournament, it is extremely important to integrate the disappointment of a defeat as quickly as possible so that ultimately, a general stress memory of the keywords "tournament", "the Olympics", or "championship", etc., does not build up. Even training can be ideally supported by means of bilateral hemispheric stimulation. To do this, focus on the entire movement sequences, ensure that the athlete feels up to all the potential opponents in the competition, and motivate him or her for the training sequences, which can be rather monotonous.

The best training results are achieved when the athlete wears or holds his sportswear during the intervention, be it boxing gloves, tennis rackets, balls, etc. Another possibility is to do the intervention at the venue of the event. Playing a recorded noise of the audience on the loudspeaker is an ideal combination. The coaching of the interpersonal dialogue, which the sportsman conducts with himself in the performance situation as we have described in Chapter 7, is also important. The more sensory-specific details arising from the experience of performance are integrated, the more resourceful the mental state will be, and, consequently, the performance capacity itself later in the situation. For this purpose, once again, look at the list of stress triggers on the issue of sports coaching.

An important area of application for wingwave in peak performance sports is coaching after sports injuries. Time and again, athletes are unable to find their way back to their full potential even after their physical injuries have healed completely. In such a case, the injury is still stored in their "pain memory" as a performance stress imprinting, which blocks, at the mental level, the recovery of the injury and the experienced pain. We are pleased that the topic of the "application of wingwave coaching after sport injuries" has been researched by the Deutschen Sporthochschule Köln within the scope of a Bachelor thesis (refer to Chapter 6), and that the first positive results are available in this regard.

9.2 A New Approach in Dealing With Overindulgence

Although this is not a classic topic of coaching, many of our clients approach us with the issue that they want to eat less and drink less alcohol or wish to quit smoking. However, in reality, a thin line should not separate these topics because peak performance is always associated with "social events" where people just eat, drink, and smoke. Think of business luncheons or parties, which are often attended willingly or unwillingly.

Moreover, it is widely prevalent that peak performers compensate for their performance stress through sensual pleasures: "I work so hard, thus I am going to treat myself to something that gives me pleasure." You must have surely heard these arguments being spoken by others or even used them yourself. However, alternatively, one knows the health-endangering effects of some of these habits, and there is a desire to reduce consumption in this regard. However, these issues are precisely where the mind and emotions drift apart strongly from each other, and where the emotions conquer the mind all too often.

In this scenario, we successfully work with the "wingwave backward" method. We let our clients describe in precise details why they love their stimulants so much, be it chocolate, red wine, or cigars. There is an abundance of answers: One feels secure, loved, proud, recognized, desired, relaxed, and has a new zest for life. We then ask our clients to precisely describe the body echo of relaxation, desire, or security. Thus, we are not searching for the body echo for the stimulant, rather the physical response to the positive emotional state.

Now, the client focuses on his stimulant *and* the positive physical emotional echo, while the processing is performed. The results are the same as in the coaching of euphoric beliefs: The clients think of their stimulant and, suddenly, they feel completely different. "A small brown square of chocolate cannot possibly give me love. What nonsense!" The clients must be demystified properly.

Naturally, using this method, even the beautiful effects of advertising become disenchanting. This is because a cigarette gives the person a feeling of freedom instead of him thinking about the miserable smoker's cough that he might get. In the case of dried, crunchy, salty potato chips, one associates the slogan, "Your friends are here" with a sense of security. Champagne or cigars are suggested as being incredibly important. In other words, the emotional promises of these stimulants are completely exaggerated by their emotionally deceptive packaging.

By means of processing, the all-too narrow associative network between the stimulant and emotion is disassociated; the feeling of greed or addiction is neutralized. All our clients experience this disassociation as liberation. There is, however, a new indulgence that emerges: People enjoy being able to say no to the old temptations.

After this disassociation, we end with a coaching on self-perception. The client visualizes his blossoming, strong, and healthy future-self, which now lives uninhibited by any overwhelming desire for stimulants. This experience becomes the new resourceful stimulant.

9.3 The Importance of a Stress Immunization

Many of our clients, who have often experienced wingwave coaching, tell us about the general effect of this method. They are increasingly experiencing that they are very often calm in situations in which they would have become immediately overwhelmed previously. "And even if I get angry or have a blockage of ideas, such a condition lasts for a very brief period. I now come out of these inner blockages on my own much more quickly", is how the Human Resources Manager, Karin, described this effect. It seems as though the brain has automated the stress experience as a trigger for the highest possible creativity, and no longer for the neural blockage. Apparently, this initiates the process, which in behavioral therapy is referred to as "stress immunization".

Consequently, there is further motivation to use wingwave coaching with regards to not just one event, but to adopt this approach as a collective training for general stress management as well. Apparently, by repeatedly experiencing this method, one develops an individual virtuous circle with the experiences that assail us every day: One remains in flow with his feelings and no longer freezes but rather reacts in a more resourceful way.

9.4 Emotions and Longevity: A Philosophical Thought

Please construe the following statements only as a play of thoughts, which have resulted from our intense, daily occupation with the possibilities of this coaching method. Of course, it sounds somewhat grandiose, when one considers: "What would happen, if every person systematically reintegrated their unprocessed stress experiences or perennially occurring thoughts and performance blockages?" In every form of processing, the Sleeping Beauty Castle Phenomenon is present. Emotional processes, which somehow come to a neurological standstill, are brought back into an emotional flow once again. The shock is no longer stuck in our system; the "mental block" disappears and an experience "no longer irritates" us.

Life and vitality are synonymous with movement. The blood flows, the heart beats, and the nervous system constantly reacts to new stimuli from the outside.

In psychotherapy, we speak of a patient's ability to change emotionally when referring to specific experiences, as opposed to having an inflexible and unchanging view of the experience. Non-movement and rigidity are the opposite of vitality. From time to time, the bold idea has been conceived that with the aid of reactive interventions, the emotional rigidity can be retransformed into a lively flow, and thus, promote health and longevity. At the end of the day, the root word of emotion means movement, not standstill. Perhaps flowing, lively emotions also promote the sense of being alive?

Accept these statements simply as an additional suggestion. All this should not be understood as a medical thesis, but rather as a philosophical thought.

9.5 The Coaching Framework

We offer the coaching methods presented in this book to our clients in a timeframe of five to ten coaching hours. This applies to a single selected goal. Most of our coaching clients also come with a targeted, individual topic: They want to be successful in a certain negotiation, achieve a performance target, or cope better and in a professional manner with their fellow human beings. However, if a coachee has several topics, together with the coachee, we choose the one which is the most important to them. For an additional topic, two to five hours of further coaching sessions are arranged.

If clients come from out of town, we arrange a half or a full day of coaching. Sometimes, we can do consecutive days too. Of course, a weekly meeting would be more ideal; however, in peak performance coaching, we have to realistically go by the calendar of the coaching clients. What is the benefit of processing the performance stress imprintings if new stress develops due to a rigid coaching time concept?

As an external setting, it is always advisable to change the everyday place of work. Many of our clients like to come to us in Hamburg. If this is not possible, we will also visit the clients. However, we insist that the coaching is always conducted at a neutral location. For "in vivo" coaching, the proximity of the workplace is always advantageous, although one should always be able to return to a pleasant place outside the everyday working area.

We are pleased that there are now more than 5,000 coaches not only in the German-speaking regions, but in many other countries as well. At www.wingwave.com, you will find, among other things, our international Coachfinder.

10

GLOSSARY

Amygdala: Two small pairs of almond-shaped nuclei in the limbic system, which show especially high activity in the case of a high arousal level in the nervous system. This happens both in the case of very unpleasant emotions (fear, anger, etc.), as well as in the case of far from pleasant emotions (greed, eating disorders, compulsive buying). The amygdala is also called the "alarm bell" of the nervous system. The amygdala controls all the incoming stimuli with regards to the criteria of "neutral stimuli", "dangerous stimuli", or "euphoric stimuli" (compulsive buying, eating disorders, feelings of being in love).

Anchor: Sensory-specific triggers for the states, which were paired (conditioned) previously, for example, a mental state or behavior, like a specific piece of music is reminiscent of a vacation. Just listening to it triggers a holiday feeling, regardless of the respective whereabouts of the person. The piece of music has thus become an auditory anchor. An image (visual anchor), a smell (olfactory anchor), a taste (gustatory anchor), or a feeling (kinaesthetic anchor) can work in a similar manner.

Arousal: Denotes the everyday state of excitement or arousal of our entire nervous system. It is predominantly organized by the limbic system. Colloquially, one also speaks of the "drive or stimulus" of a person. One can also compare the state of arousal with a transformer of an electric toy train—it powers the tracks. If it is switched off, the train stops, if one over-accelerates the speed, the train is derailed from the tracks on the bends. If the arousal is too high, even the smallest of events can throw us off our tracks.

Auditory Channel: One of the five senses and/or sensory channels, which we use during perception of (internal or external) voices, sounds, or noises: Hearing.

Auditory stimulation: The alternating right-left stimulation with the aid of sounds through the ears, usually by means of headphones. It promotes the coordination ability of both the cerebral hemispheres.

Statement tree: Systematic list of stimulus statements to locate the important events in life, which continue to linger in the stress memory and are unfavourably anchored and become activated due to coincidental experiences in the here and now. The loud voice of a colleague reminds one of a strict father, even though the colleague is nice. A presentation is reminiscent of the classroom and is unnecessarily associated with an uneasy feeling, although one has prepared optimally.

Automatic thoughts: A constant internally generated self-talk, which guides us through everyday life and with which we evaluate our experiences and comment on them as well. These sentences are predominantly subconsciously controlled and are rarely checked with regards to their emotional effect and motivational force. Automatic thoughts can demotivate and inspire at the same time, depending on how they are expressed in content and with which tone of voice.

Priming moments: Brief but important moments for our individual happiness and our successes, such as examinations, competitions, speeches, job interviews, etc. Sometimes, it is only minutes or seconds that decide the happy outcome of a priming moment. Therefore, a person should be in his best possible state in this short time window.

Abdominal brain: The complex network of nerves (emotional center) around the intestines, which is responsible for instinctive perception and behavior.

Belief: These are the automatic presuppositions of people with regards to their own personality, the "world out there", about other people, and about "fate" and "higher powers". These beliefs could also shape the reality, without the individual person being conscious of it. Here, the effect is a self-fulfilling prophecy. If a woman believes the sentence: "Women do not understand anything about technology at all", she will not dedicate herself to technology in the first place, and thus, will neglect the necessary learning skills to deal with technical things. Result: Due to the lack of experiences, the limiting and inhibiting sentence "comes true". There are inhibiting and, of course, permissive beliefs, such as, "I can be successful."

Belief mirror: The inner collection of beliefs of a person about himself, about other people, and about the functioning of the world, which have a formative effect on the externally perceptible behavior of a person. They are the internal mirrors of the external appearance. For example, someone would like to learn autogenous training, but is unable to find rest despite every effort. Perhaps he has internalized the belief "a rolling stone gathers no moss", which prohibits him from relaxing and resting.

Bilateral stimulation: Alternating right-left stimuli, for example, by means of eye movements, sounds, and touch.

Bilateral brain stimulation: The right-left stimulation of both the cerebral hemispheres to promote optimal coordination ability of the different areas of the brain.

Biographical stress: An experience, key situation, or a trauma arising from the personal life history of a person, which still triggers stress in the present, although it belongs in the past. Also see Resistant stress imprinting.

Body scan: Consciously tuning into the body to locate the "body echo" of a subjectively unpleasant emotion: Tensed-up jaws, a constriction in the throat, a queasy feeling in the stomach, weak knees, etc. The same applies to positive emotions: A joyful heart, a comfortable stomach, firm shoulders, etc.

Butterfly method: An alternating right-left stimulation, in which one rhythmically crosses their arms and taps on one's own shoulders. This touch and sound stimulation can regulate states of stress, for example, relieve a feeling of anxiety when going up in an elevator.

Coachee: The client or the customer who takes part in the coaching.

Testing of dosage: Determining the individually correct dosage of stimulants, for example, "I may eat two pieces of chocolates a day." However, neither the medicines nor the medical compatibility of substances is tested in wingwave. This test is not suitable for medical examinations or even prescriptions under any circumstances.

Disputation: A "favourably provocative dispute" to uncover restrictive beliefs and to consciously put their statement to test. For example, the coachee says, "The clever person gives in." The coach counters, "Yes, and because of this reason, the world is always ruled by the stupid." The coachee pauses and consciously tests the belief statement once again.

Dyscalculia: Problems in dealing with numbers; learning disabilities, which cannot be entirely remedied by learning and must instead be treated with professional learning therapy. This is comparable to dyslexia, which relates to difficulties with letters and words.

Interweaving: The coachee concentrates on a good feeling or emotion, a strengthening sentence, or on an "enlightening" remark from the coach. At the same time, to anchor this positive concentration, the coach slowly waves, using back and forth movements, in front of the eyes of the coachee. Since a large number of brain cells become activated with intensive eye movements, the "interweaving" helps in internalizing and stabilizing the present positive state of the coachee. Also see Cognition.

Waving-in: Slow and brief stimulation by means of slow eye movements to strengthen the results achieved.

EMDR: Abbreviation for "**E**ye **M**ovement **D**esensitization and **R**eprocessing". It is a clinical psychotrauma therapy, which was founded by the psychologist, Francine Shapiro. In EMDR, the therapist guides the eyes of the patients by means of hand movements. Francine Shapiro developed this method shortly after she had worked as an assistant with John Grinder, the co-founder of NLP (Neurolinguistic Programming). She intensively researched the therapeutic and de-stressing effects of specifically induced eye movements in NLP. However, Francine Shapiro does not make any mention of her learning history and close association with NLP in the details of her career development. EMDR was very well researched in the clinical area and is considered an effective and sustainable therapy method.

Emotions' mirror: People not only perceive their emotions, but are also in tune with the emotional experiences of their fellow human beings, which has an enriching effect on a positive wavelength and social proximity. However, some people react extremely sensitively as an "antenna" for the stress of their counterpart, and they can be "infected", "pulled down", or they do not dare to confront another person or expect anything from him. Also see Mirror neurons.

Eye Movement Integrator: An NLP intervention to internalize the beneficial coaching results with the aid of right-left movements of the eye, which is processed at all eye levels. Steve and Connirae Andreas and Robert Dilts first described it in the late 1980s.

Flow: This means the feeling of being fully immersed in an activity, like being creative or having a work frenzy, and enjoyment in the process of the activity. You have a feeling of being unconstrained, centered, and focused, without having to force it. Mihaly Csikszentmihalyi (see bibliography) developed the flow theory in 1975. Today, it is also used for purely intellectual activities. Flow can occur with the management of complex and rapidly progressing events, in the zone between overload (anxiety) and being under-challenged (boredom). The flow-access and flow-experience are individual. Nevertheless, there are general observations and principles, which always apply" (Wikipedia).

FMRT: Functional Magnetic Resonance Tomography, see MRT and brain scan.

Brain-based thinking: Ways of thinking, which takes the functional possibilities of our brain into consideration.

Brain-based formulation: A formulation of goals, which incorporates the sensory-specific aspects without negations or comparisons does justice to the characteristics of our brain, which reacts to words in fractions of a second. For example, one says: "Maintain the balance!" instead of: "Do not fall down!" Or: "It is safe here", instead of: "There is *no* danger."

Brain scan: Coloured image reproductions of the active brain, also see MRT.

Generalization: Our brain tries to simplify the process of coping with the diverse perceptual and memory tasks. For example, we have seen innumerable tomatoes in our lives. The brain does not store a special image for each individual tomato. Instead, it combines all the tomatoes that we have already seen into a representative "image of tomatoes" for our memory and orientation skills. Thus, even the unfavourable stress-learning effects can be generalized: Anxiety in an elevator is generalized into a discomfort in all possible enclosed spaces. Likewise, even positive experiences can be generalized and entail favorable chain reactions: Security and serenity during an important speech generalizes into positive self-awareness in conversations with all possible persons. The positive generalization is used in the coaching in a targeted manner.

Pleasure or "resource waving": The stimulation of pleasant or energizing emotions by hand-guided slow eye movements.

Credibility scale (belief measurement scale): Scale of 1 to 7, on which the coachee can subjectively evaluate the credibility of the assumptions and cognitions related to one's individual self before the coaching and after the coaching: How credible or true is this statement for me now? For example, "I can be successful" had a rating of 2 on the scale before the coaching, and a rating of 6 on the scale after the coaching. The assessment option is useful because the coachee can assess his own coaching effect, and the coach can assess the location in the coaching process.

Hippocampus: An area in the limbic system of the brain, which enables our short-term memory to have a general capacity for remembering and orientation. In the case of excellent performance in a well-balanced psycho-physiological state, this area shows specific activities.

Hypnosis: A technique in which the attention of the client is guided from the outside to the inside. The result is a trance state, which provides excellent assistance in learning: It results in physical relaxation and, at the same time, in an activation of the brain activity for the vivid experiences of imagination. Thus, a client can visualize a visit to the dentist calmly and peacefully. When he visits a dentist later, the brain remembers the positive state arising from the hypnosis and activates this secure feeling during the treatment.

Imaginative family constellation: The readjustment of family scenes arising from past, present, or the future in the imagination to experience the motives and attitudes of one's own and of third persons. The advantage of imaginative constellation lies in the fast and feasible possibility of work without great personal effort. Even those visualization possibilities can be chosen, which are otherwise difficult. One can imagine important people or issues floating around and visualize people much bigger or smaller than they are or were, etc. Even other systemic structures, in which people or other parts play a role, can be drawn up imaginatively: Persons in companies and organizations, personal topics with different aspects, etc.

In sensu: In the imagination; the mental experience, or running stimuli, or scenarios through the head (present, future, or past). In the coaching process, the endeavored feeing of success is experienced in the "happy-end-mode", in sports coaching, the coachee enters into his movement sequences through the mind; thus, in sensu, to optimize them through mental training.

Intoxication: Poisoning by physically harmful substances.

In-vivo: In life; the real experiencing of stimuli (for example, stimulants on the table, confrontation with one's mirror image, reaction of an audience comprising of people), testing of situations in role playing, coaching in actual context, such as on the golf course, on the stage with microphone in hand, etc.

Isolated blockage: A term used in coaching, which means that, unlike a patient who can be described as consistently ill, a coachee is basically efficient, well-balanced, and well-motivated, except for "one thing". It can be the fear of flying, lack of conflict stability, insecurity to perform in front of large groups, easy to provoke, etc. In this case, an emotional insecurity arises, which the coachee is unable to control in a self-effective manner despite excellent self-management skills.

Cognitive interweaving: See Interweaving.

Calibration: Calibrate the test instrument (here, the muscle test) on the individual personality and situation of the coachee to clearly understand and apply the test results. The calibration precedes every testing in the coaching session. In the case of the myostatic test, or O-ring test, every wingwave intervention tests whether it functions.

Clinical hypnosis: Application of a hypnotherapeutic procedure in medical treatment (in contrast to stage or show hypnosis).

Tapping technique: Tapping on energetically effective acupuncture points for the stimulation of psychological effects. There are several energetically effective procedures, such as the Emotional Freedom Technique (EFT).

Kinesiology, kinesiologic: A method, which assumes that the physical-psychological disturbances manifest as weaknesses of certain muscle groups and can be accordingly determined by means of the muscle test.

Body echo: see Body scan.

Cognition Positive: A favorable, useful, or friendly belief about one's individual self, for example ,"I am able to cope with that" or "I am likeable", etc.

Cognition Negative: An unfavorable, inhibitive, or unfriendly belief about one's individual self, for example, "I am a helpless person" or "I am a failure".

Cognitive interweaving: See Interweaving.

Short-term memory: Where information and learning contents (behavious and states) are stored for the short-term. The most important area of our short-term memory seems to be in the limbic system of the brain and in the Hippocampus.

Long-term memory: Where information and learning contents (behaviors and states) are stored for life in conjunction with an appropriate sense of time. With the help of this function, we know precisely whether a recalled image is many years old or just a few days old. The most important storage of long-term memory appears to be in the cerebrum. The prefrontal cortex plays a significant role here.

Limbic reaction: Emotionally-charged reactions. These are predominantly controlled by the limbic system, the "emotional center of the brain", and often cannot be substantiated as sensible, or as rational: Purchasing big cars or expensive clothes, without having the money to purchase them; fear of completely harmless spiders; eating chocolate, although one never wants to eat it again, etc.

Limbic system: The central part of the human brain, which plays an important role for our emotional experiences, and in its function as an incoming control, checks all the information for "danger", "safety", or an "excellent thing".

Loop: Sometimes, the processing goes around in circles in terms of contents and emotions; the coachee comes to the same point again and again despite all kinds of "waving". At this point, the coach applies the myostatic test, to test whether the focus of the perception is still on target. Or, he uses the technique of cognitive interweaving.

Magic Words: A method developed by Cora Besser-Siegmund in 1994 based on NLP to overcome the psychological blockages within minutes. In this process, the stress words are mitigated by having them written colourflly or by being spoken in the voice of Mickey Mouse. Thus, one reacts calmly to the words and consequently, also to the phenomenon, which they represent in the nervous system.

Meta-level: Describes the perceptual position with which we stand "above things" internally, and calmly perceive even unpleasant, exciting, or stressful experiences internally, and can assess them "on a broader perspective". For example, hiccups: This experience is quite intense and unpleasant on a physical level, but on the meta-level, we accept this spasmodic event quite calmly. (Exceptions are formed by the rare cases in which people suffer from persistent hiccups.)

Modalities: See Sensory modalities.

MRT: Magnetic Resonance Tomography, an imaging method to display brain activities. Colloquially, the images are also called "brain scans". Also: fMRT (functional MRT).

Muscle tone: The muscle tension, either pleasant or tense or flaccid.

Myostatic test: Muscle test in which the subject joins his thumb and index finger to form a ring and holds them together using maximum strength, whereby the tester tries to open the ring. Now, by means of the direct muscle reaction, it can be deciphered whether a stimulus (thought, word, behavior, substance) causes stress or not for the nervous system. In the case of stress, the ring becomes loose. If the subject can "cope" with the stimulus, he can hold the ring together during the test. In contrast to kinesiology and testing according to Omura, the myostatic test provides no clinical findings or data, such as diagnosis or drug compatibility. This is exclusively about the state of mental or emotional resonance within the context of everyday life management.

Negation: The linguistic negation, such as: "Look out, do not stumble!" Since the brain promptly reacts to every word, it registers the word "stumble" despite the word "not". More useful is the formulation: "Maintain the balance!" or "Place your feet safely!"

Neurolinguistic programming: NLP, an instruction manual for the human brain; a method with a more comprehensive collection to change state and behavior. "Neuro" stands for more than 100 billion brain cells, which organize our behavior and experience with numerous connections; "linguistic" stands for the linguistic mapping and accessibility of the neural structures by means of words; "programming" stands for our behaviors and mental states in the form of strategies or programmes, which, more or less, can be up-to-date and/or useful, and can even be modified. NLP is applied in all the spheres of human communication (with oneself or with others), such as in psychotherapy, in coaching, in pedagogy, and in sales and management.

Nervous system: The overall complete arrangement of all nerve cells and the nervous center in the body. One of these centers is the central nervous system, thus the human brain.

Neurobiology: Teachings on the functionalities of the entire nervous system.

Neurolinguistic coaching: NLC denotes the precise use of language, with the inclusion of a myostatic test in the coaching process. Emotionally defined words and sentences bring the coach and the coachee directly to the issue, always show the shortcut to a solution, and enable the quick testing of the effect of coaching processes. NLC can specify the process in all the effective coaching methods, not only in the context of the application of the method of bilateral brain stimulation, such as wingwave and EMDR. The application of NLC is a useful tool even when conducting a conversation, in constellation works, or in decision-making processes.

Neural Pathways: A developed connection that is stable between the brain cells by means of frequent thinking and acting, which leads to further comfortable use and supports the new habit. This is meaningful in the case of useful abilities, and disruptive in the case of action and thought patterns, which are no longer useful in the here and now.

Neurophysiology: The medical perspective on the physical and psychological state of human beings, as it is physiologically formed and reflected by the nervous system: With metabolism, muscle tone, body temperature, vascular reaction, etc.

NLC: See Neurolinguistic coaching.

NLP: See Neurolinguistic programming.

Omura ring test: See O-ring test and myostatic test. The Doctor of Acupuncture, Yoshiaki Omura, also uses the myostatic test for medical purposes, for example, for the dosage of a medicament or for the diagnosis of a disease. In this context, the said test is also called the Omura Test. However, in wingwave coaching, the test has never been used for medical diagnoses or prescriptions.

O-ring test: Another term for the myostatic test, since in this test, the letter "O" is formed using the thumb and the index finger. Explanation under the myostatic test.

Parasympathicotonic physical activation: Loose muscles, consistently permeable blood vessels, good cell supply, rather low blood pressure, favourable recovery, and regenerative state.

Performance Stress Imprinting (PSI): In the context of performance, the traces occurred in the stress memory, which continue to have a resistant effect, without the usual processing strategies, such as sleeping, distraction, time-gap, sports, speech, or rational thinking, helping one get over these traces of stress memories. The term "imprinting" should be understood as distinct from the term "trauma". It is not an injury in the clinical sense, but just an oppressive, "annoying" impression in the subjective experience in the so-called stress memory. Also see Resistant stress imprinting.

Post-traumatic embitterment disorder: A recent technical term, which describes a chronic stress reaction to social injuries– above all, caused by the significant or closely-related people, such as teachers, partners, superior officers, colleagues, etc. Also see Social pain.

Processing: The course of wingwave coaching of emotional stress leading to a resourceful stable overall state of the coachee. This is less concerned with the conversational part of the coaching, and more with the "purely" intervention part to overcome the stress-causing emotions and to develop the supporting emotions.

Procrastination syndrome: A cumbersome word for "procrastinates"; unfavourable and systematic avoidance behavior, when, for example, it comes to an examination, learning, paying bills, making important calls, etc.

Prophecy, self-fulfilling: Everyday predictions (prophetic) which come true because one subconsciously directs his feelings and behaviors toward them (self-fulfilling prophecies). For example, it is said, "That will definitely go wrong," and then the problems actually take place. The "fulfilment" materialized because, due to the negative sentence, one was uncertain and, therefore, committed the mistake. One says, "You will become famous one day!" and the person addressed feels so inspired that it has a positive effect on his charisma, which, in turn, attracts other people to him.

Psychoeducation: This term originates from classic behavioral therapy and means the inclusion of a person in theoretic models and considerations, which explain a theory behind the so-called clinical image and the meaning of psychologically well-founded interventions Education, which, among other things, also means learning or acquisition of knowledge.

REM phases: **R**apid **E**ye **M**ovement, dream phases in sleep in which the eyes of a sleeping person rapidly move back and forth.

Resistant Stress Imprinting: All forms of neurobiological traces in the stress memory that do not calm down on their own over time. Stress imprintings evoke both the emotional nad somatic stress, for example, pain. The event subsided a long time ago, but the stress memory acts as if the said stress experience has taken place just now.

Resources: Sources of a person's strength, for example, hobbies, abilities, or memories, which could trigger powerful, positive states.

Resource anchor: See Anchor.

Set: Term used for a round of bilateral stimulation, for example, the number of eye movements, which are required to achieve an emotional-physiological change in the coachee. In the classic EMDR therapy, a set comprises 20-25 back and forth movements. In the wingwave method, a set is considered as completed when a positive change occurs in the process. Then one perceives these changes, focuses on the improved state, and prepares for the next set.

Setting: The overall situation in coaching: Seating arrangement, premises, agreed time-schedule, etc.

Safe place: Before the coachee is guided into his process, the coach asks for a reference experience with a safety and stability effect. "When and where have you experienced a situation in which you felt absolutely safe and secure?" This state is then anchored (see anchor), and serves as a possibility to relocate the coachee, at any time, back into the stable and sustainable states, if it seems necessary.

Sensory modalities: Our five neurobiological perceptual channels – the five senses: seeing, hearing, feeling, smelling and tasting.

Scale of subjective experience: A bipolar scale ranging from -10 to +10 on which a coachee can assess his subjective state. This subjective self-assessment helps the coach to assess the variable states of the client in his process and even the coachee himself can conduct a before and after assessment. The coach and the coachee can find their bearings at anytime during the change process.

Social pain: Interpersonal problems and physical pain activate one and the same neuronal structures in the brain. Thus, rejection, separation, and humiliation by fellow human beings are "really painful".

Soma stress: Physical stressors, such as hunger, thirst, heat, cold, exhaustion.

SMART goals: **S**pecific, **M**easurable, **Achievable**, **R**ealistic, **T**imely. Motivational and priming factors in the brain-based target definition.

Mirror emotions: The feelings of other people, which we feel by means of our mirror neurons. When a person observes how a fellow human being is, for example, pricked with a syringe, he also winces, although he was not pricked himself. Even in the case of spectators, the activities in the pain center of the brain are demonstrably measurable. In this context, it means "to empathize"—empathy in a specific neurological sense. In the meantime, one distinguishes between empathy and compassion. In the case of empathy, we remain resourceful and capable of acting; in the case of compassion, the suffering of others drags us down and causes the blocked stress.

Mirror neurons: Specific neurons and/or cells in the brain which can reflect the emotional and physical states of other people, for example, empathy (also, see Mirror feelings).

Stop sign: The coach and the coachee agree on a "stop sign" (for example, a hand signal or a command) with which the coachee can pause the process at any time (for example, an interesting idea, unable to endure something, urge to go to the toilet).

Streamline effect: Quite frequently, central positive learning steps entail a chain reaction of additional learning steps so that one speaks of a flow effect (Also see Generalization).

Stress memory: The accumulation of resistant stress imprintings in the life of a person.

Stress imprinting: See Performance Stress Imprinting (PSI).

Stress trigger: A sensorial discernible perceptual memory (seeing, hearing, feeling, smelling or tasting), which can trigger an emotional or somatic stress reaction. For example, the mobile phone ringtone, which the coachee has repeatedly heard during a specifically stressful life/project phase can "trigger" the state of stress associated therewith even later in life (Also see Anchor).

Subjective discomfort: An unpleasant or stressful general state, which can also be measured on the scale of subjective experience with a value between -10 and 0.

Subjective wellness: An overall positive feeling, which can be measured on the scale of subjective experience with a value between 0 and +10.

Submodalities: The perceptual qualities within a sensory channel for inbound perceptions. In the case of visual, for example: Light/dark, coloured/black and white, two or three dimensional, high-contrast/blurred. Thereby, the changes in these settings only mean the type of inner image of a past or future experience. If a person says he can remember it only "vaguely", it does not mean he is unable to sharply look at it because of defective vision. The brain has continued to reorganize the submodalities of the recollected image so that the blurred representation has caused a feeling of temporal distance. Accordingly, the literal change in settings has taken place with regards to the original high-contrast stored image.

Sympathicotonic physical activation: The body is in high responsiveness: Stress hormones are in circulation, high muscle tension, vasoconstriction. This can be the case for both the subjectively negative states (anxiety), as well as positive states (euphoric enthusiasm). This activation barely allows any physical recreational opportunities, such as sleep, healing, good and steady blood circulation, etc.

Systems: In psychology, it means the social systems, such as family, organizational structures, or the inner personality system with different parts of the personality of a person.

Systemic interconnectedness: The way we are connected to one another as a part of a system (for example, a member in the family). This specific interconnectedness should always be taken into consideration for a successful coaching process. For example, a life partner must also absorb their partner's business success. He is probably suffering from failure, and, therefore, one is subconsciously afraid of depressing him further with one's own roaring success.

Tactile stimulation: Right-left stimulation with touch stimuli (for example, butterfly technique, tapping on knees, feet, and hands).

Tapping: See Tactile stimulation.

Taps: Touch stimuli in tactile touch stimulation.

Thymus gland: A gland under the sternum (breast bone), which plays an important role in supplying the general de-stressing neurotransmitters to the nervous system. The stimulation of the thymus gland by means of tapping spontaneously achieves a measureable increase in strength (muscle strength, mental power, and strength of the immune system). It has been found that healthy human beings have a pronounced thymus gland when compared with chronically sick people, where this gland has often completely deteriorated.

Tomato effect: Generalization effect.

Trigger: See Anchor.

Tunnel metaphor: A metaphor, which makes a coachee comprehend that during the process (see Processing), it is sometimes wiser to pass through the tunnel rather than apply the emergency brakes in the middle of the tunnel (also see Stop signal). Thus, the momentum of the emotional integration and regulation can be used to quickly leave the stress behind and come back into the "light" and/or the emotional security once again.

Transference: A psychological phenomenon in which the emotional reactions, which have emerged in the history of learning of a person in the past, are redirected to other people in the present, who have nothing to with the history of origin.

Vagus nerve: The tenth cranial nerve and the largest nerve of the parasympathetic nervous system (calming nerve). It controls most of the internal organs and can be put under stress easily by pressing in the area where the navel is located, which is important within the scope of calibration: The muscle test then shows the stress.

Embitterment disorder: See Post-traumatic embitterment disorder and Social pain

Visualize: Imagining something pictorially in thoughts.

Visual: The pictorial perceptions, the pictorial thinking.

Visual channel: The sensory channel, which we think and perceive pictorially.

Vita sentence: See Vita language.

Vita language: Refers to the words and sentences of a person individually defined by the life and learning history. For Columbus, "India" was an emotionally positively charged vita word, and the word "Lord Voldemort" is an emotionally negatively charged vita word in the case of Harry Potter.

Vita word: See Vita language.

Awake REM phases: The re-enactment of the REM phases (dream sleep) in the awake state, for example, eye movements performed by means of "waving".

Wellness scale: A visual scale ranging from 0 to +10 on which the coachee can assess the extent of a pleasant, positive, or resourceful subjective experience.

Wingwave music: Auditory stimulations combined with relaxing music and the sounds of nature. The rhythm alternates between the left and right ears, which promotes coordination between the cerebral hemispheres. This music represents an "auditory in-house pharmacy". It can contribute valuable help in everyday stress regulation and/or self-coaching.

wingwave mirror: Systemic intervention in which not only the emotion of the coachee is "waved away", but also the stress topics, which fellow human beings of the coachee induce and he empathizes with on the basis of the mirror neurons. Also see Emotions' mirror and Mirror neurons.

Formulation of goals: Goals can be achieved easily when they are formulated in a brain-friendly manner (sensory-specific, without comparison and negations).

Sugar test: When setting up the muscle test (see Calibration), a white sugar cube is used to provoke a stress reaction in the muscle test.

Meaning for the future: Term originating from brain research for the predilection of the brain to derive such patterns and rules from events, which are used for the spiritual and mental development of predictions with regards to the occurrence of future events.

FURTHER INFORMATION ON THE WINGWAVE-COACHING-METHOD

Wingwave-coaches in Your Area:

Visit www.wingwave.com for the national and international addresses of trained wingwave coaches in your area. You can specifically search according to the postal code areas, free search phrases, or according to the key topics, for example, "Work Life Coaching", "Presentation Coaching", "Stress Management", "Career Coaching", "Sport Coaching", "Overcoming Dental Treatment Anxiety", etc. To access the address of a coach, simply enter the corresponding term in the search field. By entering the above information, you will find the coach or therapist with the desired specialization in your vicinity.

www.wingwave.com/coach-finder.html

The Target Group of wingwave-coaching:

In this book, you have already read that wingwave is a coaching method and that this method is not psychotherapy and cannot replace it. Wingwave is a short-term coaching concept for all people in demanding professions and performance situations, for example, executives, managers, artists, and athletes. Even pupils, students, and examination candidates benefit from this method.

What is wingwave-training?

Wingwave-training is aimed at two target groups. First, certified wingwave coaches can undergo training to become wingwave trainers, and second, you, as a user of this method, can—in addition to the wingwave coaching on an individual basis—can also learn wingwave as a self-coaching tool in the group.

By means of wingwave-training, you will learn methods, which will strengthen your health and your quality of life through stress management, relaxation, and creative performance. The training offers you modern self-coaching methods for an everyday activity-relaxation-balance in a supporting manner.

The Users of wingwave-training

Do you wish to reduce stress, feel calm and stable, and be energetic in an effective way on a regular basis? Would you be pleased if, after participation in the training, you do not have to invest any additional time to derive this effect? Wingwave training enables you to easily relax and reduce stress everyday, without any additional expenditure of time. This is valuable for those who wishes to combine work and leisure time with a good attitude toward life everyday, and those who like the use of modern-day media, such as apps, tablets, and music players. The participants are:

- Professionals
- "Family managers", for example, parents
- Corporate teams
- Pupils, students, trainees

www.wingwave.com

The website offers clients the important and up-to-date information covering the overall wingwave method. There is a special info-section for the promotions offered by the wingwave trainers and master trainers for seminars, lectures, workshops, team and group work, as well as constellation work.

Wingwave is also on the social web

Facebook	Facebook www.facebook.com/WingWaveCoaching
XING	XING www.xing.com/net/wingwave
YouTube	YouTube www.youtube.com
LinkedIn	LinkedIn www.linkedin.com

Wingwave-books by Cora Besser-Siegmund and Harry Siegmund (available only in German):

Practice books

Besser-Siegmund, Cora & Rathschlag, Marco (2013): Mit Freude läuft's besser. Durch wingwave positive Emotionen fördern und Leistung steigern. Junfermann Verlag, Paderborn.

This book presents the latest results of the research on the wingwave coaching method and on the myostatic test.

Besser-Siegmund, Cora & Siegmund, Harry (Hrsg.) (2009): Erfolge zum Wundern. Fünfzig und eine Coachinggeschichte. Junfermann Verlag, Paderborn.

Besser-Siegmund, Cora & Siegmund, Harry (Hrsg.) (2003): Erfolge bewegen—Coach Limbic. Junfermann Verlag, Paderborn.

These two books provide an excellent overview of the different possible applications of the wingwave coaching, amongst other things, in the professional context, in sports coaching, in the field of medicine, or in performance coaching.

wingwave self-coaching books

The following publications by Cora Besser-Siegmund contain a lot of wingwave self-coaching exercises on various topics. In these very well written and easily comprehensible books, the author shows how many fears and anxieties or unpleasant habits in everyday life can be changed with the aid of targeted emotion management. One can easily learn to shape everyday life in a more stress-free manner, quit smoking, change eating habits, or experience relationships in a self-determined manner.

Besser-Siegmund, Cora (2013): Schnelle Hilfe bei Angst und Stress, Weltbild Verlag, Augsburg. Besser-Siegmund, Cora (2013): Nie wieder Heißhunger (e-Book at dotbooks)

Besser-Siegmund, Cora (2013): Frei von Eifersucht (e-Book at dotbooks)

Besser-Siegmund, Cora (2013): Das Rauchen aufgeben (e-Book at dotbooks)

In-depth topics:

Besser-Siegmund, Cora/Siegmund, Harry (2004): Imaginative Familienaufstellung mit der wingwave-Methode, now available in e-Pub and PDF-format at www.wingwave-shop.com

This book is about the imaginative family constellation with the aid of the wingwave method, which was successfully developed by both the authors.

Besser-Siegmund, Cora; Dierks, Marie-Luise & Siegmund, Harry (2007): Sicheres Auftreten mit wingwave-Coaching. Junfermann Verlag, Paderborn

This book specifically focuses on the topics of presentation confidence, test anxiety, and stage fright in the context of training, profession, or performance sport.

Besser-Siegmund, Cora &Eilert, Dirk W. (2011): wingwave-Coaching: die Profi-Box. Maßgeschneiderte Interventionen durch flexible Methodenkompetenz. With illustrations by Lola Siegmund. Junfermann Verlag, Paderborn

In this book, **trained** wingwave coaches will find focused interventions and suggestions to plan their own wingwave coaching.

Wingwave music:

In addition to its balancing and positive melodies, the wingwave music especially works through its left-right rhythmic beat, which, when listened through stereo headphones, "touches" both the cerebral hemispheres with its alternating beat and thus, causes optimal collaboration of all of the regions of the brain. This bilateral auditory hemispheric stimulation helps in reducing performance stress and supports the creative process. You have already learned some of the exercises in this book. For the self-coaching effect, music must be listened to with the aid of headphones.

The somewhat lively music "wingwave-movement" is used by many users, and is especially favored for activities, such as jogging, and other melodies can be put to good use for relaxation as well. You can also listen to this music for mental support during activities, such as cleaning or filing your tax return, just to name a few examples. You will then perform these activities subjectively easily and objectively in a relatively short time.

Soothing sounds of nature, pleasant or even inspiring sounds, or sounds of ocean waves (wingwave-waves) are played in the background. The rhythm is always "andante", like a heartbeat at rest. All of this together measurably reduces the pulse rate and the arousal level of the nervous system, calms you down, lets all stress flow off, increases the sense of wellbeing, and opens the broader perspective for the solution-oriented and positive perception and thinking. Actors, pupils, and students listen to the music during memorization. We offer the music "wingwave children" especially for children. The study matter is memorized very quickly and is retained for a longer period. As so often happens, it is a matter of taste as to who likes which musical track or which melody. Detailed descriptions are given for each track. On average, a musical track is 20 minutes long.

The wingwave music is directly available at the online shop at www. wingwave-shop.com. Here, you can purchase the MP3 downloads directly from the Besser-Siegmund-Institut. This music is also available at iTunes or Google play.

Feelwave – Free Download

To provide **you** with a first impression of the wingwave- music, we offer you the option **of** a free download. The track is called "Feelwave" and is eight minutes in **duration**. Note for iPhone users: Clicking on the link will play the song automatically. If you would like to import it in **iTunes**, please download it first on a computer (Mac or PC).

www.wingwave-shop.com/feelwave

The wingwave-App (Free App)

Do you want to reduce stress, achieve success, or increase your general sense of wellbeing? With the aid of wingwave self-coaching, you can noticeably strengthen your inner balance, your mental potential, and your general performance capability.

Functions:

- Use the wingwave-music for your optimal inner balance
- With "Magic Words", transform stress into positive target energy
- Learn wingwave exercises for different self-coaching topics

The free App is available at iTunes or at Google play. Depending on your taste, additional wingwave music tracks can be combined with the **App**, so that self-coaching **can be** adjusted to individual requirements.

Becoming a wingwave-coach

The four-day training for the certified **wingwave**-coach is an additional module for complete training in NLP, communication psychology, psychotherapy, training in dental hypnosis, and comparable degrees or professions, such as doctors, non-medical practitioners, **or learning education-ists**. Training content is the wingwave method **presented in th**is book. You will find your wingwave-teaching-trainer on www.wingwave.com/.

Mönckebergstr. 11
20095 Hamburg
Tel. +49 (0)40-3252 849-0
Fax: +49 (0)40-3252 849-17
info@besser-siegmund.de
www.besser-siegmund.de
www.wingwave.com

The Besser-Siegmund-Institut is Certified according to ISO 9001 for the following scope of application: Implementation and Conceptualization of Training and Advanced Training

INFORMATION ON BESSER-SIEGMUND-INSTITUT

Contact:

Dipl.-Psych. Cora Besser-Siegmund, Dipl.-Psych. Harry Siegmund and Lola A. Siegmund (Business Psychology (BA) with emphasis on Training and Coaching) appreciate your further interest in the work of their institute. For detailed information, please contact:

BESSER-SIEGMUND-INSTITUT

Mönckebergstraße 11, 20095 Hamburg

Telephone: +49 (0)40-3252 849-0 | FAX: +49 (0)40-3252 849-17

info@besser-siegmund.de, www.besser-siegmund.de

The Besser-Siegmund-Institut is located centrally in the Hamburg city center. The coaching and training take place at this location.

Additional Coach Certifications

- Work-Health-Balance Coach for Systemic Short-Term Concepts
- Business Coach for Systemic Short-Term Concepts
- Health Educationist

Since 2008, the Besser-Siegmund-Institut bears the following quality reference:

> Certified according to ISO 9001 for the following scope of application: Implementation and Conceptualization of Training and Advanced Training

This note also appears on all the training certificates awarded by the Besser-Siegmund-Institut. The certification by the TÜV Nord Cert GmbH is recognized worldwide due to the international accreditation agreement.

All the training brochures are available in the download section on the homepage of

www.besser-siegmund.de

The methodological society "Gesellschaft für Neurolinguistisches Coaching" e.V. (formerly "Bahnungsmomente" e.V.)

This methodological society promotes and certifies the training of professional coaches in neurolinguistic coaching (NLC). Furthermore, the society promotes the research pertaining to the efficacy of the short-term coaching methods in conjunction with the myostatic test to be used in the case of test anxiety, performance anxieties, and sport stress experiences, such as sports injuries and their psychological effects on performance capacity.

Wellness Management with Wingwave Music

For some of the exercises featured in this book, as well as an additional self-coaching exercise, there is the wingwave album 1 titled, *Walk at the Beach*, by Lars Linek at www.wingwave-shop.com and in the wingwave –App.

Of course, understanding the stress-relieving and soothing effects of the wingwave music may not be complete without reading this book.

You can use the following exercise as an evening ritual or simply to feel good. As already described in the book, the use of stereo headphones is important, so that a bilateral auditory stimulation can unfold.

Wellness Management With the Wingwave Music

☺ Please perceive in which area of your body you feel uncomfortable / tense/stressed.

☺ Describe the physical sensation in words: "oppressive, piercing, circling" (for example, in the case of tension or an uneasy feeling in the stomach).

☺ Using these words, develop an image, a metaphor:
- What does this feeling look like?
- What does it possibly sound like?
- Formulate words for your image: "It is as though a stone is being pressed there / as though I am carrying a backpack …"
- Or imagine the discomfort in specific terms: As an X-ray image, a reddened tissue, a tense muscle cord, etc.

♫

Now, put on your headphones and listen to the music.

♫

☺ Now, think about the described words and see or hear this image / this metaphor. Think about these contents in the rhythm of the music.

☺ When you notice a minor change, formulate words and sentences for that change, such as:
- "The feeling or sensation is sliding down."
- "It is coming up like a wave."
- "Something is being released there."

☺ Repeat these sentences or words inwardly, like a mantra to the music.

☺ Also, allow yourself to think about other things:
- "I am just thinking about my work."
- "Which emotion is accompanied by it?"
- "What kind of feeling arises in the body?"
- "What words or images describe this feeling?"
- Etc.
- Then return to your physical perception.

☺ When the first pleasant emotions, feelings, or associations emerge, continue in the same manner:

- Formulate into words what you experience and feel: "It is easy, it feels free, etc."
- Find images and metaphors.
- Perceive and think about positive words, images, and metaphors in the rhythm of the music.

☺ Continue this process until optimal relaxation / until the best possible result.

Note:

☺ The experience takes place in waves: Every up and down is allowed and felt in the described manner, focused upon using words and thoughts, and is then "released" again.

☺ Signs of the de-stressing effect:

- ☺ Deep breathing
- ☺ Distinct swallowing
- ☺ Yawning

BIBLIOGRAPHY

Bandler, R. (1985). *Using your Brain for a Change.* Lafayette, Kalifornien: Real People Press.

Bandler, R. u. (1977). *Frogs into Princes.* Utah: Real People Press.

Beaulieu, D. (2003). *Eye Movement Integration Therapy: The Comprehensive Clinical Guide".* Carmathen, UK: Crown House.

Besser-Siegmund, C. (2001). *Magic Words: The minute-long removal of blockagesords - Magic Words: der minutenschnelle Abbau von Blockaden.* Paderborn: Junfermann.

Besser-Siegmund, C., & Siegmund, L. A. (2016). *Work Health Balance.* Hannover: Humboldt-Verlag.

Besser-Siegmund, C., & Siegmund, L. (Herbst 2015). *Neurolinguistisches Coaching - Sprache wirkt Wunder.* Paderborn: Junfermann-Verlag.

Csikszentmihalyi, M. (2013). *Creativity: Flow and the Psychology of Discovery and Invention.* New York: HarperCollins Publishers.

De Jong, A. e. (1999). Treatment of Specific Phobias with Eye Movement Desensitization and Reprocessing (EMDR): Protocol, Empirical Status, and Conceptual Issues. *Journal of Anxiety Disorders, Volume 13, Issues 1 - 2,* 69 - 85.

Derks, L. (2005). *Social Panoramas: Changing the Unconscious Landscape with NLP and Psychotherapy.* Bankyfelin UK: Crown House Publishing.

Dilts, R. (2012). *Beliefs: Pathways to Health and Well-Being.* Portland, Oregon USA: Metamorpheus Press.

Goleman, D. (2005). *Emotional Intelligence: Why It Can Matter More Than IQ.* New York: Bantam Books.

Kahnemann, D. e. (1996). Kahneman D. Patient`s memories of painful medical treatments: Real-time and retrospective evaluations of two minimally invasive procedures. Pain 1996; 3-8. *Pain,* S. 3 - 8.

Kißler, J. e. (Juni 2007). Buzzwords - early cortical responses to emotional words during reading. *Psychological Science,* S. *18(06),* 475-80.

Liebermann, M. (2014). *Social - why our brains are wired to connect.* Victoria, Kanada: Abebooks.

Liebermann, M. e. (2007). Putting feelings into words - affect labeling disrupts amygdala activity in response to affective stimuli. *Psychological Science.*

Ornstein, R. (2015). *Multimind: A New Way of Looking at Human Behavior* . Los Altos USA: Malor Books.

Rathschlag, M. (2013). *Self-generated emotions and their influence on physical performance.* Köln: Promotions-Arbeit an der Deutschen Sporthochschule Köln.

Rathschlag, M., & Memmert, D. (2014). "Reducing anxiety and enhancing physical performance by using an advanced version of EMDR: a pilot study". *Brain and Behavior - DOI: 10.1002/brb3.221, Wiley Periodicals, Inc.*

Richter, M., & Weiss, T. (Februar 2010). Do words hurt? Brain activation during the processing of pain-related words . *PAIN,* S. 108 - 205.

Rizzato, M., & Donelli, D. (2014). *I am Your Mirror: Mirror Neurons & Empathy.* Torino, Italy: Blossoming Books.

Shapiro, F. (2017). *Eye Movement Desensitization and Reprocessing (EMDR) Therapy, Third Edition: Basic Principles, Protocols, and Procedures.* New York: The Guilford Press.

Singer, T. e. (2004). Empathy for pain involves the affective but not sensory components of pain. Science, 303 (5661), 1157–1162. *Science 303 (5661),* **1157 - 1162.**

Singer, T. e. (2009). The social neuroscience of empathy. The Year in Cognitive Ne 1156 , 81–96. *The Year in Cognitive Neuroscience, Annals of the New York Academy of Sciences 1159,* 81-86.

LIST OF FIGURES

ABOUT CASTLE MOUNT MEDIA

"Improving Leadership and Communication in Business, Healthcare & Education"

Castle Mount Media GmbH & Co. KG is a publishing company located in Erlangen, Germany, which specializes in print and online media dedicated to improving leadership and communication especially in the areas of business, healthcare, and education. Our mission is to inspire and empower our readers and seminar participants to achieve success through value-based, conscious leadership and generative collaboration.

For further information about Castle Mount Media, our online seminars, books, and other products please visit our website:

www.castlemountmedia.com

PRESENTATION INTELLIGENCE: HOW TO EASILY CREATE AND USE POWERFUL, BRAIN-FRIENDLY SLIDE PRESENTATIONS TO CAPTIVATE YOUR AUDIENCE

By Frowa Schuitemaker–Hartsema & Charlotte Schuitemaker

Presentation Intelligence will help you . . .

- Easily prepare an inspiring slide presentation
- Understand how your audience thinks, so you can reach them emotionally
- Inspire and motivate your audience
- Be more confident when giving presentations
- Reach your goals

Preparing a successful presentation goes far beyond just making and showing your PowerPoint or Keynote slides. However, the way you use your slides can either tremendously support or completely undermine your overall presentation. In *Presentation Intelligence*, you will learn how to master the art of presenting with slides, and you will discover which five elements collectively determine the success of every presentation you give.

Presentation Intelligence fills the gap between a book on presentation techniques and a book on presentation software in a unique way that cannot be found anywhere else. It is a handbook for anyone who wants to give presentations with more impact.

Now is the time for you to take control and make stunning, inspiring presentations!

Frowa and Charlotte Schuitemaker developed the concept of *Presentation Intelligence* together. With this concept, they have mapped out clearly and simply how to speak effectively using slide presentations. Frowa is an educationalist and has been giving presentation training courses since 1990. Charlotte is an expert in making professional slide decks and specializes in how to communicate complex information clearly to a broad audience.

ISBN 978-3-948615-05-5 (Paperback)
ISBN 978-3-948615-06-2 (eBook)

INDEPENDENT MINDS, EXPERT IDEAS: HOW TO THRIVE IN A CHANGING WORLD

By 9 International Experts

Independent Minds will help you . . .

- Better cope with the challenges of change
- Help your organization be prepared for the future
- Engage more effectively with your customers and clients
- Increase innovative thought in your organization
- Be more flexible and more able to influence the changing world around you

We are living in an extraordinary moment in human history. There is an onslaught of information, and we are expected to be present and readily available at all times. Today, many established businesses are being challenged to find new ways to deliver their products and serve their customers while keeping up with technological advancements and structural changes.

Although change is inevitable and the future is unpredictable, coping with these changes does not have to be scary. In a time of turbulence and uncertainty, we look towards thought leaders to guide our way.

Independent Minds, Expert Ideas compiles nine outstanding articles written by international thought leaders: Lindsay Adams, *Stop Selling - Start Partnering*; Laura Baxter, *The Power of Presence in an Ever-Changing World*; Christian Buchholz, *The Age of Ideas - New Skills for a Changing World*; Chris Davidson, *The Client Engagement Conundrum*; Ilja Grzeskowitz, *Transform Your Culture - Change Your Business: Change Competence as a Competitive Advantage of the Future*; Rebecca Jones, *Increasing Innovation in Your Workplace by Embracing 'Stretchy Thinking'*; Siegfried Lange, *The Laws of OUR Nature in Change*; Ogopoleng Mushi, *Breaking the System - How to Change Your Story and Transform Your Business*; Paul ter Wal, *The Role of the Value-to-Profit Model in 21st Century Organisations*.

Independent Minds, Expert Ideas introduces you to the authors' business know-how. They share some of their most valuable tips for facing the challenges of changing times head-on, and they show you how to create confidence in your business or organisation no matter what the future holds.

ISBN 978-3-948615-07-9 (Hardcover)
ISBN 978-3-948615-08-6 (eBook)

LEADERSHIP. SAFE & SECURE.

By Anton Doerig

Leadership. Safe & Secure. will help you . . .

- Find your passion in leadership
- Increase safety & security in your organization
- Master self-leadership and -management
- Find the weaknesses that may be holding you back
- Excel through integrating leadership with safety & security

Life is a journey in which you have many unique – sometimes difficult - experiences. Sometimes you win and sometimes you lose. Nothing is certain, not now and not in the future. Through his many experiences both in private and business environments, Anton Doerig is an expert in leadership and security, and in this groundbreaking book he shares his experiences with you.

Leadership. Safe & Secure. deals with self-management in combination with safety & security. The author encourages you, the reader, to reflect on and question your behavior in self-, employee- and company management. He combines this with the challenges of holistic Safety & Security and Emergency & Crisis Management as no one has done before. It is not always easy to be honest with yourself and those around you, but it is essential for a secure and sustainable success. A success that that you deserve, both privately and professionally!

Bringing Leadership Presence & Essence together with Safety & Security – for All Levels of Management!

ANTON DOERIG - Expert & Advisor | Keynote Speaker & Author - has been successful in management positions of various military, private, and public safety and security areas at regional, national and international levels for more than 20 years. Today, his focus is on coaching executives and advising companies and on giving keynotes on the connection between and the intersection of leadership, management and safety & security - all resulting in an exciting and perfect mixture for a desired change of perspective, far more than just an impulse for personal and entrepreneurial success!

ISBN 978-3-948615-02-4 (Hardcover)
ISBN 978-3-948615-03-1 (eBook)

VIRTUAL POWER TEAMS: HOW TO DELIVER PROJECTS FASTER, REDUCE COSTS, AND DEVELOP YOUR ORGANIZATION FOR THE FUTURE!

By Peter Ivanov

Virtual Power Teams will help you . . .

- Understand the process of forming and leading virtual teams
- Find excellent talent to work with you on your virtual teams
- Learn about the technology available to support you and your teams
- Create an organization to which people will want to belong
- Structure your teams so that they run efficiently and effectively

Globalization and digital transformation have brought about bew challenges in leadership and communication. Teams and projects are decentralized, usually crossing international borders, time zones, and cultural boundaries. Leading such teams requires very specific organizational knowledge including how to select qualified experts, which virtual platforms to use, and how to structure and support your team. In this groundbreaking book, Virtual Team Expert Peter Ivanov uses the engaging story of Bernd and his virtual team to show you how to organize, lead, and support your team to be not just a virtual team, but a Virtual Power Team!

Peter Ivanov is an internationally sought-after keynote speaker, business consultant, and executive coach. He has led virtual teams of 100+ people across Europe, Central Asia, the Middle East, and Africa. His teams have won multiple prestigious corporate awards.

Virtual Power Teams will help you break boundaries for the future of your organization!

ISBN: 978-3-9818472-3-9 (Paperback)
ISBN: 978- 3-9818472-4-6 (eBook)

DEALING WITH DIVAS AND OTHER DIFFICULT PERSONALITIES: A MINDFUL APPROACH TO IMPROVING RELATIONSHIPS IN YOUR BUSINESS OR ORGANIZATION!

By Laura Baxter

Dealing with Divas will help you . . .

- Remain calm, cool, and focused when dealing with difficult people
- Reach your goals with ease
- Understand how other people tick and what motivates them
- Improve relationships in your business or organization
- Better guide your team to success

In a world where having productive relationships and effective communication means the difference between success and absolute failure, you need tools that will help you remain calm, confident, poised, and focused on the task at hand so that you accomplish your goals, regardless of any conflict that may be going on around you.

This book helps you do just that. It gives you the tools you need to remain calm, centered, and focused when you are dealing with difficult people, and it gives the tools you need to better communicate with everyone on your team -- including your "Divas" -- so that you reach your goals with success.

Laura Baxter, American opera singer and performance coach, has studied the effects of the voice and the body on communication and leadership for over 25 years. The focus of her work is presence. She helps her clients master having both a strong inner presence -- even in the most difficult situations -- and a dynamic, charismatic outer presence. They own the room! In Dealing with Divas she brings this experience together to help you master dealing with your diva!

English Version:
ISBN 978-3-9818472-1-5 (Paperback)
ISBN 978-3-9818472-2-2 (eBook)

German Version:
ISBN 978-3-9818472-5-3 (Paperback)
ISBN 978-3-9818472-6-0 (eBook)

Generative Collaboration:
Releasing the Creative Power of Collective Intelligence

Generative Collaboration involves people working together to create something new, *surprising, and beyond the capacities of any of the group members individually. Through generative collaboration, individuals are able to utilize their abilities to the fullest and discover and apply resources that they did not yet realize that they had. This book is for people who want to increase their capacity* for working effectively together with others and to experience the excitement, satisfaction and power of generative collaboration.

English:
ISBN: 978-0-9962004-2-4

German:
ISBN: 978-3-9818472-7-7

Conscious Leadership and Resiience:
Orchestrating Innovation and Fitness for the Future

This book provides principles, models, exercises, and other resources to help you develop a greater proficiency and aptitude for conscious leadership – that is, to guide yourself and your team from a state of centered presence, accessing multiple intelligences and living your highest values in service to a larger purpose for the benefit of all stakeholders. You will learn how to empower, coach, stare, and stretch yourself and others in order to create a profitable and sustainable venture.

English:
ISBN: 978-0-9962004-4-8

German:
ISBN: 978-3-9818472-8-4

Robert Dilts has had a global reputation as a leading coach, behavioral skills trainer, and business consultant since the late 1970s. The author of 28 books, he has been a major developer and expert in the field of Neuro-Lingusitic Programming (NLP). Robert has provided coaching consulting and training throughout the world to a wide variety of individuals and organizations and has influenced and improved the lives of hundreds of thousands of people worldwide.